User Interface Design
for Mere
Mortals®

Eric Butow

✦Addison-Wesley

Boston ▪ San Francisco ▪ New York ▪ Toronto ▪ Montreal

London ▪ Munich ▪ Paris ▪ Madrid

Cape Town ▪ Sydney ▪ Tokyo ▪ Singapore ▪ Mexico City

The publisher offers excellent discounts on this book when ordered in quantity for bulk purchases or special sales, which may include electronic versions and/or custom covers and content particular to your business, training goals, marketing focus, and branding interests. For more information, please contact:

U.S. Corporate and Government Sales
800-382-3419
corpsales@pearsontechgroup.com

For sales outside the United States, please contact:

International Sales
international@pearsoned.com

This Book Is Safari Enabled

The Safari® Enabled icon on the cover of your favorite technology book means the book is available through Safari Bookshelf. When you buy this book, you get free access to the online edition for 45 days.

Safari Bookshelf is an electronic reference library that lets you easily search thousands of technical books, find code samples, download chapters, and access technical information whenever and wherever you need it.

To gain 45-day Safari Enabled access to this book:

• Go to http://www.awprofessional.com/safarienabled
• Complete the brief registration form
• Enter the coupon code 3UFR-YPTG-KWZT-YCGQ-UWP9

If you have difficulty registering on Safari Bookshelf or accessing the online edition, please e-mail customer-service@safaribooksonline.com.

Visit us on the Web: www.awprofessional.com

Library of Congress Cataloging-in-Publication Data:

Butow, Eric.
  User interface design for mere mortals / Eric Butow.
     p. cm.
  Includes bibliographical references.
  ISBN 0-321-44773-5 (pbk. : alk. paper) 1. User interfaces (Computer systems) I. Title.
  QA76.9.U83B88 2007
  005.4'37—dc22   2007005652

  © 2007 by Pearson Education, Inc.

Pearson Education, Inc.
Rights and Contracts Department
One Lake Street
Upper Saddle River, NJ 07458
Fax: (201) 236-3290

ISBN 0-32-144773-5
Text printed in the United States on recycled paper at RR Donnelley, Crawfordsville, Indiana
First printing, May 2007

For my family, who have always supported me and never hesitate to tell me what I need to hear.

In loving memory of three of my cats I've lost recently: Oreo, Josette, and Tigger. Life isn't the same without them, though their mother, Mewsette, doesn't mind having me all to herself.

Contents

Preface   **xv**

Acknowledgments   **xvii**

About the Author   **xix**

Introduction   **xxv**

    Who Should Read This Book   xxi

    The Purpose of This Book   xxii

    How to Read This Book   xxii

    How This Book Is Organized   xxiii

CHAPTER 1   Brief Histories   **1**

    The History of Graphical User Interfaces   1
        Xerox Alto   2
        Apple Macintosh   3
        Microsoft Windows   5
        Linux   7

    The History of Web Design   8
        The Birth of the Internet   8
        Mosaic   9
        The Netscape Revolution   9
        Internet Explorer and Its Impact on Design   9

    Differences in Look and Feel   10
        Windows GUI   11
        Mac OS GUI   11
        Linux GUI   12
        Web Pages   13
        Java and Other Web Programs   14

    Summary   14

    Review Questions   15

CHAPTER 2   Concepts and Issues   17

Computing Terms   18
    Graphical User Interface (GUI)   18
    Operating Systems   18
    Parts of a GUI   19
    Internet   23
    World Wide Web   25

User Interface Models   27
    Batch Interface   28
    Command-Line Interface   28
    The Text User Interface   30
    Graphical User Interfaces   30
    Web Interfaces   32
    Interfaces That Integrate with These Models   34
    Other Interfaces   36

Design Improvements and Aggravations   38
    Windows Vista   38
    Mac OS X   39
    Linux   40
    Web Design Improvments   41
    What's Still Not Fixed   42

Future Plans   43
    Windows Vienna   43
    Mac OS   43
    Web Browsers and Their Impact on Design   43
    Up-and-Coming Interfaces   44

Usability Terms   47
    Usability Engineers   48
    Usability Scientists   48
    User Experience Professionals   48
    Types of Usability Design   48

User Analysis Terms   49
    The Goal-Directed Design Process   49
    Testing Methods   49

User Analysis Trends   50

Accessibility Issues   51
    Section 508 Accessibility   52
    Web Site Accessibility   52

Operating System Accessibility 54

Summary 55

Review Questions 57

CHAPTER 3   Making the Business Case **59**

Gaps Between Stakeholders 60
What Users Expect 61
What Engineers or Designers Expect 61
What Sales and Marketing People Expect 62
What Managers Expect 62

Developing a Business Case Framework 63

The Benefits of Good Design 64
Long-Term Production Costs 65
Lower Customer Support Costs 66
Greater Customer Retention 67

The Case for Profitability 67

Proving ROI 69
ROI Specifics 69
Calculate the Dollar Amount 70

The Usability Engineering Life Cycle 71
Phase 1: Requirements Analysis 72
Phase 2: Design, Testing, and Development 73
Phase 3: Installation and Feedback 75
The Never-Ending Process 76

The Case Study: Mike's Bikes 76

Summary 82

Review Questions 84

CHAPTER 4   Good Design **85**

Good Design Goals 86

Are Designers Against Users? 87
User Constraints 88
Designer Constraints 88
Bridging the Gap 89

Paper Prototyping and Storyboarding 90
What Paper Prototyping Is . . . and Isn't 91

Overcoming Skepticism   92
Advantages   93
Disadvantages   95

Good Documentation Design   96
Create a Documentation Plan   97

Why You Should Care About Good Design   104

Case Study: Creating a Paper Prototype Test   105

Summary   110

Review Questions   111

CHAPTER 5   How User Behave   **113**

The Psychology of User Actions   114
Psychological Types   115
The Four Primary Temperaments   117
The Seven Stages of Human Action   121

Knowledge: Brain Versus World   122

Task Structures   124

Conscious and Subconscious Behavior   125

Transforming Difficult Tasks into Simple Ones   126

Creating a Conceptual Model   127

Case Study: Interviewing to Establish the Conceptual Model   129

Summary   132

Review Questions   133

CHAPTER 6   Analyzing Your Users   **135**

The Users' Mental Model   136
The Result   138
Implementation Versus Mental Models   139

The Experience Bell Curve   140
Different Needs for Different Groups   141

Understanding the User's Goals   143

User and Task Analysis   146
Constructing Personas   147
Watching Users in Action   152

Persona Evaluation   154

Case Study: Producing a Primary Persona   156

Summary   160

Review Questions   161

CHAPER 7   Designing a User Interface   **163**

Designing the Persona-Based Interaction Framework   164
Real-World Requirements   166
Defining the Framework   166

Interaction Design   171
Applying Design Imperatives   171
Principles   172
Patterns   172

Software Postures   173

Interface Behaviors   177
Using the Mouse Pointer   178
Window Behaviors   181

Helping Users Find Information   186
Visual Cues   186
Audio Cues   187
Pop-Up Messages   187
Search Engines   188

Communicating with the Users   189
Making Features Easy to Find   189
Online Help   190
Assistants and Wizards   190

Refining the Form and Behavior   191

Case Study: Refining the Paper Prototype Test   192

Summary   194

Review Questions   196

CHAPTER 8   Designing a Web Site   **197**

Web Versus GUI: Similarities and Differences   198
GUI Rules   198
Web Rules   199

Internet-Based Applications   200

Web Myths   200
  Usage   201
  Design   202
  Accessibility   203

Web Postures   205
  Different Types of Web Sites   205

Why You Need Web Engineering   213
  "Back-End" Programming   213
  Form Processing   214
  Databases   215

Web Standards   215
  Colors and Text   215
  Graphics   216
  Navigation   217
  Bread Crumbs   217

The Four Rules   218
  Keep It Simple   218
  Keep It Consistent   218
  Keep It Current   219
  Keep Navigability to Three Clicks   219

When Do You Break the Rules?   219
  Breaking GUI Rules   219
  Breaking Web Rules   220

Case Study: Interface Navigation Features   220

Summary   222

Review Questions   223

CHAPTER 9   Usability   **225**

Selecting Techniques for Your Usability Test   226
  Observing, Listening to, and Engaging Users   226
  Other Methods of User Interaction   227

Defining Your Usability Test   228
  Goals and Concerns   229
  Picking Your Test Participants   229
  Selecting, Organizing, and Creating Test Scenarios   230
  Determining How to Measure Usability   231

Preparing Test Materials   232

Conducting the Usability Test   233
  Conducting a Pilot Test   233
  Honing Your Observation Skills   234
  Honing Your Interviewing Skills   236
  An Ongoing Relationship   238
  Caring for the Test Participants   239
  Conducting the Real Test   239

Analyzing and Presenting Usability Test Results   241
  Analyzing and Presenting the Data   241
  The Report   243
  The Presentation   245
  Preparing a Highlight Presentation   246
  Changing the Product and Process   247

Case Study: Implementing the Paper Prototype Test   248

Summary   251

Review Questions   252

APPENDIX A   Answers to Review Questions   **253**

APPENDIX B   Recommended Reading   **265**

Glossary   **267**

References   **273**

Index   **275**

Preface

Training is everything. The peach was once a bitter almond; cauliflower is nothing but cabbage with a college education.
—*Mark Twain*

In 2005, I sat down to redesign the usability course for the Online Technical Writing Certificate Program for California State University, Sacramento. I spent a few hours researching usability-related books from a number of Web sources that included book sites and the Society for Technical Communication. Then I got up to go to the kitchen to get my credit card so I could order a large number of books. That was the beginning of my journey.

The creation of that course was a tremendous journey. I augmented my existing knowledge a great deal during that journey, and I share that knowledge to a new group of students each semester. As I put together the course, I wondered why there wasn't a book that discussed current theory and practice of not only user interface design, but also usability design and testing that ensures that the interface design is useful. I talked with Carole McClendon, my literary agent, about expanding the course into a book, and she got me in touch with Addison-Wesley.

Acknowledgments

No book can be written alone, and a successful book is the product of cooperation between a number of great people. I want to start by thanking my literary agent, Carole McClendon, for her unflagging efforts to help me write books that are interesting to me and to my readers. She shows me her professionalism and dedication every day.

Next, I want to thank Kristin Weinberger, my project editor at Addison-Wesley who inherited the book on short notice and shepherded it through the writing and editing processes. Without her steady hand, you wouldn't be holding this book in your hands.

I also want to thank the group of editors and reviewers who looked at this book and provided me with invaluable feedback. This group includes Mike Hernandez, who is the keeper of the For Mere Mortals standard. I especially want to thank my good friend Tony Barcellos, who took time out of his busy schedule (including writing his own book) to review this book and provide helpful and humorous suggestions. I would also like to thank Lawrence Smith, Ben Shneiderman, Rebecca Riordan, and David Whiteman for their technical editing.

About the Author

Eric Butow is the CEO of Butow Communications Group (BCG), a technical writing and Web design firm based in Roseville, California.

Eric has authored or coauthored eight books since 2000, including *Master Visually Windows 2000 Server*, *Teach Yourself Visually Windows 2000 Server*, *FrontPage 2002 Weekend Crash Course*, *C#: Your Visual Blueprint*, *Creating Web Pages Bible*, *Dreamweaver MX 2004 Savvy*, *The PDF Book for Microsoft Office*, and *Special Edition Using Microsoft Windows Vista*. Eric has also been a technical editor for various computing books and has written articles for international publications including SD Times and Intercom, the magazine of the Society for Technical Communication.

Eric is also an online course developer and instructor. He has developed two Windows XP networking courses—one for Windows XP Home Edition users and the other for Windows XP Professional users—for Ed2Go. Eric has also developed RoboHelp and Windows Vista multimedia courses for Virtual Training Company (VTC). In addition, he is a course developer and instructor for the California State University, Sacramento College of Continuing Education Technical Writing Certificate Program.

When Eric isn't busy writing, teaching, or running his own business, you'll find him reading, hanging out with friends (usually at the nearest Starbucks or bookstore), or enjoying the company of his family at his parents' home in the Sierra foothills or the family vineyard in northern California.

Introduction

The growth of personal computing in the past two decades of the 20th century put a new emphasis on user interface design. As part of user interface design, companies began to focus on the usability of a product. The term *usability* has its roots in the 14th century, but as computing technology became prevalent in the 1980s, the definition of usability changed toward not only making something functional and usable, but also maximizing the entire user experience with a product.

Despite the power of good user interface and usability design, you have to convince managers that usability testing is vital to the success of the company now and in the future. It's important for you to understand how managers, marketers, and users think so you can craft a proposal that will win enthusiastic support for implementing usability testing in the company for which you work.

Therefore, it's important for anyone involved in usability testing, regardless of title, to have the business acumen to create the short-term return on investment (ROI) goals while creating the framework for long-term returns.

Who Should Read This Book

You don't need a previous background in user interface design to read this book. If you're just getting into user interface design and you're thinking about developing your own user interface, this book is a good starting point for you. It's much more advantageous for you to learn about user interface design from the beginning than to learn about it from your customers when they're unhappy with your product.

If you have been working in product or documentation development and you're ready to work on a new project, you should read this book. You probably have a feel for what your customers like, but you're not sure how to maximize the usability of your product for your customers. Or perhaps you're charged with creating documentation or training and you need to know what your customers expect not only from the product, but also from the information contained in the documentation or training modules. If this sounds like you, this is a book you should read.

This book is also appropriate if you have experience in the usability and user interface design fields. Although you may already know one or more of the theories and practices contained in this book, it can serve as a refresher. You will likely find nuggets of information you hadn't considered before as well as new ideas that you can apply to your product design and beyond.

The Purpose of This Book

This book is a primer that puts together the leading practices and ideas about user interface design and usability design and testing into a "big picture" view of how people can and should design and implement user interfaces that your customers will enjoy.

The book begins with grounding in user interfaces so you understand how we got from the beginnings of user interface design to where we are today. Then the book delves into designing user interfaces and usability testing for a product; that product can be a hardware product such as a printer, a software interface, or a Web site.

After you read this book, you will know the basics of the user interface design and usability design and testing fields. This book is only the beginning of your journey into usability and user interface design. If you want to dive in and indulge yourself in one or more of the theories and practices discussed in this book, be sure to read the books listed in Appendix B, "Recommended Reading."

How to Read This Book

I strongly recommend that you read this book in sequence from beginning to end. By doing so, you will keep everything in context, and you will see the big picture that is the user interface design process.

If you are reading this book to refresh your memory about certain topics, you could read just those chapters that are of interest to you. Each chapter is designed to stand on its own as much as possible.

How This Book Is Organized

Here's a brief overview of what you'll find in each chapter.

Chapter 1, "Brief Histories," gives you an overview of the history of graphical user interfaces (GUIs) and Web design as well as the differences in look and feel between different GUIs.

Chapter 2, "Concepts and Issues," covers computing terms, user interface models, usability and user analysis terms and trends, and accessibility issues.

Chapter 3, "Making the Business Case," covers making the case for profitability and understanding what your stakeholders want so you can make that case.

Chapter 4, "Good Design," covers good user design goals, the constraints faced by users and designers, and how to use paper prototyping and storyboarding to quickly test and work out design problems. This chapter also covers good documentation design, because documentation is the first line of customer support for your product.

Chapter 5, "How Users Behave," covers the psychology of user actions, how people bring their knowledge to a task, and how they create a conceptual model of the world.

Chapter 6, "Analyzing Your Users," covers the user's mental model and where users fit on a usability bell curve so you can understand their goals and tasks.

Chapter 7, "Designing a User Interface," discusses the creation of a persona-based interaction framework that will help you identify who your users are and what they want from your user interface.

Chapter 8, "Designing a Web Site," explains the differences between an application designed for the Web and a GUI application, discusses design myths surrounding the Web, and provides Web design standards and rules.

Chapter 9, "Usability," covers usability test design and the testing process itself so you can get valuable feedback from your users about your interface.

Appendix A, "Answers to Review Questions," contains the answers to all the review questions in Chapters 1 through 9.

Appendix B, "Recommended Reading," provides a list of books that you should read if you are interested in pursuing an in-depth study of user interface and usability design.

Glossary contains concise definitions of various words and phrases used throughout the book.

1

Brief Histories

The past does not repeat itself, but it rhymes.
—Mark Twain

Topics Covered in This Chapter

The History of Graphical User Interfaces

The History of Web Design

Differences in Look and Feel

Before I discuss user interface design, there is a backstory that tells you how we got from the beginnings of graphical user interfaces (GUIs) and how that led to the advent of the Web. You will learn that, as the Web became more popular, Web design and usability became ever more important. You will also learn about the history of Web design conventions. Finally, you'll learn about the differences in the look and feel between GUIs and Web interfaces.

The History of Graphical User Interfaces

Jeremy Reimer, in his 2005 online article "A History of the GUI," (http://arstechnica.com/articles/paedia/gui.ars) traces the history of GUIs to the early 1930s when an engineer named Vannevar Bush created the *memex*, which was a device with two touch screen displays, a keyboard, and a scanner so users could search for knowledge much like the links we use today on the Web.

Bush's writings about the memex device and other user-computer issues from the 1930s through World War II inspired a young engineer named Douglas Engelbart (Reimer, 2005). Engelbart worked for the Stanford

Research Institute and received funding from the Air Force for developing the first GUI. Engelbart showed off the work by his research team to more than 1,000 computing professionals in 1968.

That demonstration of the NLS (oN-Line System) featured many of the hardware and software features in GUIs we know today: a keyboard, a mouse, networked computers and collaboration between network users, multiple windows, full-screen document editing, email, hypertext links, and video conferencing (Reimer, 2005). The system was rather primitive compared with what we use today, but the demonstration represented such a dramatic leap in computing usability that it blew everyone in the audience away.

The demonstration also concerned the Xerox engineers in attendance, because they could see that Engelbart's system was the future—a paperless future. For a company that became prominent with the development of the photocopier in 1959, a paperless future meant certain death for Xerox. Management at Xerox decided that they needed to control this new technology. Therefore, Xerox created the Palo Alto Research Center (PARC) in 1970 in Palo Alto, California. The company's mission was to develop the first commercially available GUI.

In this section, we'll talk about the first commercial GUI based on PARC research in the 1970s through the rise of Microsoft Windows during the 1990s. The rise of Windows cemented the GUI as the standard user interface for computer users and also made knowledge of a GUI a requirement for people looking for a job in the computing field. This section also discusses other significant GUI operating systems in use today: the Mac OS and Linux.

Xerox Alto

The Xerox Alto, developed by PARC in 1973, was the first personal computer with a GUI interface. The Alto was the computer that showed off the radical leaps in computing interface technology PARC developed, such as the mouse and the first GUI. The monitor was only black and white, and the computer itself was the size of a small refrigerator, but it was the first desktop computer—four years before the introduction of personal computers by Apple, Tandy, and Commodore. (However, unlike the personal computers introduced in 1977, the Alto computer unit was so large that you had to put it underneath your desk and just have the monitor, keyboard, and mouse on top of your desk—just like many of today's desktop computers, although today's computers are much smaller than the Alto.)

Unfortunately, Xerox didn't know how to market the Alto and its successor, the Star, which was introduced in 1981. That left PARC's ideas to be cherry-picked by Apple Computer in the early 1980s for the development of its new computer—the Lisa.

Apple Macintosh

Apple consulted with Xerox in the late 1970s, and from those consultations, the Apple Lisa computer was born in early 1983. The Lisa failed, but a sister project, the Macintosh, was introduced in 1984 and quickly gained a small but enthusiastic customer base. The Macintosh, commonly known as the Mac, eventually overtook sales of Apple's original computer series, the Apple II, and its successors, the Apple II Plus, the Apple IIe, the Apple IIc, and the Apple IIGS. (That list also includes the business-oriented Apple III, which initially had a 100 percent failure rate and quickly became a laughingstock.)

Despite its low market share, the Mac has a devoted following that, as of this writing, is growing thanks in part to Apple's iPod music player. The Mac OS has long been considered the superior operating system, especially over Microsoft Windows. For many years, Apple was considered the computer of choice in schools, and like many schoolchildren, I had my first exposure to using a GUI with the Mac.

However, Windows has now resolved its shortcomings to the point that Apple has adapted some Windows features for its use, such as the Dock that appears at the bottom of the screen so you can quickly access programs and documents.

The tenth and latest version of the Mac OS, called Mac OS X (X being the Roman numeral for 10), was a radical departure from all previous versions of the Mac OS. Indeed, when Mac OS X was released in 2001, it was a completely different operating system—Apple not only changed the core of the system to one based on the UNIX operating system, but it also unveiled a new interface called Aqua. Aqua sports bright colors and translucent features such as title bars and "gel" buttons that look similar to cold medicine gelcaps, as shown in Figure 1.1.

As with most everything Apple CEO Steve Jobs has touched since he returned as CEO in 1997, Aqua was an instant hit and started to affect not only Web page design, but also the design of Microsoft Windows. Indeed, the new version of Windows, Vista, uses many design styles (such as translucent title bars) that are similar to Aqua.

Figure 1.1   *Gelcap-style buttons in a Mac OS X window.*

Apple has tweaked both Mac OS X and Aqua as subsequent major "point" releases—that is, versions 10.1, 10.2, 10.3, and so on—were released. For example, Apple has toned down some of the brighter features of Aqua and has added features such as the Windows-inspired Dock. Apple named its Mac OS X point releases after big cats, and as of this writing, the next major version of Mac OS X, called Leopard, will be released in early 2007—around the same time as the release of Windows Vista. The current version of Mac OS X is Tiger, as shown in Figure 1.2.

Figure 1.2   *The Mac OS X Tiger Aqua interface.*

Microsoft Windows

Microsoft announced Windows in 1983 in response to an announcement from the makers of the VisiCalc spreadsheet (then the most popular program for business) that it would create a GUI for the IBM PC called VisiOn. VisiOn never came to be, but Windows 1.0 was released in 1985.

Unfortunately, the hardware was far from capable of managing the demands of a GUI, but as Intel released the Intel 80286 and 80386 chips, Microsoft continued to refine Windows 2.0 for use with the 80286 and 80386 chips. Even so, the GUI was still clunky, and there wasn't much of a difference in look and feel between Windows 2.0 and its preceding version.

By 1990, more businesses were using computers with the 80386 chip, and the 80386 (along with its math coprocessor, the optional Intel 80387) had more than enough power to handle a GUI. What's more, advances in video processing technology provided greater video resolution and more available colors to view than ever before. Microsoft took advantage of the situation by releasing Windows 3.0 in May 1990.

Windows 3.0 had a much cleaner, revamped interface, and it could *multi-task*, meaning that users could perform more than one task at a time. The computing media immediately proclaimed Windows 3.0 good enough, and like many users, I got a free copy with my new 386-based computer and also found Windows to be good enough. Because of the bundling of Windows with new computers and positive word of mouth, users rapidly abandoned the text-based DOS (Disk Operating System) they had been using since the IBM PC was introduced in 1981, and Windows quickly became the de facto GUI standard for IBM PC and compatible computers. Microsoft released two major point releases—Windows 3.1 in 1992 and Windows 3.11 for Workgroups in 1993, the latter of which was the network-capable version of Windows.

Microsoft revamped Windows entirely in 1995 with the release of Windows 95. This version introduced the Windows taskbar, Start button, and *visual motif* (which is a central idea or theme) that have been constant in subsequent versions, including Windows Vista. Microsoft also released three major point releases since the release of Windows 95: two versions of Windows 98 as well as Windows Me, the last release of the "consumer" version of Windows.

At the same time, Microsoft was developing its "professional" version of Windows, called Windows NT, beginning in 1993. Windows NT was built on a new core from the ground up, unlike the consumer version of Windows that built the Windows graphical interface on top of its DOS core. Windows NT was also the network-ready version of Windows, and soon Windows NT and its successor, Windows 2000, supplanted Novell NetWare as the networking software of choice.

In 2001, Microsoft released Windows XP, which was built on the NT core. This new operating system included a streamlined interface and was offered in two versions: the Home edition for consumers, and the Professional edition for businesses. The primary difference was that the Professional edition contained more network tools, as Microsoft wanted to limit the Home edition to use in small, peer-to-peer networks.

In late 2006, Microsoft released the first major release of Windows in five years: Windows Vista, as shown in Figure 1.3. The primary changes in Vista are a new interface called Aero that offers translucent features similar to Aqua, some streamlined methods in the interface for getting things done (such as changing your display settings), an enhanced address bar that lets you know your current location in relation to other windows, more immediate search features, and more security features.

Figure 1.3   *The Windows Vista desktop.*

Linux

In 1983, a programmer at MIT, Richard Stallman, founded the free software movement by developing the GNU operating system, which incorporates many features of the UNIX operating system. The goal of the GNU operating system was to develop a body of free software that people could use. By free, Stallman meant free to use, change, and redistribute. Stallman himself expanded on the movement he started by co-founding the Free Software Foundation in 1985 with the goal of making computer software free for everyone.

By 1991, the GNU operating system was only missing one component—the kernel, which is the most important component of all. Without a kernel, an operating system can't manage system resources and communications between a computer's hardware and software components. Linus Torvalds, a Finnish programmer, filled in this gap in 1991 by creating the free GNU kernel he called Linux. Linux was released in 1991 as free, *open-source* software, which means that other programmers can take the operating system and add to it. In 1993, two years after Linux was released, the first distribution was available for people to download. A *distribution* is a Linux package you can install on your computer.

The combined GNU/Linux operating system, which became widely known as simply Linux, grew popular because it was stable, and the operating system soon became a popular choice for running computer servers; today, about 25 percent of computer servers run Linux. However, businesses that ran servers were skittish about running software that wasn't supported, and the software was hard to install. Several companies offered distributions that met this need. The most popular of these distributions was produced by Red Hat, Inc. Red Hat not only provided a packaged product with installation software, but it also offered a free GUI environment developed by two Mexican programmers, Miguel de Icaza and Federico Mena, and sustained and improved by programmers around the world: GNOME.

By the late 1990s, two GUI environments were available for Linux: KDE and GNOME; the latter is shown in Figure 1.4. Both GUIs look similar to Windows and have been recognized as providing a user experience on a par with Windows XP. As Linux became a popular option for companies and users who wanted a more stable operating system, didn't want to use the Microsoft operating system, or found the Macintosh platform too expensive, having two Linux GUIs to choose from helped advance the Linux cause. Market researcher IDC predicts that Linux will have 7 percent of the operating system market share by 2008.

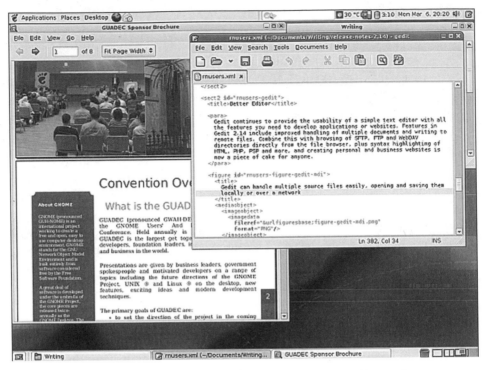

Figure 1.4   *The GNOME desktop that ships with Red Hat Linux, the most popular Linux distribution.*

The History of Web Design

Web design has had a significant effect on the design of user interfaces, in large part because many computer users access the Web. Therefore, the Web is one effective way to get your product in front of the computer-using masses.

The Birth of the Internet

The Internet was born from Sputnik, the first man-made satellite launched by the Soviet Union in 1957. After Sputnik's launch, the U.S. Defense Department immediately took steps to bring back the U.S. technological edge. One result of that effort was ARPANET, the Defense Department computer network that was launched in 1969. (ARPA stands for Advanced Research Projects Agency.) Based on the work constructing the ARPANET, the U.S. National Science Foundation constructed the first wide-area network (WAN) using TCP/IP, the Internet's standard transmission protocol, in 1983.

Mosaic

In 1989, Tim Berners-Lee created HTML, HTTP, and the first few Web pages. By 1991, the European Organization for Nuclear Research (known by its European acronym CERN) publicized the work of Berners-Lee and the World Wide Web project. To spur interest in the World Wide Web in the academic and technical worlds, where the Internet was used, the National Center for Supercomputing Applications (NCSA) at the University of Illinois at Urbana-Champaign released Mosaic, the first Web browser with a graphics interface.

Funding for Mosaic was provided by the U.S. government under the High-Performance Computing Act of 1991, which Senator Al Gore authored. (This was the basis for Gore's 1999 comment that he took the initiative in creating the Internet, which was widely lampooned.) NCSA originally released Mosaic to run on the X Window system, a toolkit for creating GUIs that run on the UNIX operating system, in April 1993. By the end of 1993, Mosaic was available on the Macintosh and Windows operating systems.

The Netscape Revolution

Mosaic spurred greater interest in the World Wide Web outside academic and technical circles. As Internet interest grew, the developers of Mosaic started their own company, Netscape, and produced the successor to Mosaic: Netscape Navigator. With the Internet's growing popularity and the introduction of community Internet service providers (ISPs) in many metropolitan areas in the U.S., Netscape Navigator became an immediate hit—so much so that Netscape's stock price went to astronomical heights when the stock went up for sale in 1996. What's more, the user interface for Netscape set the standard for Web browser design that is still largely in use today.

Internet Explorer and Its Impact on Design

Microsoft took notice of both the rise of Netscape and the World Wide Web and was determined not to be left out. Microsoft released its first version of Internet Explorer in 1995 but really didn't begin to overtake Netscape Navigator in market share until 1998. Later, a federal court determined that Microsoft had improperly bundled Internet Explorer with Windows to gain an unfair advantage over Netscape Navigator, but by the time that ruling was handed down, it was far too late for Netscape. Indeed, in 1999, America Online (now AOL) bought Netscape, and today Netscape has only a small portion of the Web browser market.

Curiously, Internet Explorer has had an impact on user interface design for two reasons: it is used by about 90 percent of Web users, and Microsoft failed to continually upgrade Internet Explorer. Version 6 of Internet Explorer was released in 2001, and Version 7 wasn't released until 2006. This five-year gap left room for other companies to innovate, and other browsers— including Netscape, Opera, and Firefox—were released between 2001 and 2006. Each of these "alternative" browsers brought improvements in the interface, such as tabbed browser pages so you can easily move from one Web page to another. Internet Explorer 7 now incorporates many of these "alternative" browser innovations. You'll learn more about the effect that Internet Explorer has had on Web design in Chapter 2, "Concepts and Issues."

There are subtle differences in HTML code between browsers, and Microsoft's Active Server Pages (ASP) technology that is used to enhance the functionality of Web sites does not work on Firefox and Opera browsers. If the Web browser market becomes more competitive over time, Web technologies may change as well, and that in turn will affect Web design going forward.

Differences in Look and Feel

The desktop metaphor implemented by GUI operating systems (where you place objects on the screen much like you place items on a desktop) is still in use today. Although all major GUI operating systems retain the power of the desktop metaphor in that they reduce the number of tasks the user has to remember, GUIs also constrain the designer by requiring the interface to conform to standards designed for that operating system. What's more, all the GUIs discussed in this section have many small differences among them.

Therefore, when you design a user interface, you have to understand how the interface works in the operating system for which you're designing it. If you're going to write a software interface for several different platforms, such as Windows and the Mac OS, you should be aware of the differences and similarities between each platform.

There's even more confusion when you design for the Web, because the Web has a different set of design parameters and constraints, as well as for Java and related Web programs, because a Java interface looks different from other interfaces, too.

Windows GUI

Microsoft has introduced several interface features that are unique to Windows 95 and subsequent versions—including Windows Vista—although other GUI operating systems have copied these Windows features in whole or in part. These features include the following:

- The taskbar, which displays all open programs as buttons and displays the Start button, which lets you open programs or view the status of services. Users display the program or document by clicking on the button.
- The Start button, which opens a menu that provides access to all programs in Windows as well as Windows functions, such as viewing a list of printers installed on the computer.
- Toolbars, which add icons to the taskbar so you can open programs quickly. For example, the Quick Launch toolbar adds icons to your toolbar so you can minimize all programs and return to the desktop and add program shortcuts, such as to Internet Explorer.

Mac OS GUI

The Mac OS GUI interface is the interface that other GUIs have tried to keep up with, and the Mac OS GUI underwent a dramatic change with the introduction of version 10, which is called Mac OS X—X standing for 10. This new version sports the Aqua interface that includes differences in look and feel as well as features:

- The Dock is a new feature in Mac OS X. The Dock is similar to the taskbar in that it lets you add programs and documents to it for easy reference. Like the Windows taskbar, the Dock appears at the bottom of the screen, not in the Mac OS menu bar.
- As with past versions of Mac OS, the menu bar appears at the top of the screen. Menu bar options change as you open new windows. For example, when you open Microsoft Word, the menu bar reflects a number of menu options available in Word. The clock appears at the right side of the menu bar just as it does in the Windows taskbar. The menu bar is similar to the Start menu in that it also provides access to Mac OS X functions, and more functions are available if you're in the Mac OS X desktop.

- The Dock doesn't provide specific toolbars as the Windows taskbar does, but the Dock does group different icons together and separates these groups with lines. The Dock groups applications on its left side and minimized windows and documents on its right, as shown in Figure 1.5. Like the Windows toolbar, you can drag program icons to the Dock to create a shortcut to that program on the Dock.

Figure 1.5 *The Mac OS X desktop with the Dock and an open window.*

Linux GUI

The two major Linux GUI operating systems are GNOME and KDE. The key to Linux becoming more widely accepted as a desktop operating system is the GUI, so it's no surprise that both GUIs are similar to Windows and to each other.

For example, both GNOME and KDE include a taskbar, toolbars, the title bar and window manipulation buttons set up the same way as in Windows, and a Start-like button just like Windows. GNOME and KDE do have some minor differences, however. For example, KDE contains a multipage taskbar so that when you click on a page number in the taskbar, you see the buttons associated with that page. GNOME is generally considered to be the most integrated and "mature" GUI, but KDE is accepted more by new users to Linux because KDE looks more like Windows, as shown in Figure 1.6.

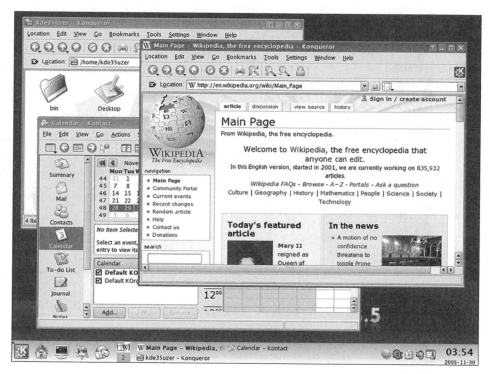

Figure 1.6   *The KDE desktop.*

Web Pages

Web pages can have many different interfaces, but they are still bound by design rules and programming restrictions, as discussed in Chapter 2. Even so, it's not hard to design a Web site that looks much like the user interface design of your software, such as hyperlinks represented as tabbed buttons on the MSN.com Web site shown in Figure 1.7.

Flash, an Adobe product that's the de facto standard for creating animated graphics on the Web, is beginning to blur the line between the desktop and the Web application. One of the uses of Flash is to create a Web application that looks more like the desktop, and integrating that interface with a Rich Internet Application System (RIAS), which uses the client's computer to perform functions. Programmers are also using AJAX, which is a combination of

Figure 1.7   *The MSN.com Web site has tabbed buttons on the top that provide a familiar user experience.*

Web technologies including JavaScript and XML, to create interactive Web sites.

Java and Other Web Programs

Programs that run on the Web may reflect the look and feel standards set by the programming language. Java is an obvious case in point. Java programs often have their own look and feel for buttons, window manipulation, and typefaces.

Summary

This chapter began with a discussion of what a graphical user interface (GUI) is, the major GUI operating systems available today and their history, the parts of a GUI, and their functions. It's important to learn about the history of Web design so that you understand how we got from the early days of GUI design to what we know and use today.

This chapter then moved on to a historical look at Web design and the complexities of the interaction between Web pages and browsers. You learned about the beginnings of the Internet and how it led to the creation of the first browser, Mosaic, and how the development of that browser led to the first commercially available browser: Netscape Navigator. Then you learned about how Microsoft developed Internet Explorer, which not only became the dominant browser but also forced competitors to innovate when Microsoft paused in further developing Internet Explorer.

The chapter ended with a discussion about the differences in the look and feel between different major GUIs, including Microsoft Windows, Mac OS X, and Linux. It introduced design issues regarding Web pages and how it's not hard to design a Web site with software interface designs, as well. Finally, this first chapter covered Web-based programs written in specific languages, particularly Java.

This brief historical look at GUIs and the Web provides necessary background for the discussion of the user interface issues covered in Chapter 2.

Review Questions

Now it's time to review what you've learned in this chapter before you move on to Chapter 2. Ask yourself the following questions, and refer to Appendix A, "Answers to Review Questions," to double-check your answers.

1. Why is it important to learn about the history of graphical user interfaces?
2. Who developed the first GUI?
3. Why was the NLS so important?
4. What was the first personal computer with a GUI interface?
5. Why did Linux become so popular?
6. What was the first Web browser with a GUI?
7. Why did Internet Explorer have such an impact on design?
8. As a user interface designer, why do you need to know how a user interface works?
9. Why do you need to know about the differences between GUIs?
10. Why do you need to know about the differences between a GUI and a Web interface?

Concepts and Issues

"If you don't crack the shell, you can't eat the nut."
—Persian Proverb

Topics Covered in This Chapter

Computing Terms

User Interface Models

Design Improvements and Aggravations

Future Plans

Usability Terms

User Analysis Terms

User Analysis Trends

Accessibility Issues

There are numerous models for interfacing with a computer. These not only include the graphical user interface (GUI) that you're probably used to using on your own computer, but also interfaces that are growing in popularity, such as touch screen interfaces.

Before I discuss models, it's important for you to get a solid grounding in the terminology that I will use throughout this book. These terms, as well as the meaning behind them, are important for you to understand before you learn about user interface design. Although some of the following terms may be familiar, it never hurts to reacquaint yourself with them. There are also other terms that you need to learn, and I will define each term as you go through this book. Finally, there is a glossary at the back of this book for use as a reference.

This chapter continues with a discussion of the history of user interface models so you can understand how you interact with a computer. Current user interfaces have recently implemented design improvements, but aggravations remain, which you will learn about. There's an exciting future in user interfaces, and this chapter discusses what's in development and how those interfaces may look different from what we're using today.

After you read about user interface models, you will learn about user design and analysis terms as well as user analysis trends. One of those trends is to design current and future interfaces to be as accessible as possible to reach the most users possible. You will learn not only about accessibility issues but also guidelines and regulations of which you should be aware before you design your user interface.

Computing Terms

I will refer to numerous computing terms throughout this book. It's important that you know about and understand these terms because they are used to express and define user interface design.

Graphical User Interface (GUI)

A *graphical user interface*, which is more popularly known by its acronym *GUI* (pronounced "gooey"), is a system for interacting with a computer by manipulating graphics elements and text. These graphics elements include windows, buttons, menus, and icons. Because all programs that operate in a GUI have many of the same elements, it's easier to use those programs, so you quickly learn to relate GUI elements to real-world equivalents.

Operating Systems

The computing world today has three major GUI operating systems. Although other operating systems are available, such as text-based systems that use a command-line interface (CLI), the following three operating systems are used by nearly all computer users today.

- **Windows**—Microsoft Windows is the de facto standard GUI operating system. About 90 percent of computer users use the Windows operating system.

- **Mac OS**—Mac OS is the operating system for Apple Computer's Macintosh computers. Unlike Windows and Linux, Mac OS is hardware-specific—meaning you must purchase a Macintosh computer to use the Mac OS. About 4 percent of computer users use the Mac OS.

- **Linux**—Linux is an operating system that is distributed for free, although you can purchase versions of Linux produced by companies such as Red Hat (www.redhat.com) and Novell (www.novell.com). Linux doesn't have a built-in GUI, but these paid versions usually come with a Linux GUI such as GNOME or the K Desktop Environment (KDE). About 3 percent of desktop users use Linux. However, because Linux is considered to be more stable than Windows, about 25 percent of network servers run Linux.

Parts of a GUI

No matter what GUI operating system you use, there are standard parts of a GUI. These parts are commonly called *widgets*, which are components that the computer user interacts with to perform tasks.

Windows

A *window*, as shown in Figure 2.1, is an area on the screen that is usually rectangular in shape and contains an interface that displays output and allows you to enter information. Different windows can contain different functionality. For example, one window contains a Web browser you use to visit Web pages, and another window contains a word processing program to type, save, and print a letter. Windows typically have a border, and they can be *minimized* (hidden) or *maximized* (enlarged to the screen size), moved around the computer desktop, and closed.

There are two different types of window interfaces: single document interfaces (SDIs) and multiple-document interfaces (MDIs). In an SDI, you can open several windows that run the same program, such as when you have several Web browser windows open, with each browser displaying a different Web site. In an MDI, there can be several child windows within a parent window, such as when you have several documents open in a word processor. Chapter 7, "Designing a User Interface," discusses SDIs and MDIs in more detail.

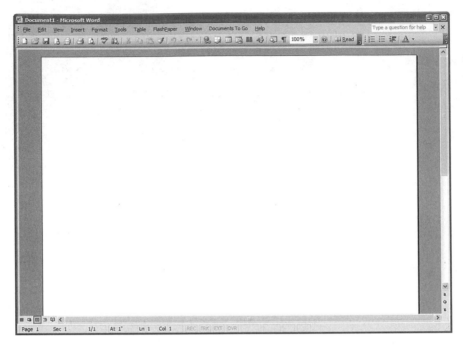

Figure 2.1 *An example of a window.*

Buttons

A *button*, as shown in Figure 2.2, is one way to issue a command. Buttons can take different forms, from clicking **OK** to confirm an action to clicking **Print** to print a document or Web page to your printer. Typically, buttons are rectangular, and when you activate or deactivate the button, the system depicts the appearance of a real-world button going up and down.

Figure 2.2 *An example of a button.*

Menus

A *menu*, as shown in Figure 2.3, is a list of commands that give you options for issuing commands to the program. The common type of menu is the drop-down menu; when you click on a menu name, the menu options appear to drop down underneath the menu name so that you can select an option. Modern operating systems also use the pop-up menu, where you click on a location in a window or on the screen (usually with the right mouse button), and a menu with options appears where you clicked the mouse button.

Menus provide access to different parts of a program or different parts of the operating system. In the example in Figure 2.3, the File menu in Microsoft Excel provides access to a number of commands, such as printing the current spreadsheet.

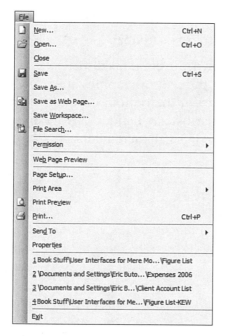

Figure 2.3 *An example of a menu.*

Toolbars

A *toolbar*, as shown in Figure 2.4, is a row, column, or toolbox that contains buttons and other widgets. When you click on one of these icons or buttons, the program initiates the corresponding function. Toolbars often appear along the top of a window below the menu bar or in a separate floating window. In the example in Figure 2.4, when you open Microsoft Excel, you see a toolbar with buttons that allows you to access commands, such as opening a new spreadsheet.

Figure 2.4   *An example of a toolbar.*

Scrollbars

A *scrollbar*, as shown in Figure 2.5, lets you view continuous text and graphics in a window if all the text and graphics in the area are too large to be displayed in that area. The scrollbar is a long rectangular area usually on the right edge (and in some cases the bottom) of the window. You can drag the scroll box up and down the *trough* of the scrollbar.

As you drag the scrollbar up and down, the contents displayed in the window move up and down with the bar. If the text or graphics are too wide for the screen, a horizontal scrollbar appears at the bottom edge of the window. In addition to the scroll box, a scrollbar usually includes arrow buttons at the ends for adjusting the scroll position in small increments.

Figure 2.5   *An example of a scrollbar.*

Taskbars

A *taskbar*, as shown in Figure 2.6, is a bar at the bottom of the screen by default (although you can move it elsewhere) that opens and monitors applications. The taskbar has been a standard in all versions of Microsoft Windows since Windows 95. The taskbar contains buttons and icons that represent your currently open windows that are not visible. Not all taskbar widgets are accessible; some widgets are only visible to provide information about a program or service.

Figure 2.6　*An example of a taskbar.*

Internet

The *Internet* is the worldwide system of interconnected computer networks that is accessible to the public. The Internet has had a significant effect on user interface design, so this book will touch on several Internet terms as well.

World Wide Web

The *World Wide Web*, also known as *the Web* or by its acronym *WWW*, is an information-sharing space on the Internet that you access through a Web browser. The Web is not the same as the Internet; it is a space where people can read and write information and share that information with others.

Web Browsers

A *Web browser*, as shown in Figure 2.7, is a software program that displays information on a Web page and lets you interact with that Web page, such as filling out a form that the Web page sends to the company hosting the Web site when you click the form's **Submit** button. Many Web browsers are available. According to the Wikipedia Web site article about Web site usage (http://en.wikipedia.org/wiki/Usage_share_of_web_browsers), between 83 and 86 percent of users use Internet Explorer for Windows and the Mac OS for Web browsing as of mid-2006.

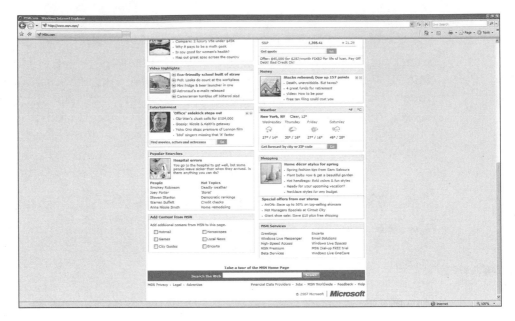

Figure 2.7 *An example of a Web browser—MSN.com.*

URL

The *Uniform Resource Locator*, known popularly as *URL* or as *Web address*, is a sequence of characters that describes the location of a Web page, site, or other resource on the Internet. A URL combines four different pieces of information to retrieve Web sites, and these pieces must appear in the exact order required for the browser to find the Web site you want. For example, the Microsoft Web site URL is http://www.microsoft.com.

HTML, Java, and Other Languages

Hypertext Markup Language (HTML) is the standard language for creating Web pages and sites. However, as a simple markup language, HTML is limited in its functionality As the Web has matured, new languages have been developed to provide more features and greater functionality to Web sites.

Java is a platform-independent programming language. *Platform-independent* means that any computer will be able to run programs written in Java. While initially widely embraced, Java has become less popular for programming Web sites, having been replaced in recent years by other programming languages, including Adobe's Flash for animations, PHP and JavaScript for programming, as well as Microsoft's Active Server Pages (ASP) technology.

The most popular of these latest technologies are PHP, Flash, and JavaScript. JavaScript was developed by Netscape, a company that pioneered the first commercially successful Web browser. JavaScript lets you add scripting language within the Web page itself, but despite the JavaScript name, JavaScript bears only a distant relationship to the Java language. JavaScript and HTML are integral components of *Dynamic HTML* (DHTML), which is a collection of technologies to create interactive and animated Web sites. *AJAX* (a term for Asynchronous JavaScript and XML) is also a popular collection of technologies for creating interactive and animated Web sites. It's so popular, in fact, that Microsoft has designed its Atlas technology to connect with ASP to implement AJAX functionality.

PHP has become the preferred Web programming language over JavaScript because it's free to use, relatively easy to learn, and recognized by all Web browsers.

Flash is a program that is owned by Adobe, a company that originally pioneered the PostScript printing language for controlling laser printers. Flash became popular in the late 1990s because it was flexible and relatively easy to create good-looking animated graphics to place in a Web site. Flash also comes with its own scripting language, ActionScript, that you can program from within the Flash program.

JavaScript, PHP, Flash, and Java are all designed to provide greater functionality than HTML, the standard language for creating Web sites. These languages not only provide animations that Web site visitors can view, but they also use their capabilities as actual programming languages to connect to other components that the user doesn't see. For example, a Web site that lets you shop for items online includes components that check the company database to see if a product is in stock, processes your credit card number, and connects to a shipping company Web site to ship the product to you.

World Wide Web

When you visit the World Wide Web using a Web browser, there are a number of features both in the browser and on the Web page of which you should be aware.

Hyperlinks

Hyperlinks are references to other documents on the Internet. You can attach a hyperlink, as shown in Figure 2.8, to one or more words in text, and you can attach hyperlinks to a graphic. In Figure 2.8, you see a hyperlink attached to the Pearson Education title at the top of the MSN.com page. Text hyperlinks are called *embedded links*, and embedded links usually have a distinctive style. (The standard embedded link style is to underline the word and color the word blue.)

An embedded link

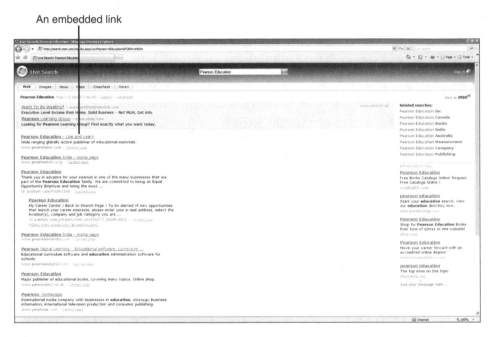

Figure 2.8   *An example of a hyperlink.*

Toolbars

A *toolbar* in your Web browser, as shown in Figure 2.9, is the same as a toolbar in any other application. The toolbar contains a row of icons that represent commonly used functions in the browser. When you click on one of the icons, the browser performs the function. For example, if you click the Back icon in Internet Explorer, the last Web page you viewed appears in the Internet Explorer window.

Figure 2.9   *An example of a toolbar in your Web browser.*

Address Bar

The Address bar appears near the top of your browser window, as shown in Figure 2.10. The Address bar is where you type the URL for the Web site you want to visit. If you navigate to subpages within a site, the URL for that page appears in the Address bar automatically so you see your exact location.

Figure 2.10   *An example of the Address bar.*

Navigation Bar/Button

Browsers let you navigate back and forth between pages using Back and Forward buttons in the toolbar, as shown in Figure 2.11. The Back button contains an icon that points to the left and displays the previous page you viewed. The Forward button contains an icon that points to the right and displays the last page you viewed before you clicked the Back button.

Figure 2.11   *An example of a navigation bar with buttons.*

User Interface Models

Eric Raymond, in his e-book *The Art of Unix Usability* (2004), categorized the history of user interface models into three distinct eras:

- Batch interfaces, which were used from the advent of the ENIAC computer in 1945 through 1968.
- The text, or CLI, in use from 1969 to 1983.
- The GUI, in use from 1984 through the present.

Use of these three types of interfaces didn't just disappear from one era to the next. Most users of IBM PC and compatible computers in the 1980s continued to use the CLI in DOS, the Disk Operating System, until many of those users migrated to the Windows GUI in the early 1990s. And the GUI has its roots in the Xerox Alto that was developed in the 1970s. Even so, computers with these interfaces didn't enter the mainstream of computing until the first year of each corresponding era.

Batch Interface

The batch interface was the first type of interface available for computers. These weren't personal computers by any means—they were used in government facilities, universities, and large businesses, and many of these computers took up large rooms. These computers had one or more interfaces that let users preprogram specially formatted cards with punch holes, like the punch holes in a three-hole punch paper. These "punch cards" were punched with specific numbers of punches in a specific pattern that the computer would recognize. Typically, the pattern of holes that composed a particular character or operator ran vertically on the card. Each card would more or less correspond to what we later would think of as a command on the command line or a line of code in a file (although some cards were used to control the batch job). The so-called job cards guided the processing of the deck of cards. The cards would be read in a card reader that supplied the information to the computer to process.

The problem with the batch interface is that you couldn't interact with the computer while the computer was processing the cards. If there was a problem with the cards, the operation would stop, and you would have to submit a new card with the corrected information. It could easily take several runs—and several days—to get your program to work.

Command-Line Interface

A CLI displays a command prompt, which lets the user know that the computer is ready for input. The user can then type in a command using the keyboard and submit the command for processing, usually by pressing the Enter key. The computer then processes the command and provides text output. A command can also call a file containing a series of commands or code to be processed.

The CLI traces its roots back to the 1950s, when teletype machines and computer monitors began to appear with newer, faster computers. In the 1970s, mainframe and minicomputer interfaces were changed over from cards to paper-based and then CRT monitor-based CLI interfaces. The CLI provided the possibility of interactivity with the computer (you could still use it to run programs in batch fashion and often did because it was cheaper, i.e., it consumed less of the processor's time, which was a precious resource at the time), which was a quantum leap in usability over the batch card interface. The biggest drawback to a CLI is that you have to learn an arcane list of commands to instruct the computer to do what you want.

DOS for the IBM PC and compatible computers was the most popular operating system with a CLI because PC-compatibles were the most popular computers. DOS included a rudimentary scripting language, called *batch programming* (not to be confused with the batch interface), that allowed users to create a small program, called a *batch file*, that included a number of commands. When the user ran the batch file, DOS would run the commands in the batch file in the order they appeared in the file.

Although Windows supplanted DOS as the operating system of choice, Windows didn't initially replace DOS. Instead, Windows was a "shell" on top of DOS that let you invoke commands without having to type anything into the DOS interface. DOS didn't go away, and you still can access an emulation of DOS from Windows by opening the command window, as shown in Figure 2.12.

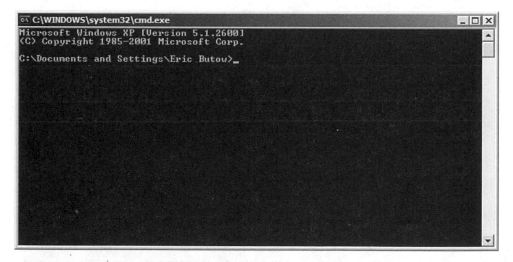

Figure 2.12   *The Windows command window.*

Even though GUIs have supplanted CLIs as the interface of choice, operating systems with CLIs are still used by many network administrators and programmers, who find that the CLI helps them be more productive. Windows XP still contains the command window, and people who have used DOS in the past will feel right at home. UNIX-based operating systems including Mac OS X and Linux also allow you to access a command window to access the operating system using a CLI. These UNIX-based CLIs also include scripting capabilities.

The development of CLIs isn't standing still. Microsoft is developing a "CLI on steroids," called PowerShell, that includes a scripting language based on Microsoft's C# (that's "C sharp") programming language and keystroke reduction features. PowerShell will be used extensively in Microsoft Exchange Server 2007, which is the next version of Microsoft's messaging and collaborative software system.

UNIX-based CLIs are also continuously under development. For example, the popular Bash (Bourne Again SHell) shell, which was first developed in 1987 and was based on the Bourne UNIX shell developed in 1978, received a major update to version 3.0 in 2004. Version 3.1 is available as of this writing.

The Text User Interface

After GUIs became popular, the term *text user interface*, or *TUI*, was coined to distinguish text interfaces from graphics interfaces, as shown in Figure 2.13. Unlike CLIs, a TUI uses the entire screen area to perform tasks. TUIs were in wide use on IBM PCs during the 1980s to provide greater functionality and usability for conducting tasks. Applications that used TUIs included word processing software such as WordPerfect, which was the leading word processor for IBM PC and compatible computers, as well as telecommunications software that allowed the user to connect to bulletin board systems through their modems.

Graphical User Interfaces

GUIs, of course, have been the standard user interface since the 1990s, and were first available for general computing use in 1984 when Apple introduced the Macintosh. However, the availability of Windows on the popular IBM PC and compatibles platform drove GUIs to widespread acceptance. Instead of typing commands, you use your mouse to click on icons and

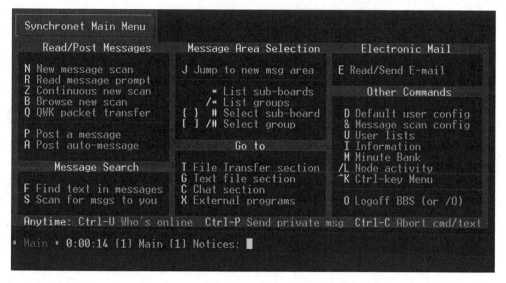

```
┌─Synchronet Main Menu────────────────────────────────────────────────┐
│        Read/Post Messages      Message Area Selection      Electronic Mail      │
│                                                                                 │
│   N New message scan        J Jump to new msg area      E Read/Send E-mail      │
│   R Read message prompt                                                         │
│   Z Continuous new scan         * List sub-boards          Other Commands       │
│   B Browse new scan            /* List groups                                   │
│   Q QWK packet transfer      { } # Select sub-board     D Default user config    │
│                              [ ] /# Select group        & Message scan config    │
│   P Post a message                                      U User lists            │
│   A Post auto-message                Go to              I Information            │
│                                                         M Minute Bank           │
│        Message Search       T File Transfer section     /L Node activity        │
│                             G Text file section         ^K Ctrl-key Menu        │
│   F Find text in messages   C Chat section                                      │
│   S Scan for msgs to you    X External programs         O Logoff BBS (or /O)    │
│                                                                                 │
│  Anytime: Ctrl-U Who's online  Ctrl-P Send private msg  Ctrl-C Abort cmd/text   │
└─────────────────────────────────────────────────────────────────────┘
 ▪ Main ▪ 0:00:14 [1] Main [1] Notices: █
```

Figure 2.13   *A sample text user interface.*

menus. Your information is organized much like a desktop—your files are located in folders and you can organize programs and other information on the screen. GUIs are typically based on a metaphor of some type where the visual elements match something in our everyday experience with physical reality. The desktop metaphor is present in the Windows, Mac OS, and Linux GUIs.

You can launch programs and manipulate objects on the screen by using the mouse, a hardware device, to move the mouse pointer on the screen to an object and perform an action, such as clicking on it or dragging it elsewhere. These objects were categorized in four areas that together formed the acronym WIMP: window, icon, menu, and pointing device. The default pointing device in many GUIs is in the shape of an arrow, but the pointing device shape can change to alert the user that he is performing a certain task, such as editing a word processing document, or to indicate that the computer is busy doing intensive processing.

Another hallmark of GUIs is the customizability of the interface. Unlike TUIs, which only let you change a few elements like colors, GUIs let you change the appearance and position of various elements on your screen, including the "wallpaper" graphic for the desktop background, icons, and in Windows, the position of the taskbar. Windows and other GUI operating systems, as well as

Web sites, offer "skins" or themes for your GUI. Skins and themes are templates that provide a custom appearance for your graphics elements in the GUI, such as the Windows Media Player 11 interface shown in Figure 2.14.

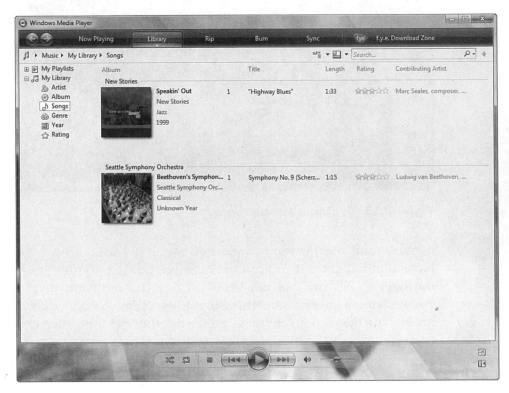

Figure 2.14   *The Windows Media Player 11 window in Windows Vista.*

Chapter 1, "Brief Histories," discussed the three major operating systems and their GUIs: Windows, Mac OS, and Linux under GNOME and KDE. There are other GUIs for UNIX-based computers, including the Sun Solaris operating system for use with Sun Microsystems workstations.

Web Interfaces

Web interfaces are based on HTML and additional technologies that work behind the scenes to let you interact with Web pages, as shown in Figure 2.15. For example, you can enter text into the appropriate boxes, click buttons to initiate actions, and click on links in text and graphics to go directly to a different Web page.

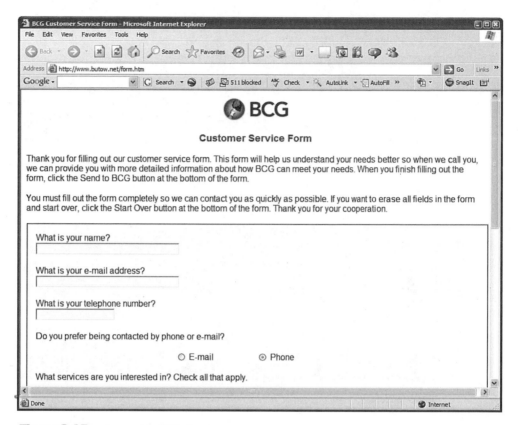

Figure 2.15   *A sample Web form.*

Web sites contain interconnected Web pages that employ a consistent user interface, and the appearance of that interface can depend on the Web browser that the user uses to view Web pages as well as the video resolution of the user's computer. For example, if a Web site is designed for users who have computers with 1024 by 768 pixel resolution, which is also called *XGA resolution* (XGA stands for Extended Graphics Array), and the user has a screen that displays only 800 by 600 pixel resolution, the Web page won't appear as you intend it to—the user will be required to scroll horizontally in the Web browser window to view the rest of the page. Figures 2.16 and 2.17 show how the Pearson home page looks in Internet Explorer at 800 by 600-pixel resolution and 1024 by 768-pixel resolution, respectively.

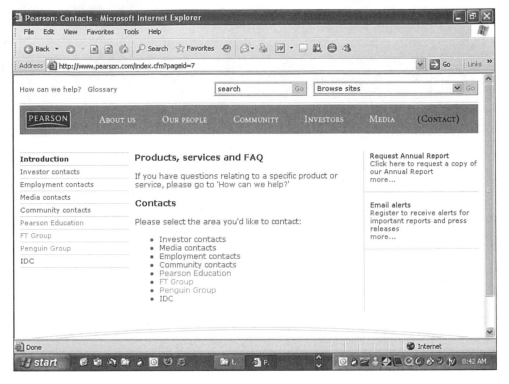

Figure 2.16   *The Pearson home page in 800 by 600-pixel resolution.*

Web sites provide some level of interactivity through links embedded in text and graphics, as well as through forms, such as an order form, that you can fill out and then submit to the company sponsoring the Web site.

Interfaces That Integrate with These Models

Security is of paramount concern with computing in general, and network computing (like the Web) in particular. Hardware interfaces that help maintain computer security are built to work with software interfaces to grant access to the computer or software application. These interfaces include the following:

- **Smart cards**, which are much like credit cards that you insert into a separate card reader. The application reads your card and compares it to the record it has on file, as shown in Figure 2.18.

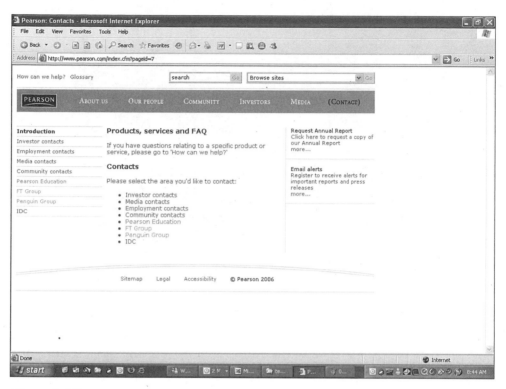

Figure 2.17 *The Pearson home page in 1024 by 768 resolution. Notice that the vertical scrollbar at the side of the page in 800 by 600 resolution is no longer needed on the page in 1024 by 768 resolution.*

- **Fingerprint scanning**, which involves placing your index finger into a small device that reads the fingerprint and checks the fingerprint against the one on file.

- **Retina scanning**, which sounds like something out of *Star Trek*. Like a lot of other devices on *Star Trek*, this device has made its way into real life. You put your face against a retina reader, and the system scans the retina in your eye and compares it to the one on file.

- **Radio Frequency Identification** (RFID) tags, which are mobile devices that interface with a computer system through the use of an RFID reader. As of this writing, RFID tags are used to track products and transport payments, such as electronic toll collection at toll booths. RFID chips are also being implanted in animals for livestock tracking, as well as in some humans. For example, in 2004, the Mexican Attorney General's office implanted 18 of its workers with RFID chips from Verichip Corp. so these workers could quickly access a secure room.

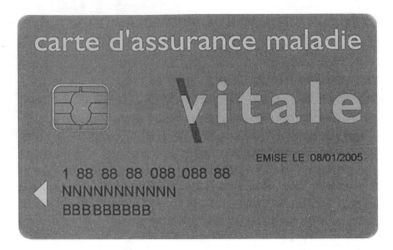

Figure 2.18   *A smart card.*

These interfaces and others designed to enhance computing security will undoubtedly have greater impact on user interface design and operating system functions. The latest version of Windows contains interface improvements that help reinforce the aspects (and the appearance) of a safe and secure operating system.

Other Interfaces

The interfaces discussed in this section are not the only ones available. Indeed, several of the new ones are widely used (or will be soon), and you may have used one of them recently.

- *Tactile interfaces* are those that rely on the sense of touch to gain feedback about what's going on with the system. This type of feedback, called *haptic feedback*, is used in simulators to more accurately project what happens in the real world. (The term *haptic* comes from the Greek *Haphe*, which means pertaining to the sense of touch.) For example, flight simulators use tactile interfaces to tell the user what's happening. When a pilot in a simulation encounters a situation on the screen, the control stick will provide the same amount of resistance that the pilot would experience in that situation.

- *Touch interfaces* are becoming popular in places like your local grocery store, ATM machines, and even polling places. For example, when I last visited my grocery store, I paid using my credit card. The grocery store has a reader at the checkout stand so that I could not only swipe my credit card, but I could also use my wand or my finger to enter my discount card code. You will also find such interfaces in cars that have a touch screen for accessing maps, radio stations, and more, as well as at kiosks to provide services, such as public Internet access or express check-in at airports.

Touch interfaces are also widely used with handheld PCs, also called Personal Digital Assistants (PDAs) and Pocket PCs. The interfaces for these devices use a *stylus*, which is a miniature wand, so you can tap icons and other objects to manipulate them. You can also use your finger to tap objects.

- *Telephone user interfaces* require you to use the telephone touch pad to interact with the program in the system. This is commonly used for such purposes as selecting the correct extension or department number when you call a company as well as accessing your answering machine voice mail system that your telephone company manages. A long session with one of these interfaces has brought about the derisive term *voice mail hell* to describe the frustration of being unable to address a real person within a certain amount of time.

  However, as the line between handheld PCs and cell phones blurs, people are also using their telephone user interface to interact with their telephone to take pictures, play games, and especially send text messages.

- *Button interfaces* include those you find on your iPod or a video game player. Although button interfaces have a lot of the features of touch interfaces, I've put button interfaces in a separate category because you use a piece of hardware to manipulate objects on the screen instead of using the screen as the interface. Button interfaces can take different forms. For example, an iPod has a button wheel that lets you navigate quickly through your playlist to find the song or video you want to play. Button interfaces can also be combined with related interfaces, such as using a joystick to move an object in a game.

Design Improvements and Aggravations

2006 saw a number of interesting developments in user interface design, starting with the most popular operating system: Microsoft Windows.

Windows Vista

Windows Vista, the sixth major version of Windows, was released at the end of 2006 to businesses and in early 2007 to consumers. This version contains some evolutionary, but not revolutionary, updates to the software. One of the biggest improvements is the Aero user interface, which includes such features as translucent windows, the capability to tilt windows, and new organizational and search capabilities, as shown in Figure 2.19. The security capabilities have also been improved, especially when it comes to controlling user accounts and who sees what in Windows.

Figure 2.19   *The Windows Vista desktop.*

The biggest issue confronting Windows is one of security. Because Windows is the most popular operating system, attacks on the system are numerous and constant. Therefore, Windows Vista has established security features that have been described in the computing media as "unfriendly." When you use a program or service, Windows Vista in its default mode opens a dialog box asking you to grant permission to run the program. This interface feature could be a deterrent to adoption of Vista for those users who are aggravated by taking the extra step to click the Allow button in the dialog box to use their system. Such features could also provide competitors like Apple an opportunity to tell Windows users that their operating system doesn't employ these security features and offers a better user experience.

Mac OS X

The Mac OS has long been considered the leader in operating system technology and usability. Previous versions of Mac OS X, shown in Figure 2.20, have included impressive improvements in searching for files and folders on your Mac, the Aqua interface that included translucent windows and "gel" buttons that sparked a lot of imitating for a while, and the Dock, which is an area at the bottom of the screen that lets you access files and folders more quickly—a concept similar to Microsoft's taskbar.

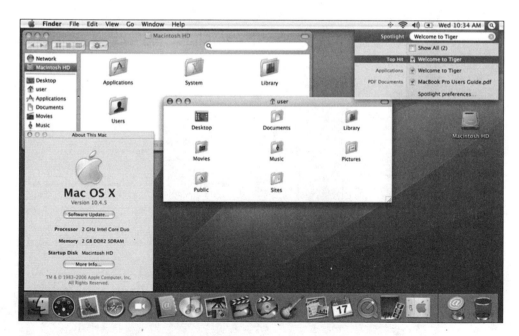

Figure 2.20   The Mac OS X desktop.

Leopard is another incremental improvement to the Mac OS that provides more evolutionary search and interface features based on user feedback. However, the Aqua interface is starting to get long in the tooth, and the improvements that Microsoft has made in its interface have put it about on par with the Mac OS. With the Intel transition complete, in 2008, Steve Jobs and company may decide to reveal Mac OS 11 (or XI or X1), which will sport a new interface.

Linux

Linux still has two major competing user interfaces, largely because Linux is an open operating system. Until Linux users settle on one interface, there may not be a concerted push to make Linux more accessible to individual computer users. As of this writing, version 3.5 is the latest version of KDE, as shown in Figure 2.21. A new version of KDE, version 4, is due for release in late 2006 or early 2007, but in terms of user interface design, it's already behind the curve. A new version of GNOME is also under development. Whether these new versions will bring these GUIs on a par with Windows Vista and the Mac OS remains to be seen.

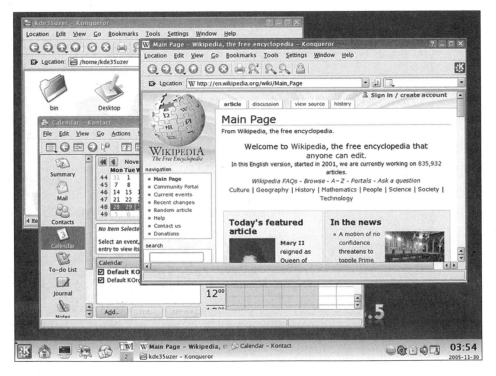

Figure 2.21   *The KDE desktop.*

Web Design Improvements

Many of the Web design improvements in the decade of the 2000s have happened "under the hood," specifically with the languages used to produce Web sites. *Extensible Markup Language*, or *XML*, is a language that is a cousin of HTML; both are built from the same ancestor: the Standard Generalized Markup Language (SGML). XML is designed to better share information between different systems on the Internet. As a result, HTML code is going away and is being replaced by sites written in a hybrid of HTML and XML, called (of course) XHTML. The difference you'll see in your browser is faster performance with database-driven Web sites.

Thanks to years of people discussing what's good and bad about Web sites, Web design has progressed beyond the days where people used dark blue text on a black background and thought it was cool—and expected people to be able to read it, too. However, new Web designers may not be aware of design requirements, and some Web sites serve as instructional aids to show new designers what *not* to do, as shown in Figure 2.22.

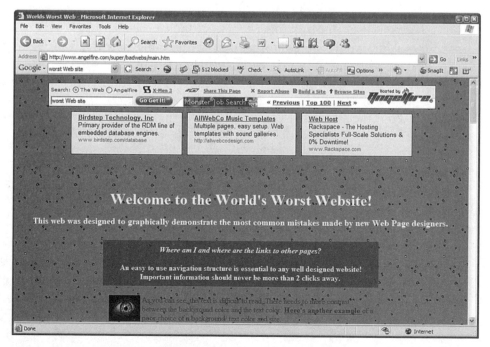

Figure 2.22   *A poorly designed Web site.*
Figure courtesy of Michelle Blowers, Owner, Gold Nugget Webs (www.goldnuggetwebs.com).

Unfortunately, there are still enough limitations in Web design that, if a designer is not aware of them, it could cause serious trouble, as I'll explain in the next section.

What's Still Not Fixed

Not all operating systems, and especially all Web browsers, speak the same language—they all like to tweak their programs to add a new feature that no one else has, ostensibly to give their product a competitive edge. However, the tweaking can aggravate users and designers.

For example, each major Web browser can display a Web page slightly different from its competitors. You also have to design a Web site using a few common fonts and a set number of colors, called Web-safe colors. This is because not all Web users have the same fonts installed on their computers or the same number of colors available, so designing a Web site according to what looks best to you may look nothing like what you intended on someone else's computer.

What's more, programs running under the same operating system may not use the same conventions, which helps undermine the idea of having similar commands across all programs to make things easier for the user. For example, I like using keystroke combinations (like Shift+F1) instead of picking a menu option with the mouse because it's faster. However, the keystroke combinations for accessing the spell checker are different for WordPerfect and Word—WordPerfect uses Ctrl+F1 but Word uses F7.

Perhaps the biggest problem with user interface design is that it's largely static—the standard GUI has been in use for nearly 35 years as of this writing, and although it has been refined over the years, there isn't a new (and hopefully more effective) way of interacting with a computer. The problem also includes GUI applications, which have been tweaked incrementally over the years, but application interfaces are similar to interfaces from older versions released 10 years ago.

However, Microsoft may have something in the works regarding a new user interface in the next major release of Windows, and there are other interfaces under development that could see the light of day during the second decade of the 21st century.

Future Plans

Whether the changes are just evolutionary or revolutionary, user interfaces will continue to change. This section provides a peak into the near future of what those changes might be like.

Windows Vienna

Vienna is the code name for Version 7 of the Windows operating system. The Vienna name replaced the new version's original name, Blackcomb. Many of the features that were promised in Windows Vista have been scheduled for individual release—perhaps as Vista service packs—between now and Vienna's release, and others have been moved back to Vienna.

One of those changes is a complete revamping of the user interface based on Microsoft research during the past decade or so. Microsoft is good at revealing hints that may or may not be included with the next version of Windows. What's more, Microsoft has a track record of announcing new features that get pushed back due to time constraints or technological issues, so it's always best to take what Microsoft says with a grain of salt.

Mac OS

In 2006, Apple's focus was more on hardware than software. It decided to migrate all its Macintosh computers from running on the PowerPC chips to running on Intel chips. This change is designed to provide Apple with more powerful portable and desktop computers.

Apple released the latest version of Mac OS X, called Leopard, in early 2007, but more significant changes may be in store now that the Intel transition is complete. Whatever Steve Jobs has up his sleeve for the next version of Mac OS, he's not letting on.

Web Browsers and Their Impact on Design

Web browsers have forced operating systems to adopt new functionality to deal with Internet issues such as blocking pop-up ads. User interface design has also integrated the use of online help directly from Web sources, which requires a presentation of that data that is easy to find and understand. And there is the issue of accessibility for all users, which was discussed in Chapter 1.

As the line between the computer desktop and the Web browser blurs with the capability for users to have always-on Internet broadband connections (such as cable and DSL), Web formatting and design restrictions are beginning to affect user interface design. Web technologies such as Flash, the de facto standard for creating animated objects on the Web as well as creating animated Web sites, have made Web sites more interactive than ever.

For example, the Rich Internet Application System (RIAS) uses Flash to create a Web interface that looks more like an interface on the user's desktop. This RIAS interface is a graphical shell that appears over the HTML pages, much as the Windows interface was a shell over the DOS CLI from the first version of Windows through the release of Windows Millennium Edition in 2000. Another example is that Windows Vista lets you search the Internet from the desktop.

A Web development area of great interest is the Web-based application, where users will be able to use applications such as word processors and spreadsheets directly from a Web site and won't have to install software on their computer. Application service providers (ASPs) are already in operation and make applications available on the Web.

Application subscriptions and rentals have the attention of larger companies such as Google, which announced the Google Spreadsheet in 2006. The Google Spreadsheet allows users to share spreadsheet data through the Web with other users, thus bypassing the need to use existing programs. In addition to the advent of open-source software, this development is a tremendous challenge for companies like Microsoft that have used the proprietary model of software design and sales, especially because these software sales provide dependable revenue for the companies that produce that software.

Up-and-Coming Interfaces

Several new and interesting interfaces are currently being designed and researched. One or more of these interfaces could make their way into our lives at some point in the future.

- **Attentive interfaces** manage the users' attention by guiding them through a process and warning them about any potential problems, such as the lack of required input from the user that will prevent the application from completing the desired task. The interface is designed to understand what the user is doing so that the interface can react accordingly. For example, the interface will watch for any change in visual attention or if the user has turned to give attention to something else.

- **Gesture interfaces** rely on hand gestures for input. If you watched the movie *Minority Report*, you saw that the computers of 2054 used gesture interfaces as users would move their hands and arms to manipulate objects on the computer.

- **Reflexive interfaces** allow users to define and control the entire system through the user interface, such as changing the command verbiage to suit their needs and expectations.

- **Tangible interfaces** give physical form to tangible pieces of information. For example, the Marble Answering Machine by Durrell Bishop (Wikipedia, 2006) has a marble that represents a message on the answering machine. When you drop the marble into a dish, the answering machine plays back the message. The movie *Minority Report* used a similar feature, where the predicted outcome of murder events was not reported on a computer screen, but in the form of a marble that had the information etched on it.

- **Zooming interfaces** is an evolutionary outgrowth of the GUI. Therefore, zooming interfaces sport the acronym ZUI, for zooming user interface. A ZUI represents objects in different levels of scale and detail. As you pan across an infinite desktop that consists of various objects in various levels of detail, you can select an object to enlarge it to view or work on it, and then you can shrink it again when you're finished. ZUIs don't use windows; instead, they use vector graphics to represent objects. One example of a ZUI is MSN.com Maps, in which you enter an address, MSN.com shows you the map, and then lets you zoom in and out as you see fit. See Figure 2.23.

- The **Archy interface** is a new interface proposed by the late Jef Raskin, a human-computer interface expert who started the Macintosh project at Apple in the 1970s. Raskin left Apple in 1982 and started his own company, where he eventually developed a product that integrated an early version of the Archy interface in 1987. That product was the Canon Cat.

This interface is text based and doesn't use GUI features. Instead, the Archy interface uses leaping, which lets you move on the screen via an incremental text search. You can also insert and execute commands at any point in the interface; all you have to do is hold down the

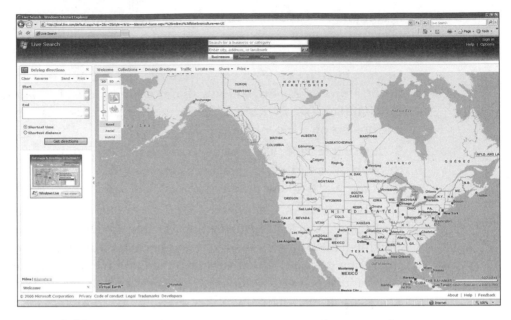

Figure 2.23 *MSN.com Maps, a zooming user interface example.*

command key (which is the Caps Lock key) and type the command. Archy also fills in the command name automatically.

The Archy interface also uses a ZUI called Zoomworld that you can interface with using a mouse. Hyperlinks are embedded in each icon, and as you move the zoom area closer to the object, the object gets bigger so you can examine more of the information and decide if you want to expand the object.

- The **brain-computer interface** is perhaps the most direct interface of all. People will not have microprocessor chips installed in their heads anytime soon, but rudimentary brain-computer interfaces have been developed that allow humans and monkeys to control a cursor on a screen. Related interfaces have shown promise in using implants that are controlled by the brain to overcome noncongenital deafness and blindness.

Usability Terms

Chauncy Wilson, a senior member of the Society for Technical Communication (STC), notes that the word *usability* can be traced back to 1382 according to the Oxford English Dictionary online (www.oed.com), and that the first reference to usability can be traced back to 1842. (Wilson, Chauncey. "Usability and User Experience Design: The Next Decade." *Intercom* (January 2005): 6[nd]9.) Today, the Merriam-Webster Online dictionary (www.m-w.com) has two rather terse definitions for usability:

1. Capable of being used.
2. Convenient and practicable for use.

These definitions do little to explain what usability is. Dumas and Redish (1999) provide a straightforward definition of what usability is: "The people who use the product can do so quickly and easily to accomplish their own tasks." Dumas and Redish base this definition of usability on four points:

1. Usability requires focus on the users.
2. People use products to be productive.
3. Users are busy people trying to accomplish tasks.
4. Users decide when a product is easy to use.

As personal computing technology became widely available, companies placed a greater emphasis on improving users' experiences with computers as more people who used hardware and software products were increasingly lay people using computers at home and in the office instead of computing professionals.

This shift in priorities gave rise to several different buzzwords related to usability, including *usability engineering*, *user-centered design*, and *user experience engineering*.

The increased focus on usability studies over the past 25 years or so has categorized those who engage in usability studies into three categories.

Usability Engineers

A usability engineer is someone who provides usability services. Usability services are any activities that improve the user experience of anything a person uses to accomplish a task. This can include the design of a software application, the creation of a user guide, the creation of training services, and the creation of a Web site.

Usability Scientists

A usability scientist is someone who has formal training in usability research and development disciplines. These disciplines include usability science, usability engineering, human factors engineering, and ergonomics. Usability scientists usually hold advanced degrees in one of the cognitive science fields.

User Experience Professionals

A user experience professional is someone who can fit into one of the other two categories, or it can be someone in a company, office, or department that isn't a formal usability engineer or works in a usability engineering department, but someone who does provide usability services.

For example, most technical writers are passionate about making printed or online documentation as easy to read and use as possible. What's more, technical writers have had to expand their repertoire to include some programming, Web design, and even software and hardware design.

As a result, more technical communicators are becoming usability engineers or are simply expanding their repertoire even more by learning about usability testing and techniques and offering these services to their internal and external customers.

Types of Usability Design

There are three major types of usability design:

- **Documentation design**, which is the design of paper and online documentation that serves as a reference for users. Technical writers lead the charge to produce documentation design and employ usability techniques, including user and task analysis, which I'll discuss later in this chapter.

- **Interface design**, which is the process of designing a software or hardware interface that users find attractive and easy to use. GUI design requirements have taken some issues of software design off the table, but GUIs do not automatically result in good software interface design.
- **Web design**, which is the process of designing Web sites, which are a number of connected pages to present information to the reader.

User Analysis Terms

As the study of usability and user analysis has matured, processes for user design and usability testing have emerged. The leading process for user design is the Goal-Directed Design Process. Usability testing falls into three categories: quick and dirty, formative, and summative.

The Goal-Directed Design Process

Cooper and Reimann (2003) produced the Goal-Directed Design Process for software engineering and user design. The Goal-Directed Design Process was designed to keep everyone in the loop, keep guesswork out of the design process, and provide a clear rationale for decisions. If you're on a product project team, it may adhere to this process. You'll learn more about the Goal-Directed Design Process and applying it to your interface design in Chapter 5, "How Users Behave."

Testing Methods

When you want to test the usability of something against the user's goals, testing falls into three different categories.

- **Quick and dirty**—This type of usability testing is usually performed after the product has been produced. These tests can be in the form of print or online questionnaires or direct feedback from the users through customer support calls or e-mail messages. If the users don't like the products, you'll know from angry customers' phone calls or low product sales.
- **Formative**—This type of usability testing occurs during the development of a product (Bias et al., 2005). You've likely heard the term *beta testers* to refer to those people who test the usability and functionality

of software. These testers provide direct feedback about the good and bad of the product. Users generally don't see printed documentation until the product is released, so any formative testing of printed documentation is usually limited to internal users. However, beta testers can test online help within software to make sure the help is usable and accessible.

- Summative—Summative testing takes place when a product has reached a certain stage of development defined by the project team and the testers want to find out how much progress has been made in the product's development (Bias et al., 2005). This type of testing uses metrics to evaluate the efficiency, effectiveness, and satisfaction of the product being tested. The draft of printed or online user documentation, if any exists, is usually available during this stage so that beta testers can provide feedback about the usefulness of the documentation.

Ideally, you should conduct user and task analysis to gain understanding about your users. *User and task analysis* is the process of learning about ordinary users by observing them in action (Hackos and Redish, 1998). Chapter 3, "Making the Business Case," covers the user's goals, and Chapter 5 discusses user and task analysis in greater detail.

User Analysis Trends

Wilson (2005) identified six trends for usability that people should pay particular attention to in the months and years ahead.

- The focus of product design and evaluation will be the total user experience. This chapter has already discussed the total user experience in some detail, and you'll learn more about it in Chapter 6, "Analyzing Your Users."
- Employers will ask usability practitioners to provide more evidence of their impact on the company's return on investment (ROI). You'll learn more about ROI and how to calculate it for your management team in Chapter 3.
- Social psychology is becoming more important in the design of new collaboration and e-commerce technologies. Chapter 6 will discuss the psychology of everyday things and how it affects users.

- Business skills and savvy will become important criteria in hiring usability and user experience practitioners. Chapter 3 goes into this concept in greater detail.

- Facilitation skills will become as important as design and evaluation skills. You'll learn more about facilitation skills starting with Chapter 9, "Usability," where you'll learn how to plan your usability test.

- The validity and reliability of cherished usability methods will be examined. There aren't many standards currently for procedures, data analysis, or reporting, so much of usability testing and research is still in its formative stages.

Accessibility Issues

Another user interface and analysis trend not on this list, but one you should be aware of, is the need to design user interfaces to meet the needs of users with special accessibility issues due to disability or age-related impairments. The following disabilities can affect computer users:

- Complete or partial blindness
- Color blindness
- Deafness or difficulty hearing
- Cognitive disabilities, such as autism and dyslexia
- Motor and dexterity limitations, including paralysis and carpal tunnel syndrome

Operating system manufacturers have incorporated numerous accessibility features into their operating systems. Some of these features work in concert with *assistive technologies*, which are hardware devices designed to meet the needs of disabled users. These technologies include alternative keyboards and pointing devices, wands and sticks, sip-and-puff systems, and touch screens.

If you're developing software or a Web site, you need to be aware of Section 508 issues that the U.S. government mandates as well as Web site accessibility guidelines published by the World Wide Web Consortium (commonly referred to as W3C). Other countries, including Australia and the United Kingdom, also have disability antidiscrimination legislation that affects user interface accessibility.

Section 508 Accessibility

Section 508 is the section that in 1998 amended the Rehabilitation Act of 1973. If you're going to develop a user interface for a government agency, Section 508 requires you to develop interfaces that are accessible to federal employees who have disabilities. Section 508 is separate from the Americans with Disabilities Act, which was passed in 1990.

For software and hardware product developers, as well as Web designers, you need to be aware of the following features to include in your product:

- **Software programs**—Programs must include usability features for the visually impaired, including the use of alternate keyboard navigation, as well as the ability to interact with speech recognition products.
- **Telecommunications products**—Include accessibility for people who are deaf or hard of hearing, such as integration with TTY devices.
- **Videos or multimedia products**—Captioning of multimedia products that appear in software or on a Web site, and the capability to turn captioning on or off.
- **Kiosks and other closed products**—These systems must include accessibility features, such as the capability to activate a speaker system so that information can be dictated aloud.
- **Web sites and applications**—Use text labels that describe graphics on the screen through the use of ALT tags, which are small pieces of text attached to the graphic that tell the user what the graphic is about. When you move the mouse pointer over the graphic, the ALT tag box appears and displays the graphic description next to the pointer.

The U.S. government lists 16 different guidelines that a Web site must meet before the site complies with Section 508 requirements. Those guidelines are available on the Section 508 Web site at www.section508.gov.

Web Site Accessibility

In 1999, the W3C passed the first version of its Web Content Accessibility Guidelines that provided recommendations for creating accessible Web sites. These guidelines include the following:

- Provide equivalent alternatives to auditory and visual content.
- Don't rely on color alone. In other words, make sure that text and graphics are understandable if you don't use color.
- Use markup and style sheets, and do so properly.
- Clarify natural language usage.
- Create tables that transform gracefully. In other words, make sure that tables use the proper HTML commands that identify the table components as a table to browsers that access pages through a Braille display or dictate pages through speech output.
- Ensure that pages featuring new technologies transform gracefully, meaning that pages should be accessible even when newer technologies such as scripts are not supported or turned off.
- Ensure user control of time-sensitive content changes.
- Ensure direct accessibility of embedded user interfaces.
- Design for device-independence.
- Use interim solutions so that older browsers display your Web site correctly.
- Use W3C technologies and guidelines.
- Provide context and orientation information.
- Provide clear navigation mechanisms.
- Ensure that documents are clear and simple.

You can review the Version 1.0 guidelines in their entirety at www.w3.org/TR/WAI-WEBCONTENT.

In May 2006, the W3C published the working draft of version 2.0 of the Web Content Accessibility Guidelines. Instead of using specific guidelines as with version 1.0, version 2.0 offers four guiding principles:

1. Content must be perceivable. For example, the foreground must be distinguishable from the background.
2. Interface components in the content must be operable. For example, help users avoid mistakes and easily overcome any mistakes that occur.
3. Content and controls must be understandable, meaning that text must be understandable and placement of text must be consistent.
4. Content should be robust enough to work with current and future user

agents, including assistive technologies. You must ensure that content is accessible or provide an accessible alternative.

The version 2.0 working draft has been criticized for being too vague, and perhaps taking a step backward in terms of Web accessibility. You can view the entire working draft at www.w3.org/TR/WCAG20/.

Operating System Accessibility

Currently, all four major operating systems—Windows, Mac OS, Linux/KDE, and Linux/GNOME—have accessibility features built in. You can activate accessibility features in the "control panel" area of the GUI that lets you manipulate operating system features. These features can include the following:

- Changing the font size, color, and size of objects on the desktop, such as increasing the size of icons and changing to high-contrast color schemes
- Enlarging a portion of the screen for greater visibility through a magnifier
- Enlarging the cursor and changing the cursor blink rate
- Enlarging the screen by changing the screen resolution
- Displaying captions for speech and sounds
- Displaying warnings for system sounds that the user should know about
- Setting window command options to have the computer read text aloud through the computer's speakers
- Changing the size and speed of the mouse pointer
- Highlighting or dragging the mouse pointer without holding down the mouse button
- Allowing users to press one key at a time for key combinations
- Moving the mouse pointer with the numerical keypad on the keyboard
- Hearing tones when you press certain keys

This is only a short list of available accessibility options; it is not exhaustive. What is more, some of these features may not be available in all operating systems. However, this list should give you a good idea of the accessibility features available in the operating system for which you design your software. Make a note of this for your customers. Check the information about accessibility on the operating system manufacturer Web site; all four operating systems contain information about their accessibility features, such as the Ease of Access window in Windows Vista, as shown in Figure 2.24.

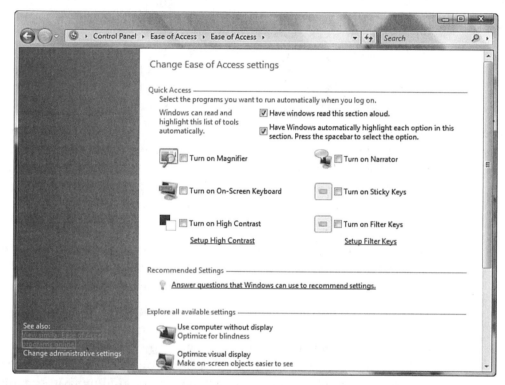

Figure 2.24   *The Ease of Access window in Windows Vista.*

Summary

The chapter began with a discussion of basic computer terminology and concepts. This was followed by the three types of interface models: batch interfaces, the command-line interface (CLI), and the graphical user interface (GUI). You learned the differences in these three interface models, and various types of hardware user interface models that work in concert with software interfaces to control access to a computer.

Design improvements and aggravations were covered next. You learned about design improvements in the latest operating systems released in 2006, the Web technologies behind the scenes and the design techniques for Web pages, and some of the issues that still need to be addressed, including the fact that the current desktop GUI is getting stale.

A discussion of future user interface plans for the three major operating systems—Windows, Mac OS, and Linux—followed. Of the three major operating systems, Microsoft's plans for the next major release of Windows are the most concrete at this point, and its plans include a major change in how we interact with our computers. You also learned about up-and-coming interfaces that could change the way we interact with computers in the future, from attentive interfaces to brain-computer interfaces.

Usability terms were covered next. You learned what the definition of usability is and what usability is designed to do from the 1999 definition by Dumas and Redish: "The people who use the product can do so quickly and easily to accomplish their own tasks." You also read about the three types of usability design: documentation design, interface design, and Web design.

Next was a discussion of usability analysis terms. You learned about the goal-directed process and how to use the process to ask a number of important questions about your users. Then you learned about the different types of testing methods available, and why you should conduct user and task analysis.

The chapter continued with trends in usability design so that you know what's required of usability analysis today. The primary trend is the focus on total user experience in product design and evaluation. Social and business skills are other trends in usability design. You also learned about the shortcomings of usability analysis and where you can find more information about usability analysis in this book.

The chapter ended with a discussion about accessibility and how it affects user interface design. You should always incorporate accessibility features into your software or hardware product, as well as your Web site, to meet the needs of your customers. You also learned about how operating systems have integrated accessibility features so that users with disabilities can access software programs and Web sites.

Review Questions

Now it's time to review what you've learned in this chapter before you move on to Chapter 3. Ask yourself the following questions, and refer to Appendix A to double-check your answers.

1. What is the definition of a graphical user interface (GUI)?
2. What are the three major GUI operating systems in use today?
3. What are the main parts of a GUI?
4. What is the Internet?
5. What is the World Wide Web?
6. What are the three user interface model eras?
7. Why is Web design still a significant challenge?
8. Why does Web design have an impact on user interface design?
9. What is a ZUI?
10. How do Dumas and Redish define usability?
11. What are the three types of usability titles or occupations discussed in this chapter?
12. When do you employ quick and dirty testing?
13. When do you employ summative testing?
14. Why is the validity and reliability of user interface methods being examined?
15. Why is accessibility important?
16. What legislation establishes statutory accessibility requirements in the United States.?

3

Making the Business Case

"Drive thy business; let not that drive thee."
—Benjamin Franklin

Topics Covered in This Chapter

Gaps Between Stakeholders

Developing a Business Case Framework

The Benefits of Good Design

The Case for Profitability

Proving ROI

The Usability Engineering Life Cycle

In the days of the Internet revolution from the mid to late 1990s and early 2000s, any company related to the Internet—or computing in general—was considered gold. Indeed, many companies without a comprehensive business plan received funding because they were involved with the Internet.

Those days are long gone. Although the go-go days are over, what's been left in its wake is a more mature realization about what's needed to survive. You need all the help you can get to beat the competition. And, as always, customer satisfaction is the key to survival and growth.

This is why usability analysis is so important—it lets you understand how your users react to your user interface so you learn what's wrong and what's right in your user interface design, as well as any other peripheral materials that ship with your product, such as the documentation. Usability analysis includes early customer involvement to gauge their reaction to and productivity with an interface. This feedback gives you the opportunity to make changes before you release your product to your customers, which can result in more satisfied customers.

User interface design, usability design, and usability testing are all strongly linked. Without good user interface design, users won't like your product, whether it's a software product, hardware product, or Web site. Without usability design and testing, you'll never know if your design is useful until you receive input from the public. If your user interface is a flop, you and your project team will have to spend time, money, and effort fixing problems that could have been fixed during the development process, not to mention that the product team will have to endure customer service headaches.

To show the benefits of good interface and usability design to your stakeholders, you need to make a strong business case. The business case not only explains design benefits to company stakeholders, but also how the company benefits from the investment, called *return on investment* or *ROI*.

The first step is to identify and understand not only the users' goals, but also the goals of the various stakeholders in your company. Then you need to create an overall plan for your project to present to your stakeholders so you can get your plan approved. The plan should not only address the benefits from good design, but the plan should also discuss who in the company benefits from good design. As part of that discussion, you should make the case for profitability. Finally, you should make an ROI study that shows just how much money you expect will be made from the investment based on reasonable estimates of time and money.

Gaps Between Stakeholders

The product creation system includes four distinct stakeholder groups (Donoghue, 2002):

- Users
- Engineers and designers
- Sales and marketing personnel
- Managers

Each group has its own stake in the success of the product, be it a hardware, software, or Web product (or some combination of the three). Therefore, each group has different expectations of what it wants the product to be. These different expectations create gaps between the stakeholders that you must bridge in your usability business case.

What Users Expect

Users expect to have a successful experience with the product or documentation the first time around. Because the users are the people who determine whether something is useful, the characteristics of your users will go a long way toward determining what is actually usable, as Chapter 5, "How Users Behave," will discuss in greater detail. However, users look for some general goals when they use a product, whether the product is a Web site, a software program, or a piece of hardware such as a cell phone (Donoghue, 2002):

- The product must be easy to learn.
- The product must solve the user's needs.
- The product help must be both easily accessible and effective in resolving the user's problem quickly.

Your customer base will likely have other criteria that define success, and these criteria will be more specific to the product. For example, if you have a Web site, your customers will want to get to the information in the fewest clicks possible.

What Engineers or Designers Expect

Product engineers and designers expect that they will largely be left alone to produce their product. They don't want to spend a lot of time fixing problems that arise after the product has been shipped, or having to answer questions from internal and external customers about how something works. In my experiences as a technical writer, I've found that during the development process, engineers and designers liked me to ask them as few questions as possible, and they liked it even more if those questions required short answers.

What Sales and Marketing People Expect

Sales and marketing people expect an outcome that makes as much money for the company as possible. There are a number of internal and external factors that sales and marketing people look at when a new product is released, including these:

- The company's client base and contacts, especially if there are good candidates to be usability test subjects.
- The public environment, such as the public and the media. The public and the media can be good or bad for business depending on the subject matter. Poor reviews of a software product can negatively affect sales, but favorable reviews can help make the jobs of sales and marketing people easier.
- Macro forces, including economic, political, and technological. For example, if you sell software to airline and trucking companies, the high cost of fuel may prevent them from spending money on your product, no matter how much they like your product. Your product may also require people to have the latest version of the operating system they use or the latest service releases installed for your program to run properly.
- Competing businesses. Businesses are always looking for every advantage, so sales and marketing people are always researching the competition to identify and exploit weaknesses, or perceived weaknesses, in competing products.

What Managers Expect

Managers expect to see how a product or initiative affects the bottom line, which is the only thing that matters in business. Therefore, managers want to see a cost-benefit analysis to gauge the company's ROI from usability testing.

Managers want this analysis to include the following so they can decide whether usability design and testing is feasible:

- How much usability design and testing will cost. These costs must not only be projected to what you plan to test in the short term, but what you want to test in the long term. For example, if you develop a software product that will be upgraded over time, you may want to include usability tests for subsequent versions.

- What will be tested. For example, will you test a software product, the associated customer support Web site, or both?

- How many other resources are needed, including people, facilities, and equipment. For example, if you need to conduct in-person usability testing using computers in your lab or on the customer site, you need to include the costs and people involved. You should also measure the amount of work people do in terms of people days that your usability project will use.

You can be sure that the higher you go up the corporate ladder in the company, executives are aware of not only the expectations of the manager making the decision, but also of other departments in the company.

Developing a Business Case Framework

Now that you have identified what the benefits are, you need to tie your usability plan to the entire production process. If possible, you should start the usability process at the same time the project design process begins.

Starting the usability process at the beginning allows you to couch the design of not only the usability tests but also the product interface and documentation in terms of the total user experience. The user experience is a five-step process (Donoghue, 2002) that encompasses the entire customer experience:

1. The process starts with the business goals. These customer goals can include, but are not limited to, converting customers, increasing retention, and increasing transactions.

2. The project team factors in the customer goals, including ease of learning, a solution that solves the users' needs, and access to help when needed. That help should also be designed to resolve users' needs quickly. Help design usually falls under the purview of the documentation specialist. Chapter 4, "Good Design," expands on the need for good documentation design.

3. The appropriate project team members design the user interface or documentation to meet both the business and customer goals.

4. When the interface is ready for testing, the team participates in the engagement and interaction processes and provides feedback. You can obtain this feedback in a number of ways, from user surveys to controlled tests. You'll learn more about creating a usability test in Chapter 9, "Usability."

5. After testing, the testers' goals are satisfied. This doesn't guarantee that you'll meet all the goals of all your customers, because testing is limited to a selected group of users. However, usability testing minimizes problems you will encounter when you release your software, hardware, or Web site to the public.

At the end of the five-step process, the satisfaction of the customer goals naturally leads into the satisfaction of the business goals. You can use this process as a framework for developing the rest of your plan, starting with the benefits of good design and how it affects your business goals.

The Benefits of Good Design

You're going to encounter skeptics when it comes to communicating the benefits of good design. For example, you may have had the following conversation with your software development team once or dozens of times before:

> You: "We need usability testing to make sure that our software is not only usable, but easy to use."

> Developers: "But the software is so easy to use—we don't need usability testing!"

A rejoinder to this argument can be hard to come by, because the developers are correct—if the developers are the only ones using the product.

Of course, other people outside your company will pay money to use your software, and if the users disagree with your developers, your company isn't only going to be deficient in the financial space, but it will also be deficient in the idea space. That is, your company will gain the perception that it doesn't meet the needs of users, and that perception can be hard to overcome.

Other people in your company may just shrug and say "so what?" in response to your request for usability testing. Without something tangible to present to other people, those people can't wrap their heads around what you're trying to convey. So what will you tell them?

You should start your business case by discussing with the company the benefits of good design (Mayhew and Tremaine, 2005). Good usability design and testing positively affect four key business areas:

- Production costs
- Customer support costs
- Customer productivity
- Customer retention

Long-Term Production Costs

Good design helps your company reduce both your short-term and long-term production costs.

Lower Short-Term Costs

The promise of popular "desktop" GUI interfaces, such as Windows and Mac OS, became popular in the 1990s. The promise was that, because users would now be using a standard interface, people would be able to use any software at all. The reality is much more complicated. The desktop GUI interface didn't solve an old problem: Application software usually brings new tasks and new ways of doing tasks along with it, and users need to know how to perform those tasks efficiently.

You will save money in production costs by focusing your production teams as early in the development process as possible on updates to existing products as well as new products. If your sales and marketing teams learn from users about faults in the product that are attributed to faults in the user design, your entire company will have to devote a great deal of time, effort, and perhaps money to fix the problems. The results could be that your company's reputation suffers, your product's reputation suffers, and any other products under development are delayed because your production team has to devote its time to fixing the existing product.

Lower Long-Term Costs

Spend less money on fixing things that users have found unacceptable, and spend more time including improvements to help make the product and your customers' lives even better. You will also take what you learned from user interface design on your current project and apply it to other projects, thus making the products produced by those projects better for your users. Better products positively affect your company's bottom line.

Lower Customer Support Costs

Customer support costs account for as much as 60 percent of a high-tech company's total costs. If users find the user interface easy to use, they will likely not need to contact customer support. Without guidance afforded by good user interface design, users will use their own judgments, for better or worse, to get something to work the way they feel it should. That guidance must also be in front of users so they cannot ignore it, because there is no guarantee that users will read the documentation that comes with the software or hardware.

For example, there are stories of users who broke CD-ROM drive trays when they used the trays as cup holders. These users used the trays as cup holders because the manufacturers didn't tell them up front that the trays weren't cup holders, not even adding a sticker on the drive tray stating something like, "Not a cup holder." Such a sticker may have saved a lot of people money and grief.

If your product is well designed, your users will rely on online help and training materials less often and be more productive because they will find your product easy to use. They won't encounter or make as many errors, but if they do make errors, good documentation and online help will get them back on their feet more quickly.

Good product design lowers training costs. Certain products are complicated and require more training, but good interface design can reduce the amount of *unnecessary* training that your company needs to provide. For example, if your software is easy enough to use that you can have online training that anyone can access from your company's Web site, you will save the time and money necessary to have one of your employees train users at your facility or another facility. If you want to have in-person training, a well-designed product will ensure that you minimize the number of days you train people so that users can become more productive more quickly.

Greater Customer Retention

Documentation is the first line of support for most customers, and customers usually use it to look for the answer to a problem they're having. The inevitable result of poor or nonexistent documentation is that more people try calling the customer support lines for help. The company tries to mitigate the costs of hiring and training customer support staff by charging for those calls.

Users, who don't want to pay for those calls if they don't have to, usually search the Internet to get answers instead. Some users visit the company Web site for those answers. Many companies not only have lists of frequently asked questions (known popularly by the acronym *FAQs*), but also have online forums to ask and answer questions. Also, there are often online forums and mailing lists not affiliated with the company that users may consult with. However, the users may still not have the answers they need, so they have two choices: pay and hope they get the information they need, or give up. The users will either call your customer support line and won't be happy about it, or they'll decide that your competitor's product is a better solution.

Any extra time that the users put into solving the problem reinforces negative feelings about your company. In the worst-case scenario, poor design can result in damage to users' computers or data and cause them to seek reimbursement from your company for those damages. If you have aggressive competitors, this isn't good news for you or your team. A popular aphorism in the business world is that it costs about 10 times more to acquire a new customer than it does to retain one.

Therefore, good design not only results in less user frustration, but it also results in more positive reinforcements of your company. Happier customers not only means that you keep the customers you have, but it also increases the chances that you will be able to attract new customers through testimonials and word of mouth, the latter of which remains the most effective marketing method.

The Case for Profitability

After you show your stakeholders how good design as well as usability design and testing will lower costs, you need to show them how design and testing will make the company money.

Usability expert Karen Donoghue (2002) has eight guidelines to successfully attach profitability to usability studies in your company. Following are those guidelines:

- **Drive the design and development of the user interface and usability design closely against the product business case.** If the production team has a business case already, be sure to integrate your interface design, usability design, and usability testing business case with the product business case as much as possible. Doing so will help make your argument that the usability design business case will positively affect the product business case.

- **Make sure all project team members (including business, technology, and design) clearly understand the business goals and how usability affects those goals.** It's important to identify the stakeholders in your project and talk with them as soon as possible about your desires and needs. Not only will this communication help stakeholders understand that you're serious about usability and good user interface design, but you'll also be able to learn what those team members want, and that will make your business case even stronger.

- **Connect financial metrics to customer satisfaction and usability metrics, and measure them in an ongoing fashion.** You'll learn about creating financial metrics using an ROI study and using usability metrics with the Usability Engineering Life Cycle, later in this chapter.

- **Make the success measurement the responsibility of one person.** Share this information with the team as an index (or set of indexes) of usability. This person can be the usability expert, someone else on the project team, or someone outside the project team whose job it is to manage company quality efforts.

- **Share knowledge among the project team, and create a learning culture so that each team member understands what other team members contribute to the user experience.** Constant communication is the key not only to meeting good design goals, but also to acquiring accurate and meaningful usability results.

- **Build the user experience for scalability.** Making the user experience scalable helps your usability efforts evolve as the business model changes and the user population expands and evolves. Also, you should make capital investments in architecture before look and feel. For example, if user needs require that your software upgrade to a new version of programming software, you need to prioritize your investment for the architecture required for upgrading the software.

- **Know the customer's needs, tasks, and goals—and make sure the user experience satisfies them.** This is where the usability design and testing comes in, but usability testing isn't the end-all and be-all of finding customer information. For example, you can bring users into the project team so they can contribute information, or you can survey users and hold focus group meetings to determine what your users want and don't want in the interface.

- **Only add features and functionality that blend value for the customer with value for the company.** This gets back to the first guideline, where you have to dovetail the design and development of a good user interface and usability testing with the product development business case. Good customer feedback before the design process starts can determine what features are important to the customer. Then you and the product team can determine what features that the user requests will bring the most value to the company.

Proving ROI

All the value propositions listed earlier in this chapter are compelling, but they lead to the most powerful value proposition of all: the ROI analysis. ROI provides a financial metric that can help crystallize the impact of usability testing on the bottom line.

An ROI study is a way of calculating payback—that is, if you're putting money into something, an ROI study lets you and other members of the business know if that something will pay for itself in a certain period of time. If you come to one or more decision makers with an ROI study in hand, you will have a far better chance of implementing your proposed usability study.

ROI Specifics

When you create your ROI proposal as part of your business case, you must write down the basics of your benefit, including (Mayhew and Tremaine, 2005) the following:

- **The cost of developing the benefit**—These costs can be based on the number of hours it will take for people to create the benefit and tangible items needed to realize the benefit, such as renting space and equipment to perform usability tests.

- **The value proposition of the benefit**—This proposition explains how the company will benefit from the investment. You can use much of the information in this chapter to show the value of the benefit.

- **The dollar amount of the benefit**—Provide your best estimate based on the amount of money your company will save as well as how much profit you expect to make. You should discuss this issue with other stakeholders in the organization, such as the customer support manager, to get some solid numbers so you can construct a solid dollar amount estimate.

- **The length of time until the benefit is realized**—This length of time is calculated in years or a fraction of a year (such as 0.5 years for a 6-month length of time). Provide your best estimate after you talk with the project team. The project timeline will greatly affect this figure. You will factor this amount into calculating the dollar amount of the benefit.

- **The interest rate for the particular business for the same length of time**—You may be able to get this information from your project team or from your company's financial officer.

Calculate the Dollar Amount

To calculate an accurate dollar amount of the benefit, you must first calculate the net present value (NPV) amount, which discounts the benefit into today's dollars. If your ROI analysis shows you'll make an amount of money two years from now, that amount of money will be less valuable today because of inflation during that period.

You can calculate the NPV amount by using the following equation (Mayhew and Tremaine, 2005):

$$\text{NPV amount} = \text{Future dollar amount} \times (n)/(1+k)^n$$

In the preceding equation, n is the number of periods, and k is the amount of interest. For example, if you're looking for returns one year from now, you would use the number 1 for n. The interest rate is a fraction of 1. In this example, we'll use a 5-percent interest rate that will be represented in the equation for *k* as 0.05.

If you project the future dollar amount to be $50,000, the NPV amount would be as follows:

$$50000 \times 1/(1+0.05)1 = \$47{,}619.05$$

Next, you must calculate the ROI value. Use the following equation to calculate the ROI value:

$$ROI = (NPV \text{ amount} - \text{cost}) / \text{cost}$$

If the cost to develop the usability test is $10,000, the ROI calculated from our example would be this:

$$(47619.05 - 10000) / 10000 = 3.76$$

So, in this example, the benefit will produce a 376 percent return, meaning that for each dollar spent on your usability design and testing, the company will get $3.76 back. If you were to send a figure similar to this example, it would likely get the attention of your stakeholders.

The Usability Engineering Life Cycle

Bias and Mayhew (2005) created the Usability Engineering Life Cycle (UEL) as a means to build a usability test plan. If you can integrate the UEL into your product development cycle at the beginning, it will provide you with a rigorous analysis and testing regimen that will help you get the most out of your usability design, analysis, and testing.

The UEL is a cyclic model that incorporates three phases (Bias and Mayhew, 2005):

1. **Requirements analysis**—In this step, you establish your user characteristics, what tasks the product requires for operation so you can determine what the users need to do, set your goals for the usability study, and determine the usability study design guidelines.

2. **Design, testing, and development**—In this step, you create a structured, top-down approach to designing the product, be it a user interface, Web site, documentation, or a combination of the three. This is the step that requires the most feedback from your project team.

3. **Installation**—In this step, you gather feedback from users during and after the development process and share this feedback with the project team to determine if you need to make any product changes.

If you and your team find that any changes do need to be made, you will likely go back to Phase 2 and design, test, and develop the changes that your project team made. However, user testing could also expose flaws in the requirements analysis that would require you to reanalyze your requirements and then go through the steps again.

Mayhew and Tremaine (2005) assert that implementing the UEL to develop a usable Web site or Web-enabled application takes 8 to 12 months to develop and provide a decent ROI, but this assertion is an average estimate. My experience has shown that it doesn't take 8 to 12 months to design and publish a Web site, depending on how much programming is included in the site.

Therefore, for a Web site that doesn't incorporate a great deal of programming, more time may be needed to market the Web site and make incremental changes as needed. Web sites that require a lot of programming, such as dynamically driven Web sites that use databases to manage and output information, will take more time to develop. This could lengthen the amount of time to realize a decent ROI or keep the amount of time the same and require less time to realize ROI. The same is true of software development.

As the car commercials say, your mileage may vary. The UEL is only a guideline, and you can adapt the UEL to suit your needs, because every project is different. You may also be constrained by tight schedules that don't permit a thorough usability test. However, it's good to have a by-the-book description of how to engineer a usability test ready to go, and the UEL is flexible enough for you to select the tasks you need to perform a solid usability test. However, you should keep the 8 to 12 month timeframe in mind when you implement the UEL in your product development processes.

Phase 1: Requirements Analysis

You can gather your users' requirements for your product in a number of ways. For example, you can use paper prototyping to give people printed representations of what your product will look like and how the system will react to user input. You'll learn more about paper prototyping in Chapter 4. You can also observe the users and see how they work; you will learn more about user observations in Chapter 9.

No matter how you decide to obtain your requirements, you should ensure that you have covered the following points in your requirements analysis. Even if you did create a paper prototype or observe the user at work, be sure to review the following points to ensure that you have all the bases covered.

- **User profile**—A description of your users' specific characteristics. There is no standard set of characteristics to measure, but you should pay particular attention to any issues that the user has with using the software, such as physical limitations.

- **Contextual text analysis**—A study of your users' current tasks, workflow patterns, work environments, and conceptual frameworks. This context will help you understand why the user reacts the way she does to the software, hardware, or Web site being tested.

- **Usability goal setting**—You need to set specific, qualitative goals that reflect the requirements you glean from the user profile. For example, you may want to have the users complete a task within a certain period and see if they can do that. If a user has some constraints that require a different method for completing the task, you should reset the goal for that user appropriately.

- **Platform capabilities and constraints**—You must define the scope of possibilities for addressing usability needs by determining the capabilities and constraints of the interface or product. This information can also be affected by the usability needs of the users.

- **General design guidelines**—You must apply generally accepted design guidelines for designing your interface. For example, there are guidelines for creating Web pages so that they appear correctly in every Web browser. You will learn more about design guidelines for user interfaces in Chapter 7, "Designing a User Interface," and for Web sites in Chapter 8, "Designing a Web Site."

Phase 2: Design, Testing, and Development

This phase is split into three levels of design work. Each level takes you from designing the concepts in the requirements analysis to developing a working product that users can test.

Level 1 Design

Level 1 design is the conceptual design level, which is where you design functionality, workflow, and rules. If you and your team have the time, you should get as much information from the users as possible before you decide how to design conceptual models. Models conceived from user input stand a far better chance of being accepted by users during the design evaluation stage in Level 3. The four steps in this level are as follows:

- **Work re-engineering**—Your project team organizes functionality and workflow design based on the users' tasks and streamlines work before you begin design. No interface design is produced in this task.
- **Conceptual model design**—The team creates high-level design rules for presenting information and interacting with the hardware, software, or Web site interface. If you have product screens or Web pages, this task doesn't go into that level of detail.
- **Conceptual model mockups**—You can create paper prototype mockups, as you will learn about in Chapter 4. You can also create wireframe versions, which are small programs that show some functionality but not the entire program, or you can even create a prototype with non-operating functionality such as small colored paper squares that represent lights on a hardware prototype.
- **Iterative conceptual model evaluation**—The project team evaluates the mockups and modifies them through iterative evaluation processes. In other words, if the team decides it doesn't like one or more portions of the mockups, it works on those portions repeatedly until it decides that the portion looks good.

Level 2 Design

Level 2 design is where you create the standards for your project. Creating standards is especially important because everyone on the team needs to understand how the project will be put together. Having people creating their own standards as you develop the user interface design is a recipe for chaos. Four steps comprise this design level.

1. **Design standards**—Now that you have settled on a model, the project team must construct a set of interface- or site-specific standards and conventions that will apply to the design of the product.

2. **Design standards prototyping**—The project team applies the interface standards to product functionality. This functionality can be presented in specific screens or Web pages that you create to test the look and feel as well as links to other screens or Web pages.

3. **Iterative design standards evaluation**—The project team conducts formal usability testing or other types of evaluation to refine the screen design standards in the interface. This process continues until major usability issues have been resolved and usability goals are within reach. You'll learn more about usability testing in Chapter 9.

4. **Style guide development**—After you have a stable and validated set of screen design standards, you document this information along with the results of the requirements analysis in the product style guide and then distribute the documented information to all project team members. Other style guides, such as a general style guide for the company and the documentation style guide, could also affect the product style guide, and vice versa.

Level 3 Design

Level 3 design is the level at which you actually design the product after making all your preparations in the previous two levels.

- **Detailed user interface design**—The project designers design the product based on the style guide conventions created in Level 2 design. The product that results is the "beta" version available for internal or external testers to use and test and for which they can provide feedback for the product team.

- **Iterative detailed user interface design evaluation**—The project team conducts formal usability testing or other types of evaluation to refine the screen design standards in the interface. This process continues until the project team validates the product against usability goals.

Phase 3: Installation and Feedback

After the product has been installed and used for a period of time, the company should gather feedback from users about what they like and don't like about the product and how they use it.

You can obtain feedback in any number of ways: by e-mail, phone, mail, or on your Web site. You can send surveys to customers, and you may want to offer prizes or special offers to entice customers to return the surveys, especially if the surveys are long. You may also want to conduct focus groups either in person at your company building or at the client, or online using a collaborative software tool that employs real time videoconferencing such as WebEx, Microsoft LiveMeeting, or Raindance.

The Never-Ending Process

One thing to keep in mind is that the UEL really never ends. Feedback during the development process will ensure that you don't have many problems to fix after the product is out the door—and good feedback is always a feather in your company's cap. You will also need product feedback from your customers after the development process ends.

In addition, you may have upgrades to your product that need to be produced—or updates to the documentation you may want to place on the company Web site. So be sure to include the additional costs of implementing continual feedback as needed, especially between product releases, into your ROI proposal and your business case.

The Case Study: Mike's Bikes

This book uses a single example as a case study to illustrate the steps involved in the usability design and testing processes. Other books in the *For Mere Mortals* series use the case study approach, which enables the author to present a process with some degree of continuity. In this book, I apply each technique to the process of designing a Web site and associated database application for use by both internal and external customers.

You may remember Mike's Bikes from *Database Design for Mere Mortals* by Mike Hernandez. In that case study, Mike's Bikes is a new bike shop located in the Seattle suburb of Green Lake. This case study picks up three years later to find that Mike's Bikes is doing so well that Mike has opened eight other shops in the greater Seattle area and now employs close to 120 employees. Given this growth, Mike has discovered that his customers now want to customize and order bikes and purchase other supplies online, and his employees want a more robust application that they can access quickly to get the information they need.

Mike has a project team of 10 people dedicated to the creation of the new Web site and database system. Following are the 10 team members:

- Mike, the owner
- Traci, the finance manager
- Jay, the marketing manager
- Laura, the production manager
- Michelle, the customer support manager
- Tony, the company Webmaster
- Maureen, the database and networking administrator
- Bruce and Travis, two database programmers
- Paul, the documentation writer

The team is excited to get going but not certain why a usability test is necessary for this project. That's why you and your assistant Evan are in the kickoff meeting with the team: to create a business case framework.

The first step in the business case framework is to interview the project team to learn what the business goals are. You let Evan conduct the interview.

Evan: "What are the business goals for this project?"

Mike: "Make more money!" (The rest of the group laughs in appreciation.)

Jay: "The recognition from customers and competitors that Mike's Bikes is the best resource for bicycles and accessories."

Michelle: "The capability for customers to order their bikes and supplies from anywhere and have that information available immediately for production."

Laura: "My workers will have easier access to more information, so they will be able to get their work done more quickly."

Maureen: "My programmers and I can work on more important things rather than enter information into the database from customers phoning their orders in."

After a discussion of the business goals, including the due date for completion of the project, the interview continues with a discussion of the customer goals, and Evan continues to ask questions prompted by the discussions. For example, the following discussion is concerned with what the users want to get out of the user interface so that all users can specify and access the information they need quickly.

Evan: "What do you think of the current database application you're currently using?"

Mike: "What do you mean, exactly?"

Evan: "I'd like to know if there's anything about the interface that drives you crazy and what you would like to improve."

Michelle: "I wish there was a page on the site that I could access from any screen in the database to show me what parts are available in what stores so a customer in one store that needs a part can find the part in another one of our stores."

Jay: "That would be huge. If a customer can't find what she needs from us, she won't come back to us."

Laura: "I think the database needs to tell us when a store is low on a part, not just tell us when the store can't send another store a part, because then that store wouldn't have a part available for its customers."

Mike: "How do you suggest we do that?"

Laura: "We need to have another column in the product table that presents a visual reminder, like a flag, to let me know that we need to order more parts to keep the pipeline filled."

Maureen: "That won't be hard."

Laura: "I also think we need to have a button next to the flag column to let me order parts. The button would open up the manufacturer's Web site so I could order from them online."

Traci: "*If* the manufacturer lets you order online."

Evan: "Laura, what happens if the Web site is down or the manufacturer doesn't let stores order from them online?"

Laura: "Hmmm. Perhaps the button could open a small window that lists contact information, and that contact information would also include a link to the company's Web site if we can access that site to order products."

Evan: "But that adds an extra step to get to the Web site. How about creating a separate button that connects to the manufacturer's Web site?"

Laura: "Good idea. If the company lets you order online, then there can be a second button with a different color that will take me directly to the Web site order page."

Maureen: "We'd have to build another module in the database to manage the contact information, but we could do it."

Jay: "But how would you get the product to the store without making the customer drive over to that store? Unless the customer needed the part right away, she wouldn't drive all the way across town to our store—she would drive two blocks to Rob's Cycle World."

Mike: "We'd need to hire people, maybe high school and college students, who would drive or bike to the store where the customer is and deliver the part. That would mean that the application would have to provide an alert for store managers that another store needs a part it has. I'll have to think about that."

The roundabout discussions provide you and Evan with a good amount of information you can use to create a list of objectives for both applications. For example, here are a few interface objectives for the Mike's Bikes Web site and database application:

- The customer must be able to find what she needs on the Web site as quickly as possible.
- The Web site must reflect accurate information, such as the number of products available for purchase.
- The customer must be able to customize her order easily and order her product(s) quickly and securely.
- If the customer gets lost, she must be able to go back to the home page quickly and start over.
- The customer needs quick access to product and support documentation.
- We need to access customer, inventory, sales, supplier, and employee information quickly.

You review the initial list of interface objectives with Mike and the rest of his team. Afterward, you and Evan refine the list and present it to the team. You and Evan present a report to the team that lists three key design objectives in bullet form:

- The product availability page must be accessible from any window in the database application. This page provides the following functionality:
    - It displays how many products are available in each store.
    - It enables employees to find parts more easily and quickly.
- The "Parts Maintenance" page should display visual cues that indicate key status points for each part. This page will provide employees with the following functionality:
    - Employees will be able to see alerts indicating that another store needs a given part that is currently in stock.
    - Employees will be able to determine how many parts are defective in each store.
    - Employees will easily be able to determine which parts need to be reordered.
- A search box must be accessible from any window in the database application. This page will provide employees with the ability to find a product, customer information, or order information.

With the initial list in hand, you then ask the team what it will take to develop the product and interface. When you talk about what development will take, include the associated costs such as combined employee hours dedicated to the project and any future anticipated costs; for example, the company may need to hire contract employees to finish the project by a certain date. You and Evan also inquire about the interest rate for the business, about the profit that the company expects to make, and about when the company will realize that profit.

Armed with this information, you and Evan create an ROI statement that you will review with Mike and Traci before your next team meeting. This ROI statement is the equation you learned about earlier in this chapter:

$$\text{NPV amount} = \text{Future dollar amount} \times (n)/(1+k)^n$$

Then you must plug the NPV amount into the ROI equation:

$$\text{ROI} = (\text{NPV amount} - \text{cost}) / \text{cost}$$

The NPV amount is the percentage return that the company will realize from its investment in usability design and testing. You and Evan received estimates from Traci of $45,000 for the future dollar amount ($5,000 per store) in 1 year at a 5.25 percent interest rate. You and Evan have estimated a cost of $12,500 for the production of test materials and the final report as well as paying testers to interview Mike's employees, create a paper prototype, and view how the employees use the current system as well as the new system as it's being built. Those costs are documented in a worksheet, as shown in Figure 3.1.

NAME_____ DATE_____

COST WORKSHEET

1. Combined employee hours dedicated to the project: __20 hours__

2. Future dollar amount: $5,000 × 9 stores =   __$45,000__

3. Years to profit: __1____

4. Interest business rate: __5.25%__

5. Costs for developing test:

   ■ Producing paper prototype test and related materials: __$2,000__

   ■ Paying note takers and observers: __$10,500__
   (3 note takers and 2 observers @ 35/hour
   for 60 hours each)

   ■ Total: __$12,500.00__

Figure 3.1   *Cost Worksheet*

Given the figures that you and Evan have, you calculate the NPV amount as follows:

$$\$45,000 \times (1)/(1+0.0525)^1 = \$42,755.34$$

Now you plug this NPV amount into the ROI equation:

$$(\$42,755.34 - \$12,500.00) / \$12,500.00 = 2.42$$

This follow-up team meeting will present not only your final list of objectives but also your ROI statement that proves your case for profitability—and in this case, a 242 percent return on Mike's usability investment should make him happy indeed.

Now that you have the ROI calculation, where do you store it? Place this ROI statement in a written report that you circulate to the rest of the team, and be sure that the written report contains the date you last updated the document. If you need to update the report, be sure to save the old report as an archive and place it in an archives directory either on your hard drive or on an external drive (like a rewritable CD-ROM) so you have a traceable record of all changes that have been made to the document. If you use Microsoft Word, another way to keep track of your changes is to turn Track Changes on.

What's more, when you distribute these changes to the team, be sure that each team member has access to the latest version of the documents online, such as through a folder on the network that is accessible only to team members. You and Evan should each keep a copy of the printed reports that you give to the rest of the team so that you have everything the team does and you have reference material easily available in case the online versions aren't available for some reason.

In the next chapter, you'll see how to apply paper prototyping to Mike's project.

Summary

This chapter took you through the steps needed to create a business case for good user design, usability design, and usability testing. The chapter began with a discussion about why you should include usability studies when you develop your user interface.

Next, the section on gaps between stakeholders discussed who the stakeholders are when it comes to your user interface design. This section also discussed the expectations that each stakeholder has regarding the interface and the outcomes from good interface design, as well as usability design and testing.

Then the chapter discussed building a business case framework and the five-step user experience process that you should build your business case around. You know that the process starts with the business goals and then factors in the customer goals. The appropriate project team members design the user interface or documentation, and then the team participates in the testing process to acquire feedback. The testers' goals are satisfied after testing, and that satisfaction leads to the satisfaction of your customer and business goals.

The section on the case for profitability listed eight guidelines for ensuring that your argument for usability studies will win over the skeptics and help your company's bottom line. The first and most important guideline is to drive the design and development of the user interface and usability design closely against the business case. You also need to bring your team members on board with the effort and share information with them constantly. You and your team need to know what the customer's needs, tasks, and goals are. From that information, you can create a scalable user experience that only adds features that blend value for the customer and value for the company. As you meet your design goals, you must make one person responsible for measuring the success of your design.

A discussion of calculating the return on investment for your usability studies followed, which is crucial to your making a valid business case for good user interface design, usability design, and usability testing. You learned how to use the net present value amount equation to calculate the ROI percentage return so you can present this return to your stakeholders and justify the usability study.

The chapter ended with a discussion of the ongoing process of usability testing and the Usability Engineering Life Cycle that places your usability testing inside a rigorous and ongoing process. Then you can incorporate the costs of that ongoing process into other product development as well as your product if it will have future releases.

Review Questions

Now it's time to review what you've learned in this chapter before you move on to Chapter 4. Ask yourself the following questions, and refer to Appendix A to double-check your answers.

1. Why is the satisfaction of customer goals important?
2. Who are the four stakeholders in a project?
3. What are the benefits of good design?
4. Why should you start the usability process at the same time as the project design process?
5. What should be the first topic of discussion when starting your business case?
6. How can you make sure that your customers' goals are satisfied by the user experience?
7. When should you add features and functionality into the product?
8. After you show stakeholders how good design, as well as usability design and testing, will lower costs, what do you need to show them?
9. Why do you conduct an ROI study?
10. Why should you use the Usability Engineering Life Cycle?
11. What are the three phases of the Usability Engineering Life Cycle?
12. Why should you get feedback during the development process?

4

Good Design

"It takes less time to do a thing right than to explain why you did it wrong."
—H.W. Longfellow

Topics Covered in This Chapter

Good Design Goals

Are Designers Against Users?

Paper Prototyping and Storyboarding

Good Documentation Design

As you put together your business case, your stakeholders may ask what you mean by good design. What does good design mean, and why should they care?

Users' desires and constraints are different from those experienced by designers. There is a disconnection between users and designers that you and your project team need to bridge as you develop your interface. Good design is presented as four goals that you should always adhere to when you design your user interface: ethical, purposeful, pragmatic, and elegant. (The next section discusses these goals in more detail.) Adopting the four goals of good design as you create the user interface design is what you need to resolve this disconnection.

One effective way to design your user interface to meet your goals is to engage in paper prototyping and storyboarding, which allow you to create mockups of the user interface designs that you and your team are discussing. *Paper prototyping* is a form of usability testing that you can work on with your team as well as with focus groups of users. Although paper prototyping lets you quickly create tangible ideas that others on your team can look at and think about, it is not the best tool for all situations. This chapter will look at what paper prototyping is and when it is appropriate.

Finally, you'll learn about good documentation design, which is another important goal if your product is to succeed. A significant amount of documentation is now available as online help. A good design for which users can find online help—or help of any kind—is your company's first line of customer support. You'll also learn the steps you need to take to develop and rigorously review the documentation before your product is released to the public.

This chapter ends with a reinforcement of what you learned about good design in Chapter 3, "Making the Business Case." It also explains why good design doesn't end with the first version of a product you're developing. In fact, if you're creating subsequent versions of a product, adhering to good design is vital if you don't want to alienate your customers.

Good Design Goals

Robert Reimann, Hugh Dubberly, Kim Goodwin, David Fore, and Jonathan Korman developed a list of the four top-level good design goals for general design work (Cooper and Reimann, 2003). These goals are important whether you're designing software or furniture. If you adhere to these four goals, whatever you're designing has a better chance of being accepted by others:

- The design must be ethical.
- The design must be purposeful.
- The design must be pragmatic.
- The design must be elegant.

So how do these goals apply to user interface design? Cooper and Reimann (2003) applied the four goals to user design as follows, and I've added a few tips of my own:

- **Ethical**—The user interface design should do no harm—that is, it shouldn't make users' lives harder than it already is. You should develop your user interface so that it actually helps improve your users' lives.

For example, an interface should not include unnecessary information that distracts the user and makes him less efficient in completing tasks.

- **Purposeful**—The user interface should help users achieve their goals in using the software. Having a purpose not only means helping users achieve goals but also understanding their limitations so that you can strengthen your users as much as possible. You can learn about the purpose of your users by understanding how users behave; you will explore this further in Chapter 5, "How Users Behave," in the process.

- **Pragmatic**—Create a user interface design as early as possible to meet the requirements of the stakeholders that I discussed in Chapter 3. By ensuring that you are aware of and regularly discuss the requirements and needs of all the stakeholders—users, engineers, marketers, and managers—you can create a design that meets all stakeholder needs. It takes time to overcome the gap between users and designers, and I discuss that gap in greater detail later in this chapter.

- **Elegant**—The user interface design must be as efficient as possible. In other words, if a function in your interface is accomplished with two clicks, try to get the function down to one click. This is especially true of Web site design, because visitors can lose interest in your site quickly if they have to keep clicking to find something.

  Elegance also means that all parts of your interface must feel like they work together as part of a whole, not disparate parts cobbled together, because incoherence can breed confusion and frustration among your users. Later in this chapter, I discuss how paper prototyping and storyboarding help you create a consistent interface for your product on paper before you start the actual building process.

You'll learn more about applying interface principles and patterns that adhere to these good design principles in Chapter 7, "Designing a User Interface."

Are Designers Against Users?

Designers and users have fundamentally different goals when it comes to design of any kind, and that includes user design. For example, designers actually design the product, and they're intimately involved with its development. Users, on the other hand, don't use the product until it's finished, and they may not agree with the designer's sense of design. Ultimately, however, it's the users who decide whether to plunk down their money to purchase the product.

These fundamentally different goals create a disconnection between users and designers that must be addressed and overcome before you can create a good user interface. Both users and designers have different constraints placed upon them that the project team needs to recognize at the beginning of the process so it can overcome them. If it's not possible to be constrained this way, the project will fail.

User Constraints

A user is faced with a number of constraints imposed by the physical world (Norman, 2002). These constraints can be grouped into five areas:

- **Physical**—For example, you can sit in a car only one way.
- **Semantic**—The meaning of the situation causing the constraint. For example, the driver's area in a car is designed in such a way that the driver can only drive the car by sitting in a certain position so she can reach the pedals, the steering wheel, the transmission controls, and so on.
- **Cultural**—For example, if you're developing a car for international markets, there are different cultural issues that have to be addressed, such as the fact that drivers in some countries drive on the left side of the road, and drivers in other countries drive on the right side of the road.
- **Logical**—For example, my father and I put together a crafting table from a kit for my mother's craft room recently, and we logically concluded that because the kit required assembly, all parts that came with that table must be used to construct it.
- **Social**—This constraint might be pressure not to admit mistakes or admit that you don't know something in front of others because you don't want to look dumb in a social gathering.

Designer Constraints

Designers have constraints of their own to deal with, which may divert their attention from users' considerations and constraints. Designer constraints include the following:

- **Time**—Designers may be facing only a limited amount of time to produce the product because of user expectations or because of an artificially imposed deadline set by others in the company.

- **Individuality**—The desire for individuality is strong within all of us, and it's easier to think about ourselves than about others even without thinking about it. Therefore, the designer may think about designing a product that he would find aesthetically pleasing.

- **Pressure from above**—Designers may be receiving directives and pressure from others in the company to create "the next iPod" and bring the company awards and recognition instead of something that he finds functional and useful.

- **Serving a different user base**—The designer may not design the product for external users directly but may only answer to internal users such as the engineering department. The designer may also deal with only one subset of customers, even though the product will be used by consumers at large.

- **The designer thinks he is a typical user**—The most important constraint is that the designer thinks of himself as a typical user; therefore, he designs to what he thinks is the best design for him. The designer doesn't think or realize that he is not in a position to determine all usability factors for all the product's current and potential customers.

Bridging the Gap

The ideal method for overcoming these issues is to bring them up when the product development process starts and resolve them before you begin design work. This is not always feasible. For example, you may come into a situation where there are severe artificial time constraints to get the product out the door quickly, and no amount of persuasion will get people to change their minds. There could also be political issues involved, where some people won't be challenged about their assumptions and directives because of their position within the company.

When you come into a situation in which there won't be many changes in the current development cycle, make sure you can obtain as much customer feedback about the product as possible. You can do this yourself, or you can talk with other departments such as marketing about what feedback they're receiving from current customers and prospective customers at trade shows.

The more information you receive, the more you'll know about whether you or the designer(s) who designed the product accurately represented users' needs. If they didn't, you can come better prepared to make your case when the product is upgraded and for the development of other products.

Paper Prototyping and Storyboarding

You may have heard or read about how movie studios create *storyboards* that show the various scenes of a potential film, particularly an animated film. A storyboard puts ideas on paper and then puts the papers in a certain sequence to provide a concept of how the film will play out. It also gives the production team an opportunity to look at the concept and make suggestions for improving the film before it takes its final form.

In user interface design, there is a more interactive version of storyboarding called paper prototyping. Paper prototyping involves creating a paper version of a software program, hardware product, or Web site so you can learn how users interact with the design before you develop the product. The paper version is easier to create, and it gives you some additional flexibility, such as the ability to move an object from one location to another on the page in response to user suggestions.

Much of the material in this section is based on Carolyn Snyder's 2003 book *Paper Prototyping*. I've also added some information about other issues that may also come up during the paper prototyping process, such as accessibility and the needs of different user segments. These differences may require you to produce several different paper prototype tests, or decide not to give a paper prototype test at all.

> **Note**
>
> You can view Carolyn Snyder's Web site about paper prototyping at www.paperprototyping.com.

Paper prototyping offers you and your design team an opportunity to test the design without expending a great deal of money. You will encounter skeptics, but this section will discuss how to overcome them.

What Paper Prototyping Is . . . and Isn't

Snyder (2003) uses the following definition of paper prototyping as a variation of usability testing, where representative users perform realistic tasks by interacting with a paper version of the interface. That interface can be anything that requires human-computer interaction, or interaction between the user and the hardware if the user is testing a hardware product.

The test is controlled and interactive. It can be given to several users at the same time or to an individual user. The test is moderated by a facilitator, who doesn't explain to the representative users how the interface is supposed to work before the test takes place; the test is designed to simulate a real-life situation.

The paper interfaces can be hand drawn, printed screen shots with additions or deletions, or even a hardware product with some added paper buttons pasted on to mimic new functionality. One of the testing team members acts as the computer or hardware product and provides feedback based on what the user does with the paper interface.

Paper prototyping contrasts with similar activities that vary in interactivity, including these:

- Producing mockups of the product you're going to produce, either on paper or in a graphics file. For example, you can create mockups that show how different elements and different pages of a Web site will look. Mockups are completely static—that is, you can only look at them, not interact with them.

- Wireframes, which can be Web site page layouts or software window layouts that show where text, graphics, links, buttons, and other elements will appear on the page. A wireframe page can include active links to other wireframe pages or windows, thus providing a more interactive idea of how the pages or windows will work together.

- Storyboarding, as discussed in the introduction of this section, where you create different pieces of paper and show how each piece of paper is related to the other, either in a linear fashion or in a decision tree structure. Storyboarding is also a static tool.

Overcoming Skepticism

Stakeholders such as your project manager and designer may wonder why you have to create a paper prototype to get user feedback. Snyder (2003) asked this question to a number of her classes she teaches in paper prototyping, and the concerns fell into one of four categories:

- **Validity**—Does paper prototyping find the problems we hope to find? And are there problems we can't solve with paper prototyping that require one or more additional or different tests?
- **Bias**—Does paper prototyping change user behavior in such a way that we can't trust the results? Will behavior change dramatically after the user tests the design on the computer?
- **Professionalism**—Will paper prototyping result in the project team or company looking unprofessional and sloppy?
- **Resources**—What's the return on this investment (ROI) of time, money, and resources?

The skeptics are not trying to make you look bad. You should show respect to them because they are sincere in bringing their concerns to you. However, be prepared to answer their questions and assuage their concerns. Snyder (2003) suggests several ways to deal with your skeptics to address questions in one or more of the following four categories:

- Create a sample paper prototype to show people how it works. After people see what a paper prototype looks like, they can better understand how the test works. After the skeptics see the prototype, they may provide feedback that could make your prototype even better. Also, be up front about the disadvantages of the paper prototype tests, and provide suggestions for additional tests that can address problems that paper prototyping cannot resolve.
- Have influential people in your company test your sample paper prototype as mock users. Walk through the paper prototype with those influential people so they can experience the benefits of the paper prototype test firsthand. Ask those people for feedback so you can make changes to the prototype before the actual test. By testing your paper prototype beforehand, you can identify any problems with bias and ensure that the paper prototype tests meet your goals.

- Seek support from sympathetic departments, and invite anyone from those departments to your paper prototyping activities. For example, the sales and marketing department (or departments if they're separate) will likely be interested in your results and may want to participate in the paper prototype tests as subjects or observers. People who are interested in your paper prototype will be willing to give you more direct feedback and also work with you to provide the best ROI figures to win over skeptics.

- Ask for feedback at the conclusion of the paper prototyping test to help assuage the concerns of any skeptics who still aren't sure about the benefits of such a test. For example, to enforce the look of professionalism with your paper prototype, use heavier paper or cardstock to make the prototype more resistant to wear and tear during testing.

Advantages

As you implement the feedback you received from the sample paper prototype test and report back to your stakeholders, be honest with them about the advantages and disadvantages of paper prototyping.

Encourages Better Planning

The biggest advantage of paper prototyping is that you will have a better idea of how your users use the product. However, you must also be aware of all your potential customer segments when you create the test, because a number of factors affect interface use (Thatcher et al., 2002, Brinck et al., 2002). These factors include the following:

- **Needs for people with disabilities**—Between 15 and 30 percent of the general population have functional limitations that affect how they use technology products—and that translates to more than 50 million people.

- **Different market segments may have different needs**—For example, there is the increasingly graying demographic in the United States as the "baby boom" generation nears retirement age. Although these baby boomers are computer savvy, there may also be functional limitations here as well (such as eyesight issues) that can affect how you design your product.

- **Cultural issues**—If you're designing your product for use in more than one country, there are cultural issues like different conventions and symbols used to communicate a concept, not to mention different languages.

If you know these factors before you create the paper prototype test, you can create a test that takes your customer base into account.

For example, if you're developing a user interface for multiple cultures, you can have the same interface on a piece of paper but have separate paper buttons with symbols attached with a piece of tape. When you use the paper prototype with people from another culture, you can detach those buttons and replace them with other buttons with culture-specific symbols, like the Cyrillic language for Russian speakers.

Resolves Problems and Encourages Creativity

Paper prototyping provides substantial advantages (Snyder, 2003). Paper prototype tests produce substantive user feedback early in the development process. A paper prototype also doesn't require technical skills; the user can simply manipulate the piece(s) of paper as necessary to perform a task. Therefore, users find the process less intimidating, and they feel more comfortable giving feedback.

You can invite coworkers from multiple disciplines and departments to participate in the test either as observers or as testers. This results in multidisciplinary communication earlier in the development process, which in turn promotes greater collaboration and the exchange of ideas.

The user feedback from paper prototyping also helps your development team by promoting communication between the development team and users taking the test, which in turn helps resolve design misconceptions and encourages development creativity produced by user interaction. For example, if the user finds a problem, the tester can quickly make changes to the interface, such as erasing a design element on a piece of paper and redrawing it somewhere on the paper. The design team can then make a note of that for further discussion.

The Results

When you approach the stakeholders, they will want to know what paper prototyping will expose in the design. Following are problems that paper prototyping is likely to find (Snyder, 2003):

- Unclear concepts and terminology.
- Problems with navigation, work flow, or task flow.
- Content issues that can lead to refinement, which leads to a better design that sends the right message.
- The way the user expects to find and use product documentation.
- Functionality issues.
- The layout of objects on the screen on the hardware product. Objects can include text, windows, and buttons.
- The effectiveness of the product. If the product isn't easy to use, it won't be effective.

Disadvantages

Paper prototyping is not appropriate for all situations. Some situations may call for a different type of usability testing or for further testing.

Different Testing

The following list of situations should be indicators that you may not want to promote paper prototyping but a different type of usability testing instead (Snyder, 2003):

- There are only a few people working on the project, or there aren't enough people in the company to conduct a paper prototype test.
- Everyone is familiar with the technology used in the product.
- The development team is close by or can test the product remotely.
- You can easily set up a test environment to create a different type of usability test in the early stages of the development process. For example, you may be testing an upgrade to a software program that's already set up in your company's training room, so it will be no trouble to install the upgrade version.
- The development team can control everything the user sees.
- The user doesn't have to sit through long delays (a minute at most).
- Usability testing can wait until the middle or end of the development process. For example, if your team is producing a software upgrade, the testing for that upgrade doesn't need to be done early in the development process.

Further Testing

Unfortunately, paper prototyping is somewhat static, and you can't replicate some dynamic features such as scrolling in a paper prototype test. You should also point out to your stakeholders that paper prototyping is not a substitute for full user testing of the actual software product, hardware product, or Web site. It is, quite simply, a first-phase development tool.

When you report to your stakeholders, you need to identify what other questions need to be answered through further usability testing and inspection (Snyder, 2003). These issues include the following:

- Scrolling and link rollover issues. A paper prototype test doesn't show dynamic responses such as what happens when you scroll down a list or what happens to a button when you move the mouse pointer over it.
- Long documents and lists. For example, if you have a long list of options available, wait until you have the entire list finalized in the software, hardware, or Web site so the user can scroll down the list.
- Keystroke, mouse, and other input errors that the user makes when using the product.
- Keyboard or mouse preferences. For example, your users may have different ideas for keystroke shortcuts, such as pressing Ctrl+S to save a document.
- Long download times, screens that take a long time to load, or a function that takes a long time to perform. For example, if a Web site takes a long time to load, you can't replicate that in a paper prototype test.

Good Documentation Design

In Chapter 3, you learned that documentation is not only part of the complete user experience, but it's also part of the first line of customer support for your business. Users who run into problems usually turn to the documentation first for help. If they can't get help, they may call your company for answers, and poor documentation factors directly into customer support costs that account for as much as 60 percent of a high-tech company's total costs.

Unfortunately, your development team can fall victim to the same argument about documentation that it does about usability testing. That argument usually goes something like this:

> You: "We need documentation for our software so our users will know how to use it."

> Developers: "But the software is so easy to use that we don't need documentation!"

Just like usability testing, a rejoinder to this documentation argument can be hard to come by, because the developers are right—if your development team members are the only people using the software. That, of course, is part of your answer: Documentation is for other people —the users.

Create a Documentation Plan

The financial benefits of having good documentation make for a powerful argument, but that argument isn't enough. You need to have a complete documentation plan developed and ready to present to your stakeholders before you approach them. When you promote documentation, you will need to identify who you will work with to develop the documentation as well as what documentation you need to develop for your users.

Just as when you start a road trip, you need to put together a map and plan ahead. For documentation creation, there are eight steps that compose a documentation map.

Step 1: Create Your Documentation Team

Before you know what to create, you need to build your team. Your team not only includes more than one or more technical writers, but you also have to know who your subject matter experts (SMEs) are. Many of those SMEs will be on your project team, but some won't be. For example, you may have other engineers who have knowledge you need but aren't on the project, and you may want to consult people in the sales or marketing departments.

After you identify the technical writer(s), if any, as well as your SMEs, you need to do some scouting by talking with them or their superiors to find out if they will be available to help you construct documentation. If so, you should determine when those people will be available (some may be working on different projects that have a higher priority than yours) and how they prefer to be contacted so you can get the fastest response possible to your queries. Some people like to be contacted by phone, others by e-mail, and others like to meet face to face.

If the people you want to bring into your project won't be available, you should bring up this issue with the rest of your project team, and perhaps some executives, about how you should get around the problem.

Step 2: Create a Checklist for Your Project Team

After you have identified your documentation team, you need to work with that team as well as members of your project team to create a documentation checklist that answers two questions:

- What type(s) of documentation does your company need to create?
- What information do you need for the documentation?

Documentation comes in many forms:

- **Paper documents**—In an October 2000 article in *Scientific American*, Steve Mirsky reported that people have an easier time reading paper documents than online documents because reading online requires different brain skills. However, there is a generational aspect to paper versus online documentation, because many younger people have grown up reading online and may have better developed skills for reading online documents.

  The advantage of paper is that you can hold it in your hands, as shown in Figure 4.1. This is important if the user wants to read the documenta-

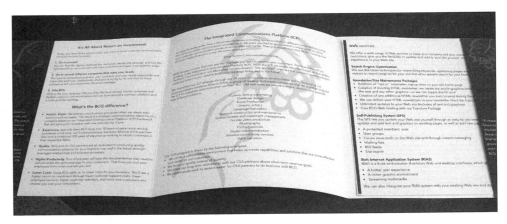

Figure 4.1   *A print documentation sample.*

tion when a computer is not available or wants to use tangible, interactive tools like a highlighter or a bookmark. What is more, if you have a hardware product, paper may be the only media you can provide for your documentation. The disadvantage of paper is cost. Paper prices keep rising; therefore, the costs for printing (and perhaps binding) documentation at a print shop also keeps rising.

- **Portable Document Format (PDF) files**—PDF is the de facto format for sharing, displaying, and printing formatted documents. Adobe System developed PDF and currently maintains the standard. Adobe allows anyone to download the free Adobe Reader program to view PDF documents on many platforms including Windows, Mac OS, Linux, as well as major handheld PC operating systems such as the Palm OS.

PDF is a good way to provide documentation that looks like a printed document that users can print on their printers without having you print the documentation yourself, as shown in Figure 4.2. PDF files are

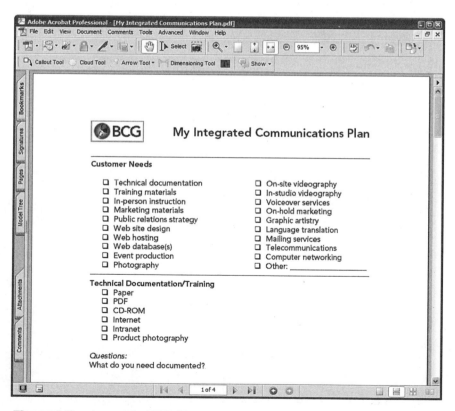

Figure 4.2 *A sample PDF file.*

also portable, so you can put them on your software product CD-ROM as well as make the PDF file available on your company's Web site.

- **Online help**—Online help can take different forms. It can be incorporated into a software program, or it can be a standalone file that is accessible on the Windows desktop or from the Web, as shown in Figure 4.3. Help creation software such as RoboHelp can create one help system and then convert that system to a number of formats including WebHelp, which is HTML-based help that you can view in any modern Web browser on any computing platform. You can also create help desk support modules from your online help for use by your customer service staff.

The disadvantage of online help is that it usually isn't designed to provide quick access to the specific information that people require. Many companies also don't realize that online help has different design challenges; therefore, those companies simply create a user manual in

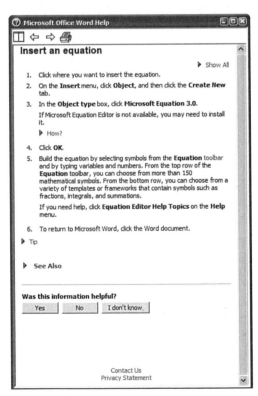

Figure 4.3   *A sample online help window.*

online help. Furthermore, for those who like to view paper documentation, online help usually doesn't format well when printed, unlike PDF documents.

- **Web site**—A Web site can be one that is available to the public, a private Web site that is accessible only by entering a user ID and password, or an intranet that is available only to customers within the company. Many company Web sites, such as the Adobe product support Web site shown in Figure 4.4, have additional customer support information available, including documentation files, technical support issues, and frequently asked questions (FAQs), which list commonly asked questions and answers. It is tempting to replace customer service with a Web site. The disadvantage is that if the user can't find the answer to her question, she feels like she wasted money on your product.

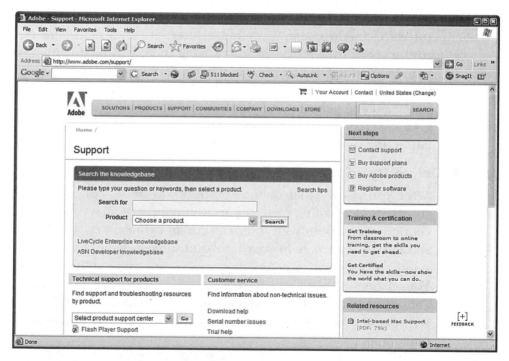

Figure 4.4 *The Adobe product support Web site.*

© 2007 Adobe Systems Incorporated. All rights reserved. Adobe, the Adobe logo, Flash and LiveCycle is/are either [a] registered trademark[s] or a trademark[s] of Adobe Systems Incorporated in the United States and/or other countries

It's important to understand what sort of documentation to include that meets the needs of your audience. To do that, you need to interview your users as often as possible.

Step 3: Interview Your Users Often

You may need to create different types of documentation to meet the needs of your audience. For example, your documentation may include a printed "quick start" guide, online help that's accessible from the Help menu in the software, documentation that can be printed or published to a PDF file, and multimedia training simulations.

However, you won't know what types of documentation you need until you understand the needs of your users. You need to know who the software, hardware, or Web site user experience level is before you determine what needs your users have. You'll learn more about user experience levels in Chapter 6, "Analyzing Your Users."

As you go through the design and development process, you'll likely have preferred users test your product as you develop it and provide feedback. (In software development, these preferred users are called *beta testers*.) Take advantage of your testers by also having them review the documentation as you develop it and send you feedback. The testers will provide invaluable feedback that you can use to create better documentation before it's released to the general public. For example, you can ask your testers how many graphics and screen shots to include, how to present information in the documentation, and how well they find information (or not) in the documentation.

Step 4: Define Style Sheets and Formatting

After you know what documentation you need, you should define style sheets and formatting conventions. Defining style sheets and formatting conventions helps both your internal staff and your users. A defined style sheet and formatting will help your team and subject matter experts (SMEs) understand how you will structure and present information in the documentation. Your users will benefit by seeing a clean and structured presentation that is consistent in tone, style, grammar, and layout. The company may already have style and formatting conventions that you can use in the creation of your documentation.

Step 5: Create an Outline

After you create the style and formatting guidelines, create a high-level outline for each component of the documentation. For example, create outlines for online help, printed documentation, and any training modules. Then circulate these outlines to SMEs as well as the marketing and sales staff for feedback and possibly other technical writers for peer feedback. High-level outlines include header topics that provide a broad view of each document you're creating. After you receive the feedback, send the revised outline to the original reviewers for a final review.

Step 6: Draft a Table of Contents

When the outline is complete, create a table of contents from it. In the table of contents, you "drill down" by adding subtopics underneath the broad headlines that you created in your outline. It's always a good idea to include sections for a glossary of terms and an index in printed or PDF user guides and online help. You may also want to add appendixes that users can refer to in a hurry, such as an appendix that contains answers to FAQs. When the draft is ready, circulate it to the appropriate stakeholders for review.

Step 7: Acquire the Information

As you write the documentation, you will have to interview SMEs to fill in any gaps that present themselves. If you do your homework about the contact preferences of your SMEs in step 1, interviewing will be far less difficult than it would be otherwise. As you gather information, it's likely that you will refine the table of contents to best present that information.

Step 8: Review Thoroughly

Users will recognize a poorly reviewed document right away. Therefore, it's important to have a structured, rigorous review process as you refine drafts of your documentation. The review team should include members of your project team, at least one person outside the team (for example, a sales engineer), as well as beta testers.

Review your documentation in multiple stages to catch as many problems as possible with accuracy, style, grammar, and the amount and appropriateness of information. You may want to include a printed or online form with your review copy so the reviewers can see what they need to check for, indicate their approval, and write down changes. Be sure to tie all review stages to strict deadlines so your document arrives on time and is as accurate and useful as possible.

Why You Should Care About Good Design

In Chapter 3, you learned about the business reasons you should care about good design. In sum, those reasons can be boiled down to three:

- **Save money you would unnecessarily spend trying to fix problems caused by poor design**—These problems not only include users contacting your customer support department asking how to use the product, but they can also result in users using the product incorrectly, which can lead to even greater problems.

- **Convince users that they should use your product**—Users determine if your software will be used. Even if users are required to use a software product in their workplace, the usability of the software you design can go a long way toward determining whether your customers will keep making your software product, hardware product, or Web site.

- **Keep your existing users, and bring in new ones**— If your product solves the user's problems, she will feel that your company knows what it's doing and feel more confident in your company and your product. If the product doesn't help her, she will let others know through word of mouth that your product isn't good enough.

  Today, the Web makes it easier than ever to share good and bad information through such media as sites that let people share opinions about products and services, as well as *blogs* (short for Web logs). When you're *blogging*, you're sharing your ideas with hundreds or thousands of other users on blog sites such as Blogger, WordPress, and MySpace.

These rules, and the rules of good design, aren't just for the first version of your software, hardware, or Web site. If your company produces software and Web sites, chances are that you update these products often to add new functionality in response to what competitors are doing, and to prevent your customers from gaining the impression that your products, and therefore your company, are stale.

However, good intentions for the next version can go awry. How many times have you upgraded your software to a new version that promised a better user experience only to find that the feature you were used to no longer works the same way—or isn't included at all? You need to care about good design and good design goals not only for your first version, but also for subsequent versions. That not only includes the design of the product—be it hardware, software, or the Web site—but also any documentation you create for the product. You'll meet all three of the preceding guidelines, and you and your company will be better for it.

Case Study: Creating a Paper Prototype Test

Now that the ROI statement is completed, Mike has given you the go-ahead to construct the usability test, starting with updating information in the existing database application. Mike has decided to work on upgrading the existing application first so he can have all the internal issues worked out first before making the capabilities available to his customers through his Web site.

Therefore, it's time for you and Evan to start walking the project team through the changes in the database application interface by using a paper prototype.

Evan purchased Susan Snyder's *Paper Prototyping* from the neighborhood bookstore to get more information about what's needed to create a paper prototype, including materials and steps for completing tasks.

You and Evan decided on the following office supplies to be purchased at the nearby office supply store:

- White poster boards, which provide fixed backgrounds onto which prototype session participants can place other elements.
- Blank paper for drawing larger prototype pieces and taking notes.
- Unlined index cards for smaller prototype pieces such as dialog boxes and menus. Get 4 × 6-inch and 5 × 7-inch index cards in case you need to cut them into several large pieces or if you need to write a lot of information on one index card.
- Markers and pens to hand-draw parts of the prototype, such as new buttons.
- A highlighter pen to make a highlighted element on the screen.
- Scissors to cut screen shots into pieces as well as create smaller prototype pieces from pieces of paper and index cards.
- Restickable glue to keep elements of the prototype in place on the page but which allow you to move those elements when you need to.
- Removable tape to write on and represent small amounts of text that change, disabled buttons, and list elements.

- Transparencies used with overhead projectors so you can hand-write data on the transparencies without altering the prototype, which is useful when you have a large number of fields to complete and you don't want to use a large amount of removable tape.
- Transparency pens for writing on the transparencies.
- Paper towel or cloth to wipe the transparencies.

The good news with this project is that you and Evan can print current screens, perhaps by taking screen shots and then enlarging them on a piece of paper. These screen shots will serve as a basis to show what the interface looks like, but you and Evan will also have to hand-draw parts of the prototype (see Figure 4.5).

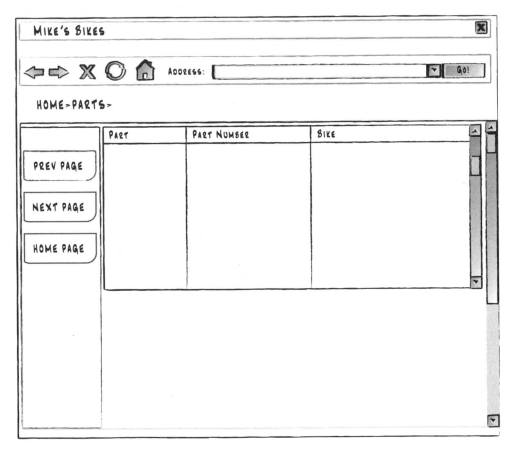

Figure 4.5 *A mockup of the application screen.*

The user interviews that you and Evan conducted that were discussed in Chapter 3 resulted in a list of specific goals for the upgraded database. (For example, the Parts Maintenance page should display visual cues that indicate key status points for each part.) Each task must show a specific example of meeting this goal.

Each task should be large enough for a user to achieve his goals but also have a finite and predictable set of solutions with a clear end point. The task should take only a few minutes for an expert to complete. For example, in the Mike's Bikes database application, one task could be to order a product online by clicking the appropriate button in the product availability page.

Each task should be written down using the following template:

- The task number and task name.
- The goals or output of the task.
- Inputs and assumptions. For the Mike's Bikes database application, you need to list all the tangible and intangible information and resources that the user needs to complete the task, such as a user ID and password to log into the application.
- The screen-level steps needed to complete the task. Each step will let you and Evan know how many prototype pieces you need to create for each screen in your prototype.
- The amount of time it would take an expert to complete the task.
- Instructions for the user to complete the task.
- Notes about the task, such as what you and Evan need to be aware of as you conduct the test.

Using the template should yield a document like that shown in Figure 4.6.

The tasks should be written down as bullet points or as tersely as possible so the tester learns only as much as he needs to know to complete the test and so you and Evan can quickly refer to the steps in the task.

As you prepare the prototype, you need to prepare not only the blank screens but also the data that will be associated with them. For example, you will need to prepare a dialog box that contains the error that the user will see if he does something wrong. Conversely, you will need to add the elements that will appear if something works correctly. Because you're updating an existing application for Mike's Bikes, it's easy to see what sort of errors the application returns by using the program. Mike has given you and Evan access to the application to see how it works.

NAME _____ DATE _____

TASK WORKSHEET

■ Task Number/Task Name:

_____

■ Task Goals and/or Output:

_____

■ Inputs and Assumptions:

_____

■ Steps:

_____

■ Amount of time:

_____

■ Instructions:

_____

■ Notes:

Figure 4.6 *Documenting the tasks.*

Note that if you have dummy text in the paper prototype that's not important to its functionality, such as content that will appear on the page, you can "greek" the text by drawing lines that represent the text on the page.

Organizing a paper prototype can result in a lot of clutter, so you and Evan must decide on a strategy to organize all the paper prototype materials in one place. You will place all the tasks and screens in a binder with dividers so you can keep everything in check. The binder will also include a "pieces page" (see Figure 4.7), which is strips of tape with data that stick to the page. You and Evan will be able to remove the page from the binder, unstick the pieces as necessary to place on the paper prototype, and then return those pieces to the "pieces page."

Figure 4.7   *A pieces page.*

All 10 team members will participate in the paper prototype test. Before you perform a dry run of the test with yourself and Evan, you need to add more information about the users' conceptual model and apply it to the tasks you want to offer in the paper prototype test. You'll learn how to do that in the next chapter.

Summary

This chapter began with a discussion about good design goals. You must implement four good design goals into any user interface: to implement ethical, purposeful, pragmatic, and elegant designs. The benefits of user design include lowering long-term production costs, focusing your energies on improving the product instead of fixing problems after your users have complained about them, and applying your design processes to other projects.

You learned about the constraints that users and designers face, and the gap this causes in producing well-designed user interfaces. You should try to bridge this gap as early in the process as possible, but if you can't, you should acquire as much information from the users as possible about whether the designer's outlook for the product matched the users' outlook.

Paper prototyping and storyboarding were covered next. You learned about the issues involved in creating a paper prototype, why it's the most effective means of developing and testing a user interface before you start developing that interface, and the limitations of paper prototyping. You also learned how to address skeptics' concerns, including being up front with the disadvantages and making paper prototyping look more professional through the use of stronger paper material so the prototype is more resistant to wear and tear.

You then learned about good documentation design and why it's important not only to good design overall, but a good user experience. Creating good documentation is an 8-step process similar to a road map that takes you from building your documentation team to reviewing the documentation thoroughly so you have documentation that looks good to your users, because users will spot poorly reviewed documentation right away.

The chapter ended with a discussion about why you should care about good user interface design. There are three primary reasons for good user interface design: good design saves you and your team time and your company money, convinces prospective customers to use your product, and keeps your existing customers happy. Note that good design goals for your product and your documentation don't end with the first version; they continue with subsequent versions of your product that your company releases.

Review Questions

Now it's time to review what you've learned in this chapter before you move on to Chapter 5. Ask yourself the following questions, and refer to Appendix A to double-check your answers.

1. Why should you resolve conflicts and constraints before you start the design process?
2. Why does a user interface need to be elegant?
3. How do you bridge the gap between user and designer constraints?
4. Why should you use paper prototyping?
5. How do you give a paper prototyping exercise a professional look?
6. What are the advantages of paper prototyping?
7. What are the disadvantages of paper prototyping?
8. Why does a product require good documentation?
9. Why is good documentation design important?
10. Why is good design important?

How Users Behave

Those who cannot tell what they desire or expect, still sigh and struggle with indefinite thoughts and vast wishes.
—Ralph Waldo Emerson

Topics Covered in This Chapter

The Psychology of User Actions

Knowledge: Brain Versus World

Task Structures

Conscious and Subconscious Behavior

Transforming Difficult Tasks into Simple Ones

Creating a Conceptual Model

Now that you've learned about good user design and what it takes to build both a good user interface and good user documentation, you need to understand how users behave so you can build a software product, hardware product, or Web product to meet your users' needs. When designers approach the design of a product or documentation unaware of their users' mindset, a product can become unusable very quickly. Only users who have more experience with the way something works can figure it out.

There are plenty of stories about the trials of technology. In the olden days before TiVo and digital video recorders, the "gold standard" of poor usability was the VCR machine, where children often had a better grasp of how to use one than their parents. If you have a great deal of experience with technology, you also know that you're the person who's the live-in technology repair department, especially within the family. Recently I visited my grandmother, and she asked me to fix her radio. She unintentionally pushed a button and lost her preprogrammed station (programmed by someone else in the family) and the time on her clock. I got it working in a couple of minutes because I'm used to playing with electronic gadgets that have a lot of buttons.

To understand your users' needs, you're going to have to delve a bit into psychology. Users bring their experiences to a new task, and they bring those experiences packed into a conceptual model of how they think the world works. Users also bring their various personality types into every situation.

People have to manage their knowledge in their brain versus knowledge that's already in the world. Most of us deal with imprecise knowledge in our brains, but we're often reminded about knowledge that's also in the world. Sometimes we look for that world knowledge in other places, such as on the Internet. Users' perceptions of the world are reinforced every day as they interact with it, and context affects perceptions, attitudes, and solutions. There are trade-offs using knowledge in the brain versus knowledge in the world.

According to Norman (2002), when people are presented with a new task, they adhere to one of three different types of task structures. They also adhere to previous information they've encountered and make their choices based on this information on both a conscious and subconscious level.

You'll see how to develop a user interface design by using several steps to transform difficult tasks into simple ones and create a conceptual model of what you're creating.

The Psychology of User Actions

Everyone who has ever used anything or has tried to perform a task and failed has felt helpless. Indeed, many people find reasons they can't perform a task using a product or object (Norman, 2002). These reasons include the following:

- **Blaming oneself**—For example, I received a bill from my health insurance carrier, so I believed that I had to pay it. However, I forgot that I had signed up for the carrier's automatic payment feature, so I was paying twice. I blamed myself for the error, but the health insurance company never printed anything obvious on the bill, such as "do not remit" in the payment line. Instead, the bill contained small print saying I didn't need to pay by check. The product, the bill, failed to impart this information, and I paid twice as a result. (Fortunately, the insurance company refunded the money I sent them by check.)

- **Adhering to misconceptions**—You could adhere to misconceptions because that's what you're comfortable with and decide to blame the product or company because that's easier than reading the user guide or finding information on the Web. For example, I had a router that I thought wasn't working, and I blamed the company. It was only later after talking to the company's technical support rep that I realized I'd plugged the broadband network cable into the wrong router port.

- **Blaming the wrong cause**—Recently, my dryer was taking longer and longer to dry. This dryer is part of a combination unit with the washer on the bottom and the dryer on the top, and the dryer didn't indicate where the lint filter was. I adhered to a misconception and thought the dryer automatically expunged lint because there wasn't anything to indicate where the filter was. It turned out that the dryer did have a lint filter—it was just made to look like one of the vents at the back of the unit. There was no mention of this anywhere on the dryer unit, and when I searched the manufacturer's Web site, I discovered that the combination washer/dryer was obsolete and, since I live in an apartment, I didn't receive information from the management either. I was amazed the dryer didn't catch fire.

- **Helplessness**—The user learns this after he keeps failing at something or learns it from past failures or poor design. For example, if you have customers who want to do something on your site (such as make a payment) and you don't follow the three-click rule for Web site design, they may give up before they reach their destination because they've encountered similar problems elsewhere, and they don't have the tolerance to keep clicking and searching. However, people doing research on the Web are more patient than people who are trying to perform a specific task, so the three-click rule may not be as important to a person doing research.

Psychological Types

You may be familiar with the Myers-Briggs Type Indicator (MBTI) method of identifying and understanding personality type preferences. It was developed during World War II by Katherine Briggs and her daughter, Isabelle Myers

(Eisenberg and Eisenberg, 2006). The MBTI has been adopted by many companies over the years as part of human relations training to show employees what types of personalities are in the workplace and how to best get along with people of each type. I remember going through the same type of mandatory MBTI training years ago.

The MBTI was based on psychological types pioneered by Carl Jung, and Hippocrates before him (Eisenberg and Eisenberg, 2006). These psychological types were split into four areas that Jung called feeler, thinker, sensor, and intuitor.

Briggs and Myers expanded each of these four areas into two different dichotomies, because people use their left and right brains to make decisions. The use of these personality dichotomies reflects the dichotomy created by the left brain, which is more logical and rational, and the right brain, which is more creative and emotional. The current version of the test asks a person 93 forced-choice questions, which means there are only two possible answers. The tester then scores the test and places the information into one of four dichotomies (Wikipedia, http://en.wikipedia.org/wiki/Myers-Briggs_Type_Indicator):

- **Introversion and extroversion**—This dichotomy identifies where people get their sources of energy. Introverts get their energy from an internal view of ideas and impressions, and extroverts draw energy from the outside world. An introvert can be worn down by long periods of social activity, whereas an extrovert is energized by it. The distinction does not reflect how much you like people or like to talk.

- **Intuition and sensing**—This dichotomy identifies how people acquire information from the world. Sensing people get their information from concrete information they acquire from the world. Intuitive people get their information from hunches and emerging patterns based on their experiences. Sensing is more of a conscious activity, and intuition is more of a subconscious activity. You'll learn more about the conscious and subconscious later in this chapter. Often, a sensing person is more mathematical in nature, whereas an intuitive person is one who can better interpret literature.

- **Thinking and feeling**—Thinking people organize information logically and make decisions about people and tasks subjectively. Feeling people rely on their "gut" feeling, or instinct, about a person or task. However, this doesn't mean that thinking people don't feel or feeling people don't think—it's more of a preference of whether people want to think things through first or go with their instincts when they make a decision.

- **Judging and perceiving**—This dichotomy describes how people organize and structure their lives. If you like living an organized life with a routine and only a few changes to keep a little variety in your life (like going to a movie once in a while), you're the judging type. However, if you like to live a largely unstructured life and see where life takes you during each day, you're the perceiving type. Judging types like making a decision; perceiving types like to gather information and explore all the possibilities, so they take longer to make a decision.

Myers and Briggs combined these four dichotomies into 16 different personality types because not everyone adheres to every type of personality characteristic associated with the left brain and the right brain. For example, a person can be an introvert but rely on her feelings when dealing with people and tasks. Indeed, with eight different personality characteristics, there are people on the extremes of the personality scale—those people who have completely left-brained characteristics and those who have completely right-brained characteristics—but most people are somewhere between both extremes.

These personality types are not always predictive of how people will behave in different situations, because context also drives behavior. For example, people who are participating in a usability test may react differently because they know they're participating in a test. Those people may be more interested in providing feedback about the product's usability than they would be in the real world, where they may just ask for a refund if they find the product's usability lacking.

The Four Primary Temperaments

Bryan and Jeffrey Eisenberg (2006) also discuss the development of temperament and character types by David Keirsey and Marilyn Bates, who were more interested in long-term behavior patterns. These studies were later merged with the Myers-Briggs personality tests to show how people put their personality types to work when they make decisions. In Chapter 6, "Analyzing Your Users," you will learn how to create groups of user models called *personas* that will include one or more of these personality types. From these models, you will learn who your primary users are and determine what interface suits those users best. For example, if your primary users are sensing people and also the judging type, you may want to create an interface that is consistent with interfaces that don't introduce anything unfamiliar and provide visual cues for completing tasks.

Keirsey and Bates identified the sensing and intuition types as the first type of preference that people apply when they approach a task or situation, because people want to know how to process information from the brain and the world. (You'll learn more about knowledge in the brain versus knowledge in the world later in this chapter.) Keirsey and Bates then applied this preference criterion against the four left-brain personality types to create four primary temperaments (Eisenberg and Eisenberg, 2006):

- Sensing/judging
- Sensing/perceiving
- Intuitive/feeling
- Intuitive/thinking

Eisenberg and Eisenberg (2006) give each of these four primary temperaments intuitive labels that provide a good idea of the behavior that each type of user temperament exhibits when the user is faced with a new task or situation. These four types are as follows:

- Sensing/judging: methodical
- Sensing/perceiving: spontaneous
- Intuitive/Feeling: humanistic
- Intuitive/Thinking: competitive

Note

If you've been through personality training, you may recognize these personality types as being associated with different types of animals. When I went through personality training as a contractor for a large high-tech company, these four personality types were associated with different types of birds. A methodical personality was associated with an owl, a spontaneous personality with a peacock, a humanistic personality with a dove, and a competitive personality with an eagle.

Methodical

Methodical people are logical, and they approach a new situation slowly. They exhibit the following characteristics (Eisenberg and Eisenberg, 2006):

- They have a detached attitude and are detail-oriented.
- They are disciplined about their time, and they methodically pace tasks so they can get as much done during the day as possible.
- They want to know how a task or solution solves their problem. They want to see hard evidence of that, and they want to see testimonials and other evidence that you provide excellent customer service. In the case of a user interface, methodical people want to see that you don't waste their time with unnecessary clicks.
- They believe that completing a task is its own reward.
- They despise disorganization and inefficiency.

Methodical people want you to answer the *how* questions:

- What is the process to complete this task?
- What are the details involved with completing this task?
- What proof do you have that this task will work?

Spontaneous

Spontaneous types live in the moment, which makes them impulsive when they take action. They wish to make an immediate impact—they skip many of the details and make a gut decision quickly. Spontaneous types exhibit the following characteristics (Eisenberg and Eisenberg, 2006):

- They have the personal touch, and they're activity-oriented.
- They use time spontaneously and keep up a fast-paced lifestyle.
- They want to address immediate needs and want to be presented with relevant and credible options so they can solve the problem right away. They never read instructions.

Spontaneous types want you to answer the *why* and *when* questions:

- How can you get me what I need as quickly as possible?

- How can I narrow down my choices to make a decision as soon as possible?
- Can I customize how I work with your product?

Humanistic

Humanistic types put others before themselves, and they're uncomfortable with allowing anyone else to do work (or anything else) for them. Humanistic types highly value relationships and enjoy helping others. They fear separation, are creative and entertaining, and are good listeners, so it's not surprising that they have a wide circle of friends and acquaintances. Humanistic types prefer to look at the big picture. They greatly value human development in themselves and others.

Humanistic types exhibit the following characteristics (Eisenberg and Eisenberg, 2006):

- They have the personal touch, and their lives revolve around relationships.
- Their time is open-ended, and they like to go at a slow pace. Humanists generally are averse to deadlines.
- They want to know who else has used a solution to solve a problem, and they want to learn what others' experiences have been through testimonials and other means of user feedback.

Humanistic types want you to answer the *who* questions:

- How will your product make me feel?
- Who will this product help?
- Can I customize how I work with your product?
- Can I trust you?
- Who is working on your staff to develop this product?

Competitive

Competitive types seek competence in themselves and others and desire not only to understand life, but to control it. They enjoy overcoming challenges and learning new things and look for methods to achieve their goals. Competitive types are highly motivated and persuasive. They usually come to decisions quickly after they feel they have all the information at hand.

Competitive types exhibit the following characteristics (Eisenberg and Eisenberg, 2006):

- They are power-oriented and businesslike.
- They are disciplined when it comes to time; they strategically manage their time to get the most out of each day.
- They want to know what a proposed solution will do for them, and they want you to provide rational options for overcoming challenges.
- They despise disorganization and inefficiency.

Competitive types want you to answer the *what* questions:

- Do you have a credible product backed by a credible company?
- How can you help me be more productive?
- What are your product's competitive advantages?

The Seven Stages of Human Action

Many everyday tasks aren't planned, but they're opportunistic—on most days, people simply decide to use something when they think about it. No matter if you've used a product before or not, you may experience difficulties with that product because of simple misunderstandings and misinterpretations.

These misunderstandings or misinterpretations can occur anywhere along what Norman (2002) described as the seven stages of human action when performing a task:

1. **Forming the goal**—For example, if you have a Web site with information that the user wants, the user will consider the goal to be to find the information on the site.
2. **Forming the intention**—If the user believes that the Web site contains information she needs, she will make a decision to find that information.
3. **Specifying the action**—The user needs to identify which link to click on that she believes will get her closer to reaching the information on the Web site.
4. **Executing the action**—The user clicks the link to get to the next level in the Web site.

5. **Perceiving the state of the world**—The new Web page appears in the user's Internet browser, and the user reads the page and perceives what has happened as a result of executing the action.

6. **Interpreting the state of the world**—The user processes the information on the new Web page and determines if the information on the Web site is the information she seeks.

7. **Evaluating the outcome**—The user determines whether clicking the link met the desired outcome. If it didn't, she must decide whether clicking another link on the new page will get her closer to the desired outcome.

People can use one, some, or all of these stages when performing a task, and there is a continuous feedback loop. Misunderstandings and misinterpretations can come from people who are not using all of the stages for some reason, such as confidence that they've used a similar product in the past and belief that their actions will work for a new product just as well. Other misunderstandings and interpretations can come from poor design that fails to account for how the user perceives the state of the world.

Knowledge: Brain Versus World

People rely on a dichotomy of two different preferences: sensing and intuition (Eisenberg and Eisenberg, 2006). Sensing is based on knowledge that people bring with them from information they gather through the world, whereas intuition is based more on information they've stored in their brains, such as patterns they've noticed from similar tasks.

Most people rely on imprecise knowledge to get around in the world. For example, people know what a 10 dollar bill looks like because they see the number 10 in the corners of the bill. However, if you ask a group of people who the person is on the front of the bill or what the structure is on the back of the bill, you won't get many correct answers. People don't need precise knowledge in many cases. For example, if I see a $10 bill in my wallet to pay for lunch, as shown in Figure 5.1, I don't care who the person is on the front of the bill because that information isn't necessary to complete the transaction. However, I need to know that the number 10 is in the corners of the bill so that I use the right currency to pay for the transaction and get the food I need to survive.

Figure 5.1 *Can you name the person on the 10 dollar bill?*

Our brains can only accept so much information in our memories. Because of that, we require constraints that break information up so our brains can process it. For example, there are seven digits in phone numbers because our human brains can process only seven digits at a time. As we perform more complex tasks, we break up each task into smaller ones so we can keep track of everything, such as when we're assembling a new computer desk that has a large number of parts and tasks.

People are also reminded about knowledge from the world—that is, from external sources. If you're like me, you use a calendar program like Microsoft Outlook to remind you to perform tasks at a certain time. (And, like me, you may have your calendar synchronized with your Palm Treo or other handheld PC calendar.) There may also be instructions for a product that tell you how to do something, such as the controls on your stove showing you which knob controls the appropriate burner.

How much knowledge you use in your brain versus the world depends on the context of the situation. For example, if you're presented with a new Windows program, you know how Windows works, so you're likely to use more of what's stored in your brain about the use of Windows products to guide you in the use of the program. There are trade-offs to using knowledge in your brain versus knowledge available in the world. For example, knowledge available in the world is easily retrievable as long as it's visible or audible and within your visual and auditory range. However, if you rely on your memory, you may have a difficult time remembering or become distracted by something else. Yet, after you do remember something, you're efficient because you know how to do the task. If you're relying on instruction from the world, such as from an assembly diagram that comes with a product, you're learning; therefore, you're inefficient.

When you create personas in Chapter 6, you'll learn more about how your users see knowledge in their brains and in the world. Then you'll use that information to design an interface that helps your users complete tasks quickly and efficiently.

Task Structures

So how do people manage others' knowledge in their brain versus knowledge in the world to communicate as effectively as possible? They structure tasks, which is something you learned in school. There are three types of task structures that people face when performing tasks (Norman, 2002):

- **Wide and deep structures that contain a large number of choices when performing a task, such as in a game**—For example, the game of baseball involves many possible outcomes in every situation. If a hitter comes up to hit, he could hit a home run, or he could hit within the field of play. If he does hit within the field of play, he could hit a single, double, or triple. Or he could try to stretch a single into a double and make it to second base safely—or be called out. Or he could hit a foul ball that will be caught by the opposing team—or not. Or he could pop up or fly out to one of the nine defensive players. Or he could strike out.

  And these are only *some* of the possible outcomes.

- **Shallow structures that offer a few choices after a top-level choice**—For example, a restaurant menu contains several top-level choices for you to choose from, such as appetizers, salads, entrees, drinks, and desserts. Underneath each top-level choice, you have a choice of other options, such as beef, chicken, pork, fish, and vegetarian meals under the entrees section. And under those options, you can decide what type of side dish and vegetable you want. A menu bar on a window on your computer is a shallow structure.

- **Deep and narrow structures, such as a recipe that requires many steps to be followed to complete the task**—These structures are commonly used in user documentation when you're teaching the user to do something. A former boss of mine referred to this approach as the "cookbook style" of documentation where you give the reader short, step-by-step instructions for completing a task.

In general, people find wide and deep structures the most challenging and the most time consuming when completing a task because there are so many options available. The reason for that lies in how people behave consciously and subconsciously.

Conscious and Subconscious Behavior

We handle a lot of our everyday behavior subconsciously (Norman, 2002). After all, we've brushed our teeth, showered, dressed, and driven to work and back many times. Sometimes we can't even remember driving through an intersection to get to work, even though we realize that we drove through that intersection because we're obviously at work! Subconscious work depends on patterns and regularity, and our subconscious mind completes tasks every day based on these patterns.

Sometimes our subconscious mind takes over unexpectedly. When I was in grade school, I was so comfortable taking a spelling test that my conscious mind decided to take a vacation for a couple of minutes, and I didn't remember those two minutes. However, when I looked down at my paper, I found I had written two more words, and both of them were spelled correctly.

Subconscious behavior can be fast, relies on longer-term memories, and can make it seem as though solutions pop into your head instantaneously. Now that I'm an adult, I find that my subconscious comes up with answers I thought about days earlier but had forgotten about, but then an answer suddenly popped into my head and I wrote it down. Subconscious behavior can also be the source of hunches about behavior or how something is supposed to work, as opposed to the conscious method of acquiring information.

By contrast, conscious behavior is slow, serial, and relies on short-term memories, which are limited and can be unreliable. When you perform tasks using your conscious mind, you have to be deliberate and go through the seven stages of human action to perform a task, as you learned about earlier in this chapter. The conscious mind also relies on the subconscious to see if there are patterns it can apply to the task. This assumption of patterns can lead to mistakes.

Transforming Difficult Tasks into Simple Ones

So how does a designer create something that's as usable as possible before talking with users? Suggest to the designer that he follow Norman's (2002) principles for transforming difficult tasks into simple ones:

- **Realize that users use knowledge in their brain and in the world**—People need to use both types of knowledge to get an accurate sense of what's going on around them. When a user approaches a user interface, he brings information with him from related tasks (the brain) and gains feedback from the user interface itself (the world) to make an accurate assessment of the task at hand. As a designer, you need to observe what information the user brings to the task in the usability test and learn how he responds to the feedback from the interface.

- **Simplify task structures**—If you have an interface in which it takes two clicks to get to a piece of information that could be reduced to one click, reduce the work for the user.

- **Make things visible**—If you can make user interface options visible without adding to clutter on the screen and overwhelming the user, do so. This is a real balancing act, but you will gain the right balance after you see how users react to the interface in your usability tests, as you'll learn about in Chapter 9, "Usability."

- **Ensure that the mappings are correct**—A user's perceptions that a product is quick to use is based more on the speed at which the user finds information than the speed at which the interface or Web site loads (Eisenberg and Eisenberg, 2006).

- **Exploit constraints to make a better product**—User interfaces can be constrained by the operating system, such as your interface being required to reside within a window.

- **Design for error**—Think of all the ways users could use the program for destruction, and then plan for that. One way to do that is to write use cases, which are written forms that include every conceivable way the user could cause errors, and then plan around those. You can mitigate many of these errors before you conduct your usability test.

- **When all else fails, standardize**—Fortunately, in the case of user interface design, the constraints imposed by the operating system on your design also provide you with a great deal of standardization.

If you have a Web site, the design rules are more fluid, but books and Web sites are available that provide examples of good and bad design practices so you can learn about standards for usable and effective Web sites.

Creating a Conceptual Model

When you're exposed to a task for the first time, you bring your life experiences, your beliefs, and your own set way of doing things to try to complete that task. The same is true of other people, and as this book has mentioned before, it can be hard for designers to realize that fact.

These life experiences, beliefs, and other methods that a user has built up over the years—even if it's asking another family member for help—build a conceptual model for her. A conceptual model is a person's idea of how she should perform a certain task.

When a person tries to perform a task for the first time, she goes step by step through creating this conceptual model by asking three questions (Norman, 2002):

1. What affordances does this product provide? Norman refers to the perceived and actual properties of something as *affordances*. Affordances give you clues as to perform fundamental tasks using an object. For example, as I look at a cup with a handle on it, I can see that my options are limited. I can see that the handle is there to grasp. The handle is an affordance.

2. What constraints are there? When I put my fingers into the cup handle, I find that I can put in only so many fingers, which is a *constraint*. (It could be argued that you can leave your pinky finger free to extend it in an elegant manner, which could be an affordance.)

3. How do you map the possible operation? As I put my fingers in the cup handle, I learn that the fingers I use don't affect the use of the cup, but the handle does suggest how the cup is to be used.

Contrast the example of using a cup with using a cell phone, which is far more complicated. The small LG Electronics phone I previously used has several buttons on top of the numeric keypad, and I don't have any idea what they're used for without looking at the phone documentation. What's more, the star, zero, and pound buttons at the bottom of the keypad contain different symbols, and I don't know what they mean just by looking at them.

I traded in my LG Electronics phone for a Palm Treo 650. This handheld PC is much more powerful and versatile than my old cell phone, but it's also much more complicated. For starters, there is a screen at the top that's blank, and there is no indication about how to turn on the unit until you look further down the front of the unit. The front of the unit has six buttons plus a center button ringed with four arrow buttons. There are also a couple of buttons on the side that don't have labels, so that's even more confusing. The buttons on the side are small and don't give much of an indication about what to do, although some buttons *do* provide clues. One small button has a picture of a home on it, and another has an envelope on it, so that likely means these are buttons to go to the home page and the e-mail program.

Yet these buttons don't tell you how to turn on the device. There are two buttons that have pictures of a telephone handset on them. However, if you're unfamiliar with the on-off symbol, which is a letter O with a line going outward from the center beyond the top of the O, you wouldn't know that the right phone handset button, which is red, is also the button that turns on the Treo.

My guess is that few people would consider the Palm Treo a good match for the user's conceptual model. Given that the Treo is an example of what *not* to do when you want to create a good conceptual model, how do you design a product that *does* create a good model? Norman (2002) suggests four features that designers should consider as they create a product:

- **Keep things simple so that users can form a good mental model that maps the use of the object to perform a task**—For example, in a user interface, you shouldn't overwhelm the user with buttons if at all possible. This is especially true in Web design, where good designers adhere to the three-click rule. This rule states that if the user has to click more than three times to get to his desired location, he'll lose interest and won't revisit your site.

   However, Albert Einstein once said that you should make things as simple as possible, but no simpler. It's easy to make things so simple that users won't be able to understand how to use it—or even find where the tool is. For example, when I visited my sister and brother-in-law and wanted to use their shower, I didn't know how to switch the water flow from the bathtub spigot to the showerhead. There was no knob, lever, or anything. My brother-in-law finally discovered that there was a ring around the lip of the spigot that switched the water flow once you pulled the ring down. I had never seen anything like that before.

- **Keep things visible**—For example, if you make a phone call to someone and you don't want to be interrupted by call waiting, you may be unpleasantly surprised if you don't see anything on your phone that informs you that call waiting is on and you don't remember to turn it off.

- **Provide good mapping between the object to be manipulated to perform a task and the results of that manipulation**—However, you can easily overlook this mapping process because you're so intent on keeping the experience consistent. That's true with Apple's iPod. Despite the iPod's popularity, users have fielded interface complaints about it. One problem is that if you want to change the volume if you're in another part of the interface (like the calendar), there isn't a way to quickly go back to the main menu and access the volume controls. You have to go back through one or several menu screens to get back to the main menu so that you can change the volume.

- **Provide good feedback continuously about the results of actions that the user takes**—This can be as simple as showing if the unit is on or off, as in the case of the Palm Treo. Clicking most of the buttons on the front of the unit won't turn the unit on, so the user can determine how to turn the unit on by trial and error. Programs also emit an audio or visual warning if you click a button or perform an action that you can't do.

Case Study: Interviewing to Establish the Conceptual Model

Now that you've put together a template and organizational model for your paper prototype test, you need to interview team members about the conceptual model they construct when they use the database application. This conceptual model will help you and Evan determine what tasks to add to your paper prototype list.

Your team's model may also result in changing the existing user interface application to make things work more efficiently. You and Evan noted in your initial interview in Chapter 3 that there were several suggestions to change the existing application to integrate the new features and make the interface as a whole more usable.

The two of you decide to begin by scheduling a meeting in which all 10 team members take the MBTI test, which you find on an MBTI site on the Web. You give the test to the team members because you want to create personality types for the primary user persona that you'll develop in Chapter 6. You also ask the team members about their conceptual model and correlate their answers to their psychological model.

After you and Evan give the MBTI test to all 10 members and analyze the results, you find that you have a good cross section of personality types:

- Mike is an extrovert, is intuitive, and is a thinking and perceiving person; the acronym for this personality type is ENTP.
- Traci is an introvert, is intuitive, and is a thinking and judging person (INTJ).
- Jay is an extrovert (which you would expect from a marketing person) and is a sensing, feeling, and perceiving person (ESFP).
- Laura is an extrovert and is an intuitive, thinking, and judging person (ENTJ).
- Michelle is an extrovert and is a sensing, feeling, and judging person (ESFJ).
- Tony is an introvert and is an intuitive, feeling, and judging person (INFJ).
- Maureen is an introvert and is an intuitive, thinking, and perceiving person (INTP).
- Bruce is an introvert and is an intuitive, thinking, and judging person (INTJ).
- Travis is an introvert and is a sensing, feeling, and judging person (ISFJ).
- Paul is an extrovert and is an intuitive, thinking, and perceiving person (ENTP).

As shown in Table 5.1, these 10 members fall into eight different categories (with each category denoted by an acronym that describes each employee's personality types).

Table 5.1   *Team Members by Psychological Type*

ENTP: Mike, Paul	ESFP: Jay	ENTJ: Laura	ESFJ: Michelle
INTJ: Traci, Bruce	INFJ: Tony	INTP: Maureen	ISFP: Travis

Now that you and Evan know what your users' psychological types are, you can ask the following questions of each user in the project team:

- What application features do you feel make it easy for you to do your job? (This question will give you and Evan information about what the users think the application affords.)
- What features in the application do you feel constrain you when you're trying to do something?
- If you feel a constraint, how would you change the operation so that it works better for you? (This question will give you a good idea about how to better map tasks.)

When you're finished asking questions, group the answers into different areas. For example, from your questioning, you discovered that Laura, Michelle, and Traci want to make it easier to call product companies directly from within the application because they're the three people who are most likely to call these companies for information. You can then alter the tasks and add more features in your paper prototype to fit.

For example, you may want to add a link to the phone number in the contact information that will call the company via the stores' voice over IP (VoIP) phone system when the user clicks the link so the user doesn't have to dial the number. You can then add a mockup of the phone in the paper prototype test so that the project team members can see that if they click the phone number in the database application, the VoIP phone system will activate and dial the number.

In the next chapter, you'll ask more questions of the team members so that you can understand their needs and goals. You'll learn how to take all the information you've gleaned from these interviews and create a primary persona for your application.

Summary

This chapter began with a discussion about the psychology of user actions and user misunderstandings and misinterpretations and how and why they happen. It also covered how personality types identified in the Myers-Briggs Type Indicator can affect users' actions and how those temperaments can affect the type of questions they ask when being persuaded to do something.

Knowledge in the brain versus knowledge in the world was covered next. You learned how most people rely on imprecise knowledge to get through a situation. This is largely because our brains can accept only so much information, and we break up more complex tasks into smaller ones so we can keep track of everything. You also learned how people are reminded of knowledge by the world, and what the trade-off is using knowledge from the brain and from the world.

A discussion of task structures followed the topic of breaking up tasks. It talked about the different types of task structures: wide and deep structures that provide a large number of choices, shallow structures that offer a top-level choice and a few subchoices, and deep and narrow structures that provide step-by-step instructions for completing a task. Our conscious and subconscious behavior determine the type of task we use.

Next, this chapter covered transforming difficult tasks into simple ones to allow digestion of a user interface. It discussed seven task simplification principles that you can use in any design situation. The seventh and final principle is the most important one: When all else fails, standardize.

The chapter included a discussion on how computer users bring a conceptual model with them in their brains when they approach a new user interface. That conceptual model is based on the users' past experiences, beliefs, and ways of doing things. The chapter concluded with the step-by-step process that users go through when they create a conceptual model.

Review Questions

Now it's time to review what you've learned in this chapter before you move on to Chapter 6. Ask yourself the following questions, and refer to Appendix A to double-check your answers.

1. What are affordances?
2. What are constraints?
3. Why do people consider themselves helpless when they fail at a task?
4. What does the MBTI test do?
5. What are the seven stages of human action?
6. What are the trade-offs between knowledge in the brain and in the world?
7. What task structure is the most challenging for people?
8. Why must you be deliberate when you're using your conscious mind?
9. Why do you transform difficult tasks into simpler ones?
10. What makes up a person's conceptual model?

Analyzing Your Users

*"Observation more than books, experience more
than persons, are the prime educators."*
—Amos Bronson Alcott

Topics Covered in This Chapter

The Users' Mental Model

The Experience Bell Curve

Understanding the User's Goals

User and Task Analysis

In Chapter 5, "How Users Behave," you learned about how users behave as well as the personality types, experiences, and behaviors that they bring with them. This users' mental model is the user vision for your user interface—what they expect the interface will look like and how it will behave. The closer you come to this vision in your interface design, the happier your users will be.

If you plotted user experience levels on a graph, you would find that they adhere to a bell curve. Most of the users on this bell curve have an intermediate level of knowledge, and you can design your user interface to meet the needs of this large group of users.

To create a good interface or product design for your users, you need to have goals. Therefore, this chapter discusses the Goal-Directed Design Process promoted by Cooper and Reimann (2003). This process is composed of five phases for understanding the users' goals. You can get an idea of what you're looking for by answering a series of questions during the design process. You will also learn where the Usability Engineering Life Cycle from Chapter 3, "Making the Business Case," fits into the Goal-Directed Design Process.

Users have goals, but how do you find out what those goals are based on their situations? You do this through user and task analysis, which also fits into the Goal-Directed Design Process. Then you can create *personas* of your users, which are representations of specific types of individuals with specific needs. After you have personas in place, you can prioritize them to determine the personas for which you want to design your user interface.

The Users' Mental Model

As Cooper and Reimann (2003) point out, the software development process has gone through four phases. When computers first came about, people who knew how to program them were *hackers*. Originally, programmers did everything when it came to designing computers. This was also true as the first home computers—such as the Commodore PET and 64, Atari 400 and 800, Radio Shack TRS-80, and Apple II—became popular in the late 1970s and early 1980s.

The advent of VisiCalc for the Apple II, and later the acceptance of the IBM PC and compatibles in business, forced the programming industry to fall under the rubric of business processes, where managers drove new software projects. Much of the work that the managers did involved specifying a list of features and then watching as all the features specified for version 1 still didn't make it in time for version 3.

As graphical user interfaces (GUIs) became standard in the 1990s and more people bought computers for the home to connect to the Internet, more companies became interested in the look and feel. In part, that was because they found that a lot of people were calling them to complain about usability features, and they wanted to keep their customer service costs from rising. The use of *beta testers* (preferred customers who test the software and identify bugs before general use) as well as usability testing became common during this period.

In the past 5 to 10 years, the issue of good design prior to the coding period has been gathering steam. Unfortunately, despite the introduction of design in the software development process, most engineers still design software from the point of view of adding features and functionality, because the functionality is what's important to engineers. As a result, many software programs either clumsily implement or don't implement digital-age improvements to mechanical-age structures.

Take the calendar as an example. Early Windows programs simply showed the calendar one month at a time and didn't provide any other functionality, such as the ability to scroll month by month or even year by year. My calendar in Outlook 2003 is better, as you can see in Figure 6.1, but it's still functionally limited. For example, for the next three months, I can see the calendar summary in the upper-left corner of the Outlook window, but I can't see a yearly calendar in Outlook. I can view only one month at a time.

The point is that software engineers are still building to mechanical-age standards. They're only slowly building in technologies that help extend the functionality of familiar systems such as the calendar.

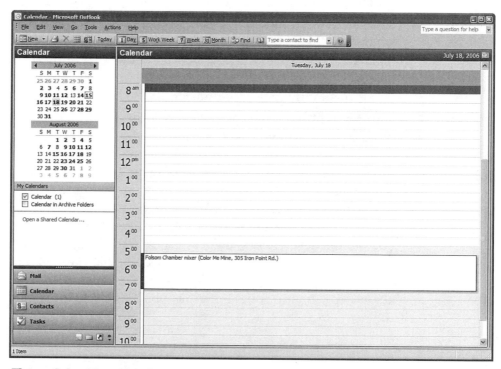

Figure 6.1   *The calendar in Outlook 2003.*

The Result

The result of this mechanical-age design is that you have four primary bad behaviors that still haven't been fixed (Cooper and Reimann, 2003):

- **Software makes assumptions about the user's ability to understand why something needs to be done**—If the program doesn't tell you why something is being done, you could make a mistake that could cause you to lose a lot of work. For example, if you presume that the software saves your work before you close it, and you decides not to save the file when prompted because you think the file is saved automatically, you'll get a rude surprise when you try to open it.

- **Software is often rude to the user; it blames the user for problems that are instead the fault of poor design**—How many times have you received an error message that doesn't tell you anything about why the problem occurred? (See the one in Figure 6.2, which asks for installation media even though it's installed.)

- **Software is obscure**—Many of the error messages that you find in Windows are obscure and don't provide information about how to fix the problem. The only "improvement" in this regard that Microsoft has implemented is to include a list of programming codes that show where the problem is, ostensibly to help the technical support people determine what's causing the problem. (Few users take the time to contact technical support.) This information is largely useless to anyone but the developers (and perhaps even to them), but that's not entirely the case. With some error messages, you can look up the error code on the Web and see if there is any information about the problem associated with the code. Hopefully, you'll find suggested solutions to the problem as well.

Figure 6.2 *Software behaving badly.*

- **Software behavior can be baffling**—For example, when I check the word count in a document in Microsoft Word, which is a task that doesn't change anything in the document, Word asks me to save the file again. This behavior hasn't changed in subsequent new versions of Office. WordPerfect, however, closes the program without asking me to save it.

Implementation Versus Mental Models

Cooper and Reimann (2003) differentiate between the implementation model and the users' mental model:

- **Implementation model**—The representation of how a product actually works.
- **Users' mental model**—Stipulates that users don't need to know all the details about how something works to use it. For example, you don't need to know how your CD-ROM drive burns data onto the CD—all you need to know is how to put the disc into the drive properly so that the computer will write the data to the disc (and not use the CD-ROM drive as a cup holder).

Unfortunately, most software designed by engineers follows the implementation model because the interface conforms to the logic within the software. For example, a separate dialog box represents every user action (Cooper and Reimann, 2003), and the user is prompted for information when the program needs to receive it instead of when it's natural for the user to provide that information.

Because people form mental models that are simpler than reality, designers should always strive for simplicity—one of Norman's (2002) principles for transforming difficult tasks into simpler ones. (You may have heard of the acronym KISS, which means Keep It Simple, Stupid.) Users don't care about how something works, and they don't care if their perceptions are accurate or even true. They understand what they interact with, and they expect the interface to reflect their own model as much as possible. The closer that the implementation model is to the mental model, the easier the interface for the user.

The Experience Bell Curve

Chapter 5 discussed the experiences, behaviors, and other personality traits that people bring with them, and the previous section discussed how the users create a mental model from all these components. If you polled several different groups of users and plotted their experience levels on a chart, you'd find that most of them fall into the range that Cooper and Reimann (2003) describe as *perpetual intermediates*. Cooper and Reimann call intermediate users perpetual because most of them have neither the time nor the interest to learn more about the program than they need to know to complete their regular tasks in a timely manner.

The chart would look like a bell curve, as shown in Figure 6.3, with the bulk of the curve being populated with perpetual intermediates, and beginners and advanced users on either end.

The bell curve is not an accurate representation of every computer user for every user interface through all time. People who are beginners don't stay that way for long, in part because people don't like to feel incompetent. Also, users are likely interested in learning how to use the interface because it will benefit them. People can also transition from the intermediate to the advanced stage if they use enough features for a certain period.

The curve can also be skewed depending on how you define experience. For example, if you have a large number of people using a program for the first time, the curve will be skewed so that most of the people using the program

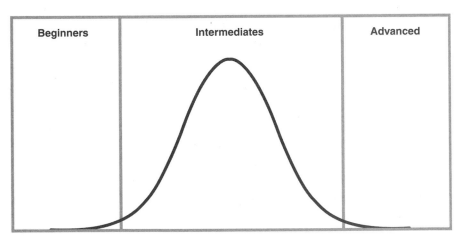

Figure 6.3 *The experience bell curve.*

are beginners, and a much smaller group in the graph (usually the developers) are in the intermediate to advanced stage. However, if all the users in the test are proficient in Windows, the chart can skew the other way to show that there are no Windows beginners in the group—just intermediates and advanced users at different stages of knowledge.

Different Needs for Different Groups

The three groups of users—beginners, intermediates, and advanced—have different needs (Cooper and Reimann, 2003). If you design your user interface (as well as peripheral information such as your documentation) to meet these needs, all these groups will be more satisfied than if you design primarily for one group or the other.

Beginners

Beginners know they're novices when they start using a program, and they don't want the program to reinforce that feeling. Users want to be treated as intelligent people, and they want to learn as quickly as possible. Therefore, instruction needs to be delivered quickly and effectively. This is a good reason to design your user interface as closely to your users' mental models as possible. You'll learn how to analyze your users' mental models later in this chapter.

Beginners have questions that are more basic and broad:

- What does this product do?
- Where do I begin?
- What do I need to do to complete the tasks?

Some pieces of software simply refer to online help as their only means of support, but online help is not designed to be a tool for getting beginners up to speed. If online help is designed well, it is for intermediates and experts to get quick information about a question or issue. A better method for getting beginners up to speed is a demonstration that shows them basic tasks and how to use the program to complete those tasks. This demonstration should be interactive whenever possible so that the tutorial can reinforce the steps needed to complete a task. There are programs that provide interactive tutorials. You can even design an interactive design tutorial in PowerPoint if you want (see Figure 6.4).

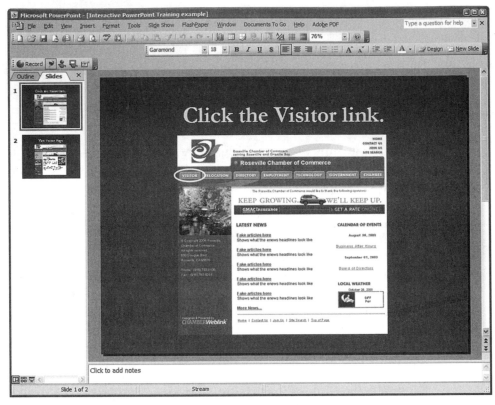

Figure 6.4   *A sample interactive PowerPoint tutorial.*

Intermediates

Intermediates are looking for specific answers to questions, including these:

- Can you remind me how to perform this task?
- How do I find this function?
- What new features are in this upgrade?
- Can I undo my last action?
- What's the command to perform this task?

These users want access to the tools they need to use, so it's important to design your user interface to get them those tools right away. You can do a lot of this in the user interface. Intermediate users depend on online help that's easily accessible from within the program and provides answers quickly.

Intermediates don't need to know about advanced features, but they like to know they're there in case they need them at some point in the future. However, many intermediates are assured by having the Microsoft Word advanced features there in case they ever need to use them in the future.

Advanced Users

Advanced users use the user interface constantly, so they develop an instinctive feel for its nuances after a certain period. Therefore, their questions are about connecting their actions to the program behaviors:

- Are there shortcuts for completing this task?
- Can I automate this task?
- How can I customize the interface for my needs?

Some experts are also looking for specific information about a feature of the program that they use regularly but most people don't use, such as the equation editor in Microsoft Word (as shown in Figure 6.5) or Adobe FrameMaker.

Figure 6.5 *Word's equation editor.*

Understanding the User's Goals

The Internet has changed the way people think about interfaces and the way companies market to users (Eisenberg and Eisenberg, 2006). This is both a problem and an opportunity for user interface designers. The problem is that users are now driving not only the marketing of products, but also the user interface design. The opportunity is that the designer(s) can get a better grasp of the disconnections between the users' goals and the user interface design.

Cooper and Reimann (2003) identified the problem as being a disconnection between research performed by market analysts and the design of the interface performed by designers. To fill in the gaps, Cooper and Reimann created the Goal-Directed Design Process for software engineering and user interface design. These gaps are in the forms of three new primary activities between the research and refinement stages.

The entire five-step Goal-Directed Design Process combines *ethnography* (a method of studying and learning about a person or group of people), research, modeling, and design into five phases, in the following order (Cooper and Reimann, 2003):

1. **Research**—This phase uses observational and contextual testing as well as interviews to learn more about potential and actual users of the product. One of the primary outcomes of research is the discovery of usage patterns, which suggest the goals and motivations for using the product. For example, if you do research on word processors, one motivation is to write and edit documents more quickly than doing so by hand. You will learn more about observational and contextual testing in Chapter 9, "Usability."

2. **Modeling**—After the research is completed, the modeling phase analyzes the research for user and workflow patterns, and from that creates user models based on those patterns. Those models are based on groupings of user goals, motivations, and behavioral patterns. From these user models, or *personas*, the project team determines how much influence each persona will have on the interface design. You'll learn more about personas in the next section.

3. **Requirements**—In this phase, the project team creates requirements that meet the needs of one or more of the personas you identified in the modeling phase. To meet the requirements, you need to learn more about the user in the environment in which he would be using the interface. That takes user and task analysis, which you'll learn about later in this chapter. The result of this phase is a requirements definition that balances the needs of the user, the business, and the technical necessities.

4. **Framework**—Designers create an interaction framework that produces a structure for the program so they can add the remainder of the code later. This framework melds general interaction design principles with interaction design patterns to create a flow and behavior for the product. Parts of the framework include input methods, views, data elements, functional elements and groups, and group hierarchy. You'll learn more about creating an interaction framework in Chapters 7, "Designing a User Interface," and 8, "Designing a Web Site."

5. **Refinement**—This phase refines the framework and includes detailed documentation of the design as well as a form and behavior specification. This phase defines what the design should do to meet the goals of each persona identified in the Modeling phase as well as the business that employs the persona. For example, you should identify a problem that both the persona and business are having, such as having inadequate tools to gain customer feedback, and then identify the solution that your interface will provide to the persona and the business.

The Goal-Directed Design Process also includes important questions that project teams should ask during the process (Cooper and Reimann, 2003):

- How do I find out who my users are?
- How do I learn what my users are trying to accomplish?
- How should my product behave?
- What form should my product take? For example, should the product be GUI-based or Web-based?
- How will users interact with my product?
- How can my product's functions be most effectively organized?
- How will my product introduce itself to first-time users? In other words, how will first-time users know where to start?
- How can my product put an understandable and controllable face on technology?
- How can my product deal with user problems?
- How will my product help infrequent users become more expert?
- How can my product provide sufficient depth for expert users? For example, how can I automate things so that expert users can become more productive?

Note

In this list, the use of the word *product* doesn't just include your user interface; it also includes all contact with the user through the program, including error messages and online help. You will only be able to answer all these questions effectively if you take into account all the messages that your interface sends your user.

The Goal-Directed Design Process was designed to keep everyone in the loop, keep guesswork out of the design process, and provide a clear rationale for decisions. Note that this process is not linear. You will likely go back and forth between different phases as required to obtain as much information as possible to create an effective user interface.

If you're on a product project team, it may adhere to this or a similar process. You should not only be aware of this process, which is similar to discovering information from users and refining documentation, but you should also strive to dovetail all related efforts, such as documentation and training, with this process. Dovetailing your efforts will ensure not only that all on the team understand the process, but also that they perform some joint research to gather information and give you an opportunity on the product's interactive processes.

User and Task Analysis

The users' mental model is based on many factors, including their experiences, behaviors, beliefs, and situations. As you analyze your users' mental models, what you're really doing is marketing to them. As mentioned in the previous section, users are now driving the marketing and acceptance of user interfaces, so it behooves you to make every effort to find out what users are thinking about.

The Research phase of the Goal-Oriented Design Process involves researching how users behave in a number of ways using qualitative and quantitative research (Cooper and Reimann, 2003). Quantitative research is the most objective type of information, but there are numerous ways to interpret statistics to fit a certain point of view. In addition, quantitative research can't capture the complex interactions between a human being and a user interface.

Qualitative research is research based on the characteristics of something rather than a number or measurement. This book has been building up to this point by discussing the questions you need to ask as well as the different user types. To answer these questions and learn what sorts of users you have, you need to employ qualitative research techniques. These techniques include the following (Cooper and Reimann, 2003):

- Reviews of competing products.

- Reviews of market research, such as computing media Web sites and technology white papers.

- Researching market demographics in the area you're developing in. That research can include analyzing demographic, geographic, or behavioral variables to see if any patterns emerge.

- Interviews with stakeholders (such as the sales and marketing department), developers, subject matter experts (SMEs), and other experts as needed.

- Ethnographic interviews, in which one or more members of the project team interview a group of users. This group is based on a hypothesis about what the team wants to get out of an interview, such as learning what needs users have.

- Conducting focus groups in a room and asking the groups to answer a structured set of questions or make certain choices.

- Engaging in usability and user testing. The most effective means of user interface testing is user and task analysis, which is done by observing the user as he works in his natural environment. That environment is usually the workplace, but it is more than just the user's cubicle or office—it's about the user's work day and how he employs the tasks every day.

Constructing Personas

Part of user and task analysis is constructing personas, which is also part of the modeling phase of the Goal-Directed Design Process. Before you engage in user and task analysis, you need to learn who your users are by constructing personas. As you read at the beginning of this chapter, personas are user models based on groupings of different user characteristics.

Eisenberg and Eisenberg (2006) discuss the creation of personas in terms of sales, which is essentially what you're trying to do with your user interface: persuade the user that the interface is worth using. Personas connect three different dimensions of information into one cohesive persona:

- **Demographics**—This segments some of the persona features. For example, demographic data shows such data as the user's gender, location, and income.

- **Psychographics**—This segments some of the persona needs and determines questions that each persona may ask. For example, a spontaneous type and a competitive type will ask different questions and will want different types of information.
- **Topology**—This allows you to segment by determining how complex the persuasion process is; that complexity is based on a customer's perceptions and experiences.

Regarding the topology dimension, Eisenberg and Eisenberg mapped a four-dimension model for the process of persuasion in sales:

- **Need**—This is the urgency that a user feels for a product or service.
- **Risk**—This is the amount of risk the user is willing to accept regarding such features as a career or self-esteem.
- **Knowledge**—This is how much knowledge the user has about the product, which can affect need and risk. For example, if someone feels he doesn't have enough information about a product or service, the risk factor for that user is higher.
- **Consensus**—This is the understanding during the persuasion process of how many people need to be convinced and when.

The information from the three dimensions of information—demographics, psychographics, and topology—begins to reveal the motivations of your persona types so you can learn what motivates your users to do something.

The Advantages of Personas

Personas overcome several problems that you have at the start of the user design process (Cooper and Reimann, 2003). As you develop personas, you communicate with developers, designers, and other stakeholders to learn what their understanding of user needs are, which encourages more collaboration. The project team uses that input to determine what a product should do and how it should behave. Then it builds several design choices for prospective users to test.

Learning about your users through personas helps minimize or eliminate four design issues that can arise during product development (Cooper and Reimann, 2003):

- The *elastic user*—that is, the definition of the user in the mind of the designer, developer, or other project team member that allows the member to design the interface and claim he is serving the user. By identifying the typical users of the software, the project team can design the interface to the users' needs as shown through research, not what's in a particular team member's head.

- *Self-referential design* involves designers or developers projecting their ideas onto the project and claiming that this is what the user wants. In other words, the designer or developer thinks he is a typical user.

- Designing for *edge* cases, meaning that the project team will design for every eventuality that *could* happen but probably won't. With a list of personas available through research, the project team can focus on tasks and functions that will be most important to the majority of users.

- Targeting people who are not end users. There is a tendency to target people who review the software or people in your IT and customer support departments who will be administering and supporting the software. However, by knowing who your real end users are, your project team will be able to design for those users.

The project team then measures the effectiveness of the design by testing design choices on different personas. The feedback from those choices helps the project team build a consensus about and a commitment to the final design.

Personas are also useful for other product-related development efforts, because you can apply what you learn in creating personas for one project to other projects.

Fusing Behaviors, Characteristics, and Goals

Constructing a persona requires you to fuse the behaviors and characteristics of your users with the goals of your users to create a narrative that explains the persona (Cooper and Reimann, 2003).

This chapter has already discussed the project team goals as part of the Goal-Directed Design Process, but users have their own goals and motivations. These goals include the following:

- **Life goals**—These are met through personal motivations such as wanting to become the president of the company or learn all there is to know in a particular field or area of software.

- **Experience goals**—These are met by a deep desire to feel competent by not making mistakes, avoid feeling stupid, and enjoy oneself as much as possible.
- **End goals for using a specific product**—These can include finding the most "bang for the buck" when it comes to the best combination of features and service, finishing tasks quickly and efficiently, and finishing short-term and long-term goals such as fulfilling a customer service request or completing development of a product.

User goals are not the only ones you have to consider when you create your personas. You must also manage the goals of other stakeholders who are both inside and outside your company. In addition, there are three other goals that you have to consider in design (Cooper and Reimann, 2003):

- **Technical goals**—These goals include ensuring that the program runs in all modern operating systems and that it is secure from viruses, worms, and other malware. If you have a hardware product, your product team must ensure that the hardware is reliable and performs as expected. If your product is not reliable and secure, no one will buy it.
- **Customers' goals**—Customers are different from users in that they are not going to use the product, but they will give the product to someone else to use. Therefore, customers are very interested in ensuring that the recipient is satisfied by the customer's purchase. Customers may also manage products but not use them regularly, such as a product that manages a network server. In these cases, the customers are more interested in the program's stability and security.
- **Business goals**—Examples are decreasing costs and increasing profits for the company that is developing the product. Satisfaction of business goals can also show stakeholders that there is a return on investment (ROI) for user interface design and usability testing, which can ensure that such techniques are valid and should be used with other projects,

These goals should never supersede the users' goals, but in the case of the customer goals, they may require you to create a new persona, as you'll learn about later in this chapter. You can also use these goals as part of your approach to stakeholders for good user design so that you can show them how good design addresses those goals. See Chapter 4, "Good Design," for more information.

Interviewing Your Users

Personas are represented as individuals and are synthesized from observations of real people. Those observations take the following forms (Cooper and Reimann, 2003):

- Interviews with users outside of the context of their jobs, such as interviews in conference rooms.

- Interviews about users by other people in the company who can supply that information, such as sales and marketing personnel, executives who meet with users, as well as other stakeholders such as subject matter experts (SMEs).

- Market research data, such as surveys, and other forms of direct feedback, such as feedback at tradeshows, literature reviews, market segmentation studies, and other studies, such as white papers. Figure 6.6 shows a white paper.

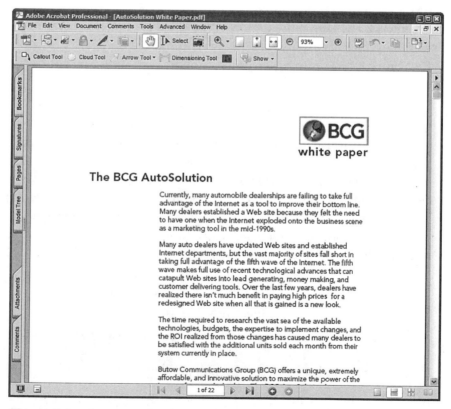

Figure 6.6 *An example of a white paper.*

As you interview your users, map those subjects to behavioral variables, as discussed in Chapter 5, "How Users Behave," as well as any other demographic data that you or your project team wants to find out, such as age groups. Then you will begin to see patterns in the data to compare against the persona hypothesis and determine if the hypothesis needs to be changed. For example, if your data patterns show something unexpected, you may need to account for these unexpected behaviors by holding new interviews or adding these behaviors to a new persona that you weren't expecting to add.

This "drilling down" for information about your persona obtains a deeper understanding of your users than a high-level profile, which provides only small amounts of information about the user, such as the user's name and some demographic data you find in market segmentation studies.

Watching Users in Action

Interviewing your users in a conference room doesn't give you the opportunity to see how their perceptions and ideas mesh with an impartial view of their work environment and how they react to changes there. The work environment doesn't just include the work that users do in their cubicles, but how they interact in their larger environment. That includes contact with other people in the company through meetings, phone calls, and e-mail, but also the physical environment.

Therefore, it's important to perform user and task analysis "in the field" to get the answers to questions about how users operate in their work environment. *User and task analysis* is the process of learning about ordinary users by observing them in action (Hackos and Redish, 1998). Only by observing users of your products will you be able to obtain a clear picture of how they use your products and how to minimize their problems as much as possible—a condition called *extreme usability* (Donoghue, 2002). User and task analysis will enable you to understand the following:

- What users' goals are and what they are trying to achieve
- What users do to achieve those goals
- The personal, social, and cultural characteristics that users bring to the task(s)
- How the physical environment affects users
- The influence that users' previous knowledge has on how they think about the work, and the workflow they use to perform their tasks

- What users value that will change the interface or make the documentation more usable for them

JoAnn Hackos and Ginny Redish (1998) formulated a list of questions that you will want to have answered about your users before you begin your observations. These questions include the following:

- How do your users think about their relationship to their work? For example, do they like their work, or do they dread coming to work each day because of problems they continually face?
- What motivates your users in their jobs?
- Is the product you're developing related to the users' primary work, or will they use it only occasionally?
- What and how much do users know about the subject matter you're designing for? You may be designing a new interface for a type of product they already know, or this may be a program or type of program they have never used before.
- Have the users had any experience doing similar jobs or tasks?
- What technical skills and tool knowledge do the users bring to the job?
- Do your users embrace or run from technology? There are people who use technology because they like it, and there are those who use technology only because they have to.
- Do your users prefer learning from written documentation or via other methods? People react differently to different types of media and training. Some like to learn on their own, and others like to learn in groups.
- What languages are the users comfortable using? If you're creating software for a multicultural audience, language is a significant factor to consider in your user interface design.
- Do the users like new experiences, or do they adhere to the "if it ain't broke, don't fix it" philosophy? Some users like using the products they have now and are more irritated about having to learn something new than learn how the new product will improve their workflow and the business at large.

You should strive to view as many users in their "natural habitats" as possible. This may require you to work with more than one person to get as much information as possible. For example, you may interview a group of users and then perform an onsite user and task analysis for a different group of users. Another person will perform an onsite analysis of the group of users you interviewed, and interview the users for whom you performed an onsite analysis.

You will likely encounter resistance to onsite user and task analyses both during the Modeling phase as well as usability testing during the Refinement phase. You'll learn how to resolve those objections in Chapter 9.

Persona Evaluation

After you learn about users' behaviors and goals from your research, it's time to review your data and form the personas (Cooper and Reimann, 2003).

As you form your personas, be sure to check your data for completeness and distinctiveness. If there are gaps in the data, such as missing data that needs to address the concerns of your stakeholders, you need to fill them in. If you find that you have two personas that are very similar, you may want to eliminate one or change one enough so that they are distinct enough. Each persona must differ in at least one significant behavior.

When you have your list of personas, it will help your project team and stakeholders to develop narratives for each persona that show what this type of person is like. These narratives help your team get to know your users. For example, "Lisa is a nurse who manages eight patients a day. She's very busy, and she becomes aggravated easily when the interface doesn't get her to where she wants to go within two clicks. Her goal is to get reliable information about her patients quickly." Lisa's sample persona appears in Figure 6.7.

You can also add a stock photograph of this typical user to give people a visual cue about what the persona is all about. For the Lisa persona, you could select a stock photo of a frazzled-looking nurse in her uniform. Be sure you select the right stock photo for the right persona, because if you don't, you'll create confusion among your team members and stockholders.

Prioritizing the Personas

A persona is only a candidate for the design you want to create. Don't try to design a product to appeal to every possible persona. After you have your set of personas, you need to determine which comprise the target group for your design. After you create designs tailored for each person in the target group, you can combine those designs into a balanced composite that appeals to the broadest cross section of your likely or potential users. That carefully balanced composite will be the final design for your user interface.

Lisa

Lisa is a nurse who manages eight patients a day. She's very busy, and she becomes aggravated easily when the interface doesn't get her to where she wants to go within two clicks. Her goal is to get reliable information about her patients quickly.

Figure 6.7 *A sample persona without a photo.*

You need to prioritize your personas by placing them into one of six categories (Cooper and Reimann, 2003):

- **Primary persona**—This is the primary target of an interface. If the primary persona is the target for the user interface, all other personas are at least minimally satisfied with the interface. If there is no clear primary persona, the product might need multiple interfaces for multiple personas, or the program or Web site might be trying to do too much. If you identify more than one primary persona, your product might have too many features.

- **Secondary personas**—These are personas that would be satisfied with the interface features if one or two specific needs were added. If you have more than two secondary personas, your program might have too many features.

- **Supplemental personas**—These are completely satisfied by either the primary persona interface or the secondary persona interface.

- **Customer personas**—These address the needs of customers, who won't be using the product but want to make sure the person who uses the software likes the user interface.

- **Served personas**—These are personas that are directly affected by the use of the product. Lisa the nurse's patients aren't direct users of the interface but are served by a good interface because of the improved care that Lisa provides for them.

- **Negative personas**—These are people who are not users of the product and shouldn't be the design target for it. For example, a candy striper probably won't use the interface that Lisa is using.

How many personas should you create? That depends on your situation. For example, you may have stakeholders who have concerns about certain user characteristics, and you should have personas that address these concerns. At the very least, you should have two personas (Eisenberg and Eisenberg, 2006). One of these personas should be the primary one, but the second one can fit into any one of the other five categories.

Now that you have learned how to prioritize the personas, you need to translate your goals and the users' goals into design, as you'll learn about in the next chapter.

> **Note**
>
> Don't apply personas to all products in your product line, as tempting as this may be. Although you can use many of the things you learned in creating a persona in one product, the primary difference between personas from product to product is the context in which the users use the product. For example, if users use a Web browser and an e-mail program, you may think those activities are tightly linked, but you will likely find that the context in which users use both programs are different.

Case Study: Producing a Primary Persona

Your personality type and conceptual model interview questions were only the start of the interview process. You and Evan now need to ask some follow-up questions of each user about individual behaviors and goals so you can produce a primary persona for your group.

You put together a list of questions patterned after the list proposed by Hackos and Redish as follows:

- Do you like your work? Why or why not?
- What motivates you in your job?
- Is the database product related directly to your primary job? That is, do you need to use this product every day to get your job done?

- How much do you know about the subject matter you're designing for?
- What technical skills and job knowledge do you bring to the job?
- How do you approach technology? Do you love it or put up with it?
- Do you prefer learning from written documentation, or do you prefer online help? What do you think of the documentation of the current system?
- Do you like new experiences, or do you think if it isn't broken you shouldn't fix it?

Because none of the employees are using different languages with the software, you and Evan decide not to ask this question but save it for later. After all, when you broke up from your first interview, Mike told you that Mike's Bikes plans to go international in the future, and at that point, multiple language support will become an issue.

You and Evan decide to ask these questions in person instead of giving the users a list of questions to fill out on their own because you want to see the users' nonverbal behaviors and listen to their tone of voice as they answer their questions. Users may also qualify their answers with some additional information.

For example, when you interview Jay, the marketing manager, he tells you that he likes his job, but you can tell from his tone of voice and his gestures that he's clearly frustrated with it. He also tells you that he thinks Mike could be doing more to market Mike's Bikes to a wider area, but his tone of voice and gestures mellow out when he talks about the changes to the database application and Web site because he believes these changes are going to help meet his goal. Therefore, the answer to the question, "Do you like your work?" is no, but you understand that the new database application is motivating him to like his job more in the future.

With the information about personality types, conceptual models, and individual behaviors and goals, you and Evan review your information and place each of the 10 project team members into different categories based on the following characteristics:

- The personality type of the respondent
- The conceptual model
- The individual behaviors and goals

As you place people into these three categories, a significant number of respondents have the same characteristics, and these people become your primary persona. Your primary persona ends up looking like the following:

- You give the persona the name "Bob" (after all, Bob is a friendly name). He's someone who knows the system inside and out.

- Bob is an extrovert and is an intuitive, thinking, and judging person. Therefore, he enjoys his job and how technology can make it better.

- Bob is someone who already knows the system and likes new experiences, but only if they make his job easier. Bob also knows his own division intimately and can tell you exactly how his division helps the company.

- Because Bob uses the system every day, he's come up with a list of ideas for improving the system, and he's made a lot of judgments about what works in the system and what doesn't.

- Bob likes the fact that the database is interconnected and that the system affords him a real-time view of what's going on.

- Bob doesn't like the fact that he can't search for a product or term instantly on the site. He considers the current system search functionality to be tedious to nonexistent, which he feels is a constraint.

- Bob wants to have more immediate methods of finding information on the system presented in the appropriate place. For example, the search function should be on all pages so he can immediately find anything he wants on the site. Also, the search function should return relevant results, and there should be functionality on the search results page to quickly go to the previous page or any other page in the system.

Place this information along with a mockup of Bob's picture and the bulleted persona text on a piece of paper. Make a copy for all the team members to share during the paper prototype test (see Figure 6.8).

In the next chapter, you'll learn about applying user interface features such as visual and audio cues into your paper prototype test.

OUR PRIMARY PERSONA: BOB

- You give the persona the name "Bob" (after all, Bob is a friendly name), and he's someone who knows the system inside and out.

- Bob is an extrovert and is an intuitive, thinking, and judging person. Therefore, he enjoys his job and how technology can make it better.

- Bob is someone who already knows the system and likes new experiences but only if they make his job easier. Bob also knows his own division intimately and can tell you exactly how his division helps the company.

- Because Bob uses the system every day he's come up with a list of ideas for improving the system and he's made a lot of judgments about what works in the system and what doesn't.

- Bob likes the fact that the database is interconnected and that the system affords him a real-time view of what's going on.

- Bob doesn't like the fact that he can't search for a product or term instantly on the site, and the current system search functionality is tedious to non-existent, which he feels is a constraint.

- Bob wants the system to have more immediate methods of finding information on the system presented in the appropriate place. For example, the search function should be on all pages so he can find anything he wants on the site immediately. The search function should also return relevant results and there should be functionality on the search results page to quickly go to the previous page or any other page in the system.

Figure 6.8   *Bob and the persona text.*

Summary

This chapter began with a discussion about a users' mental model by differentiating between the implementation model, which is a representation of how the product actually works, and the users' mental model, which stipulates that the user doesn't need to know everything about how the product works to use it. The users' mental model requires that designers design user interfaces for simplicity.

The experience bell curve was covered next. You learned that users fall into three categories of experience: beginner, intermediate, and advanced. Most users fall into the intermediate range of knowledge. These "perpetual intermediates" are most interested in specific answers to questions about the product. Beginning users want to know answers to questions such as where to start, and advanced users want to know how they can work more efficiently with the product.

Next, this chapter covered the Goal-Directed Design Process. You learned what the five phases of the Goal-Directed Design Process are, why the process helps fill in the gaps in user interface development, how the process provides a clear rationale for decisions, and what questions the process answers. The Goal-Directed Design Process is not a linear process; you may have to go back and forth between the different phases as needed to create an effective user interface.

The chapter ended with a discussion about user and task analysis and how you use it to obtain as much information as possible to generate personas, which are representations of specific types of individuals with specific needs. You learned about constructing personas and how personas minimize four key design issues: designing for the "elastic user," creating a self-referential design, designing for "edge" cases, and targeting people who are not end users. You also learned the way that personas fuse behaviors, their characteristics, and goals to create a narrative that explains the persona. Finally, you learned to prioritize your personas by placing them in one of six categories: primary (which is the most important and is populated by one persona), secondary, supplemental, customer, served, and negative. The number of personas you should create depends on your situation.

Review Questions

Now it's time to review what you've learned in this chapter before you move on to Chapter 7. Ask yourself the following questions, and refer to Appendix A to double-check your answers.

1. Why are designers still building to mechanical-age standards?
2. Who are perpetual intermediates?
3. What questions do beginners always have?
4. What questions do intermediates always have?
5. What are the five phases of the Goal-Directed Design Process?
6. Why should you conduct user and task analysis?
7. What three dimensions of information do personas connect together?
8. What types of goals do users have?
9. Why should you perform user and task analysis "in the field"?
10. Why should you prioritize your personas?

Designing a User Interface

"Let it be your constant method to look into the design of people's actions, and see what they would be at, as often as it is practicable; and to make this custom the more significant, practice it first upon yourself."
—Marcus Aurelius

Topics Covered in This Chapter

Designing the Persona-Based Interaction Framework

Interaction Design

Software Postures

Interface Behaviors

Helping Users Find Information

Communicating with the Users

Refining the Form and Behavior

This book has been taking a step-by-step approach to understanding the process and your users and has included the following topics:

- Learning the issues related to user interface design (Chapter 2, "Concepts and Issues")
- Making the business case to your stakeholders (Chapter 3, "Making the Business Case")
- Learning about the tools necessary to create good design (Chapter 4, "Good Design")
- Obtaining information about and understanding your users (Chapters 5, "How Users Behave," and 6, "Analyzing Your Users")

Now that you've made the business case and you know about your users, it's time to take that knowledge about your users and begin defining the requirements of your user interface. You'll begin by designing the interaction framework based on user personas that were discussed in Chapter 6.

Then you'll learn about interaction design and what you should do to make your interface ethical, purposeful, pragmatic, and elegant—four features of good design discussed in Chapter 4. Part of the interaction design is the type of posture you want to use. You'll learn about the four different GUI postures and when they are appropriate.

Finally, you'll delve into interface behaviors and how you should design the interface so that you can effectively communicate with users and help them find the information they need. When you have finished determining what the users need in the framework and how elements within the framework should behave, you're ready for the fifth and final step in the Goal-Directed Design Process: refining the form and its behaviors to create a final design.

Designing the Persona-Based Interaction Framework

The third phase of the Cooper and Reimann (2003) Goal-Directed Design Process is the Requirements phase. You need to define the requirements of your plan based on your personas before you can design a framework. Cooper and Reimann define obtaining requirements as (yes, it's another) five-step process.

- **Create problem and vision statements**—Based on your understanding not only of the persona but also of the company goals, create the objective of the design in terms of a problem statement and vision statement.

  The problem statement defines what the persona faces currently and how the business is affected, if at all. For example, "Nurses can't get the patient information they need quickly enough; therefore, nurse morale is lower, which results in more nursing mistakes and patients staying in the hospital an average of an extra day."

  The vision statement should explain how the new user interface will help both the users and the company. For example, "The new design of the user interface will give the nurses the ability to perform tasks A, B, C, and D and result in higher morale for nurses, fewer nursing mistakes, patients being released earlier, and greater bed turnover."

- **Brainstorm**—Having one or more brainstorming sessions with your project team will help your team understand what biases exist among your team members after looking at the persona data. One or more brainstorming sessions will also uncover ideas that your team can implement now or sometime later. Brainstorming sessions should be centered on a topic. For example, a brainstorming session can center on what user interface elements will meet specific goals.

- **Identify persona expectations**—Each persona has its own mental model of the product. You must identify each persona's desires and the expectations, behaviors, attitudes, biases, and other factors that affect them. Some of the information that the personas mention or don't mention, such as tasks they want to perform, can provide a guide to what each persona wants.

- **Construct context scenarios**—These stories about personas and their activities will help you understand how each persona gets through a typical day using the new and improved system, which includes the new user interface. The scenarios don't discuss the form and function, but only the behaviors of the user and the interface.

  In each context scenario, you need to identify not only the environment and organization in the persona's daily scenario, but also touch on the points that each primary and secondary persona has with the system and the other personas that it may interact with through the system. For example, the primary persona is a nurse who works with one persona, but the secondary persona is an administrator who works with a completely different persona from the nurse. This difference may show that each persona uses the system differently.

- **Identify needs**—After you create the context scenario, analyze it to determine what the needs are for each persona. Personas have three types of needs: data, functional, and contextual.

  Objects and information in the system comprise data needs. For example, the letters you see in a word processing document are objects you need to see as you type those letters.

  Operations that need to be performed on objects in the system comprise functional needs. For example, if you want to make a block of text in a word processing document bold, there is an operation to do that.

  Firm and possible relationships between sets of objects or sets of controls comprise contextual needs. For example, when you save a favorite Web site in the Favorites list in Internet Explorer, Internet Explorer must update the list with the new favorite as well as list all your other saved favorites.

Note that this process is not a linear one-time process, but iterative. For example, you may want to go through the process once, go through a brainstorming session, and then refine your persona expectations, context scenarios, or needs based on the results of that session.

Real-World Requirements

When you've finished developing the creative side of your product requirements, it's time to focus and learn about your real-world requirements for the product. These other requirements include (Cooper and Reimann, 2003) the following:

- Business requirements that include business development models, timelines, and pricing structures.
- Customer and partner requirements that include installation, configuration, customer support, and licensing agreements.
- Technical requirements that include the operating system you use and the form factor that the product requires. For example, the product may be a Web site that needs to be displayed at a certain video resolution so that all users can read the information on each Web page.

These other requirements may force you to rethink or refine some of the ideas that you generated in the requirements process. They may even spur more brainstorming.

Defining the Framework

When your requirements list is ready, it's time to define the framework. Creating a framework is a six-step process (Cooper and Reimann, 2003):

1. **Define the form factor and input methods**—Are you creating a user interface in a desktop computer operating system, like Windows? Are you creating a Web interface? Or are you creating an interface for a handheld PC operating system? The answer defines your software *posture*, which you'll learn more about later in this chapter.

   You also need to find out how people will interact with the interface. For example, will people use a keyboard and mouse, voice interface, or a wand that you use with a handheld PC to touch the screen? There are plenty of input options available for which you may need a plan.

2. **Define the views**—You need to determine what the user will see based on the context of where he is in the system so he can properly organize the information on the screen. For example, you may need to have separate views for different tasks, such as opening a Print dialog box to print a spreadsheet. However, if you have elements that are related to each other, like a spreadsheet and a chart generated from that spreadsheet, you can define a view that incorporates the spreadsheet and chart in the same view.

3. **Define the functional and data elements**—After you construct a list of views, you need to know how objects, such as onscreen windows and controls, buttons, and icons, will be viewed onscreen. The type of input devices that your users will use will affect what functional and data elements you will have on the screen. An example of input devices in Microsoft Word is shown in Figure 7.1.

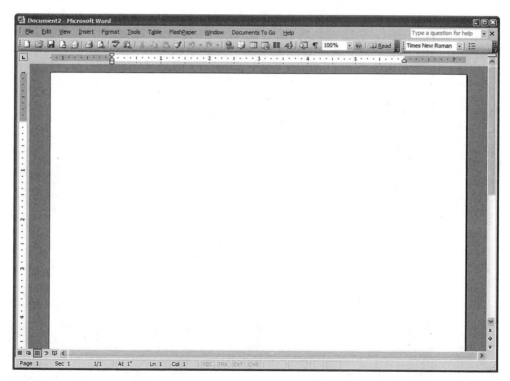

Figure 7.1 *Microsoft Word has many types of input devices to manipulate it.*

4. **Determine the functional groups and hierarchy**—Now that you know what your functional and data elements are, you can begin to group these features together, arrange containers, and establish hierarchical relationships between each group. Use the persona types as a guide for organizing your functional and data elements. A menu bar is one example of functional groups; there is a group name in the bar with the individual menu options underneath the name. Some features in the list are groups themselves that open a second-level feature list in the hierarchy, such as when you can add a closing salutation from the AutoText option within the Insert menu, as shown in Figure 7.2.

5. **Sketch the interaction framework**—You can sketch rough drawings of the top level ("the big picture") of the user interface design and write notes about the relationship between different objects in the interface. You don't need to drill down into certain sections of the interface at this point; doing so can end up distracting you and your other team members.

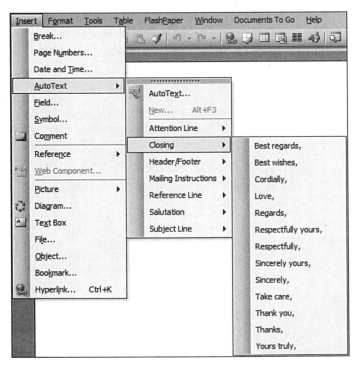

Figure 7.2   *A menu example of functional groups and hierarchy.*

6. **Construct key path scenarios**—This is where paper prototyping and storyboarding techniques that you learned from Chapter 4 come into play. Work with your team to develop scenarios of what users will see in the interface based on your personas, and then create storyboards to show the path of each interaction as the user completes a task, as shown in Figure 7.3. Each storyboard represents a screen and shows what the screen will look like as the user initiates an action, such as clicking a button.

Note that this process is also iterative. As you refine and finalize your key path scenarios, you can create paper prototypes based on those scenarios discussed in Chapter 4 so that you can determine whether your scenarios match up with direct user manipulation of the prototype. If they don't, you will likely have to revisit one or more steps in this process to resolve problems revealed by the paper prototype feedback.

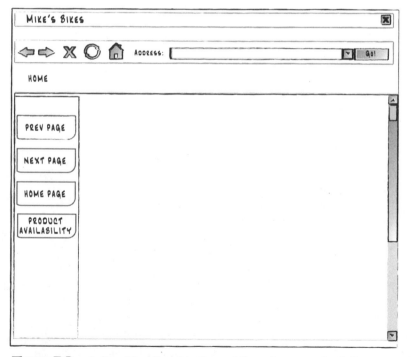

Figure 7.3   *A sample of a storyboard that shows a draft framework and scenarios. (continues)*

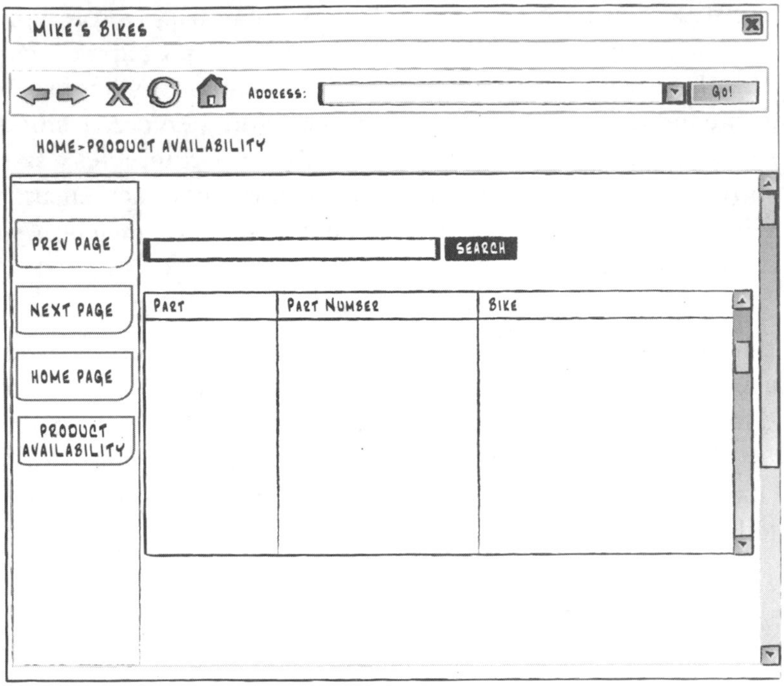

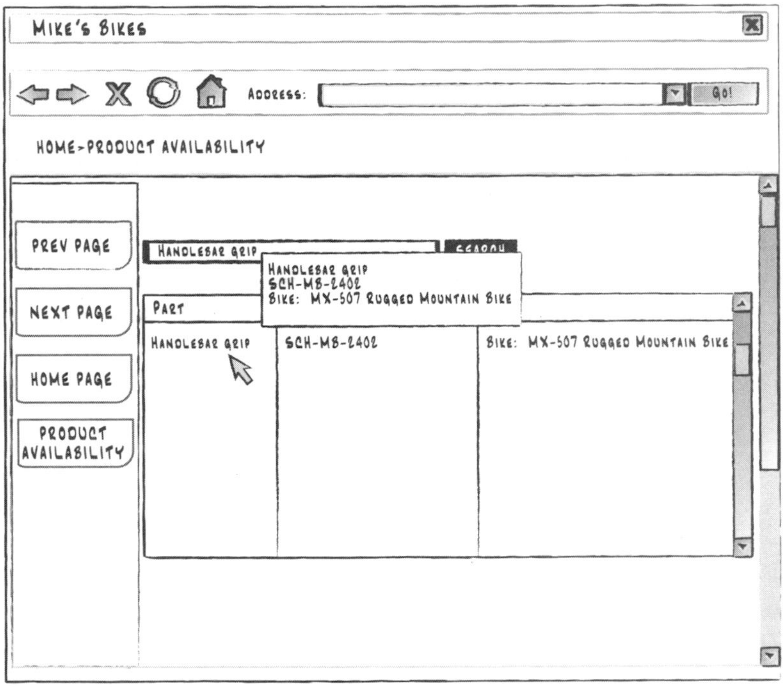

Figure 7.3 *(continued)*

Interaction Design

When you create a persona-based interaction framework, Cooper and Reimann (2003) recommend that you suspend reality and believe that the operating system is human. That's a sound strategy, because an interface that seems more human and is more responsive to human needs results in a happier user experience.

To help meet the goal of user interface design that is more human, you need to adhere to design imperatives by following principles and patterns of interaction and interface design.

Applying Design Imperatives

In Chapter 4, you learned about the four design imperatives. Keep the following design tips in mind as you develop your user interface (Cooper and Reimann, 2003):

- **Ethical**—Ethical design is considerate and helpful and actually improves human situations. In interface design, you can improve communication between your user interface and the people who use it, which leads to improved understanding and effectiveness.

- **Purposeful**—The goal of this entire book, as well as the reference books I've cited, is to create user interface design that has the purpose of serving your users well by making them stronger and more effective in their lives.

- **Pragmatic**—You must create and build a good user design for it to be of value. However, there are always other considerations requiring flexibility and communication between company departments for a design to see the "light of day" and experience success.

- **Elegant**—Elegant design should represent the simplest complete solution, possess internal coherence, and stimulate cognition and emotion to get the user involved. If your user interface is unnecessarily cumbersome and inconsistent, it's unlikely that the user will be interested in using it, and your company will be left wondering why no one wants to use your product.

Principles

Principles are guidelines that address issues of behavior, form, and content (Cooper and Reimann, 2003). These principles are designed to minimize the work of the user as part of elegant design.

There are three levels of design principles that you have to design for:

- **Conceptual-level principles**—These define what a product is. In Chapters 5 and 6, as well as in this chapter, you learned about how to bring your project team and your users closer together to define a product that users will want to use.

- **Interaction-level principles**—These define how a product should behave, both generally and in specific situations. This chapter will discuss interaction-level principles for graphical user interfaces (GUIs), and Chapter 8, "Designing a Web Site," will discuss interaction-level principles for Web sites.

- **Interface-level principles**—These define the interface look and feel. This chapter and Chapter 8 discuss these principles.

If your company has a style guide already established, it's likely that you can use some of its principles to help guide you in creating your design principles. However, in most cases, companies don't go into the level of detail that you and your project team need to develop user interfaces. (You may be able to augment your company's style guide with principles you learned during the development process. In fact, if you keep this in mind as a secondary goal, you are more likely to create a user interface that is compatible with your company's preferred "look." A subsidiary benefit is increased acceptance by your superiors of a product that fits well into the company line.)

Note, too, that these principles are only guidelines and don't provide a complete guide as to how to create your design behaviors. For example, you'll use feedback from your users as another means to guide you and your team in the design process.

Patterns

As you develop your product, you will begin to create patterns that solve problems you encounter in the design, which you can then apply to problems in your current project. You can also address these problems in your development principles/styles guide as a means of educating and applying these patterns in other projects. Cooper and Reimann (2003) list three types of interaction design patterns:

- **Postural**—These help determine the product stance in relation to the user. You'll learn more about software postures in the next section.
- **Structural**—These solve problems that relate to the management of data in the program, including how information displays and how users access and manipulate data and options in the program. For example, you have probably noticed that Microsoft has been working on organizational issues with successive versions of its Office software programs, such as Word.
- **Behavioral**—These solve specific interactional problems with individual data or functional objects, or groups of objects.

Software Postures

As you create your user interface design, your personas will give you a good idea of how they will use the program, and you can design an interface with a posture that reflects how your primary personas work. Note that your users will likely not use only one of these postures, but may use more than one, depending on the task they are performing.

There are four desktop-based GUI postures (Cooper and Reimann, 2003):

- **Sovereign**—The *sovereign application* is a full-screen program that keeps the user's attention for long periods of time. For example, sovereign applications include programs in Microsoft Office, Microsoft Word (as shown in Figure 7.4), as well as graphics programs such as Adobe Photoshop and Illustrator.

  This program uses the entire screen most of the time, so sovereign applications are designed for full-screen use. These applications use that space to add functions for manipulating objects. The Microsoft Word window is a good case in point, with a menu bar, toolbars, and a task pane on the right side of the screen. This results in rich feedback to the user as well as rich input mechanisms.

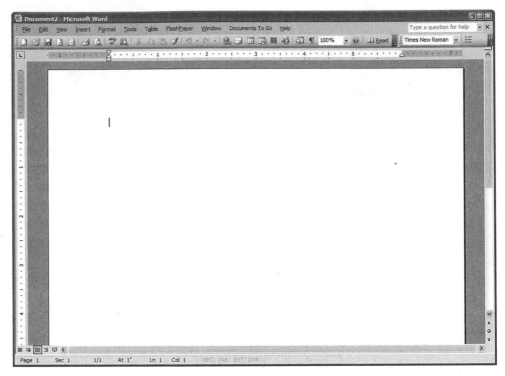

Figure 7.4 *An example of a sovereign posture.*

- **Transient**—The *transient application* is one that comes and goes when the user needs to perform a specific task, such as using the Windows Character Map to view a list of available characters in a font set. Transient programs don't take up a lot of real estate and aren't used very much.

Because transient applications aren't used as often as sovereign applications, they should be simple to use and should communicate well to the user. You should minimize your use of scrollbars and other complex interaction features in the window and just add them when necessary. In the Character Map window, as shown in Figure 7.5, the user sees a visual presentation of the characters so she can see what she wants quickly and easily. This program contains a scrollbar to scroll down the list of characters. If the user needs help, she can click the **Help** button at the top of the window.

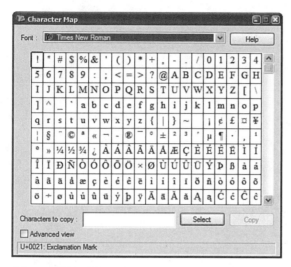

Figure 7.5 *The Character Map window is an example of a transient posture.*

- **Daemonic**—The *daemonic application* is one that doesn't normally interact with the user. Such programs include driver programs that support your printer, monitor, and mouse. If you need access to these programs, operating systems provide "control panels" like the one you can access in Microsoft Windows. The Control Panel window in Windows provides a list of daemonic programs you can change, as shown in Figure 7.6.

  Windows has also placed access to some of those daemonic programs in the system tray at the right side of the taskbar in the form of small icons next to the system clock. Some programs that include utilities (such as a driver for the trackball I use) also place icons in the taskbar so you can access those utilities when you install the program.

- **Auxiliary**—An *auxiliary application* is one that combines the characteristics of sovereign and transient applications. Microsoft has developed auxiliary programs with its Office suite of programs as well as Internet Explorer and Microsoft Outlook. Microsoft Word can also display an auxiliary posture. For example, you can have the task pane open on the right side, or you can close it. Adobe's interfaces for its graphic design software like InDesign go Microsoft one better by having their transient programs in the forms of tabs at the right side of the window that you can click to open and close, as shown in Figure 7.7.

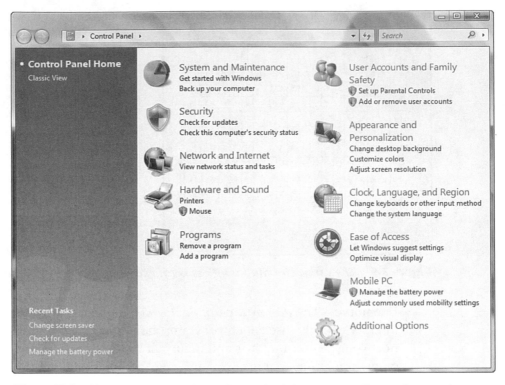

Figure 7.6 *The Control Panel window, which lets you configure daemonic programs.*

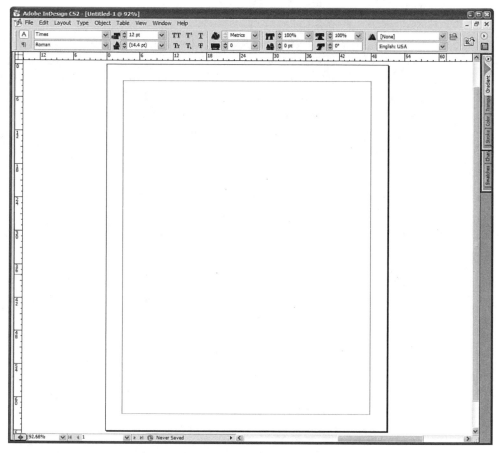

Figure 7.7   *InDesign contains tabs at the right side of the window.*

Interface Behaviors

GUI interfaces for desktop interfaces exhibit behaviors of two of the most commonly used means of accessing and viewing information: the mouse pointer and the window. These two features are universal in a GUI. You can find mice or mice equivalents on any computer, such as a touch pad on a laptop. In this section, you will learn about the behaviors of some of these features and some of the issues surrounding them—some by Cooper and Reimann (2003) and some from my own experiences.

Using the Mouse Pointer

A *pointer* is a GUI graphic feature, usually an arrow, that you manipulate directly using a *mouse*, which is a device that typically looks similar to, and has similar dimensions to, a bar of soap. The mouse pointer is your control device to manipulate different objects and control mechanisms (called widgets) in the GUI. You can also use alternative manipulation devices such as a trackball or touch pad instead of a mouse if you find that a mouse isn't that comfortable. For example, I use a trackball to move the mouse pointer around my computer screen. Many notebooks have mouse pads built in.

You must be aware of mouse behaviors and how a GUI uses them, because your users expect your user interface to follow the same rules as all other programs in the GUI.

Moving Around

A mouse has a ball or laser guidance system on the bottom so that when you move the mouse around on your desk, the mouse pointer moves in the same direction that you move your mouse.

As you move around, the mouse pointer may change shape in response to a program's requirements. In Microsoft Word, for example, when you move the mouse pointer over a document page, it changes to an I-shaped bar, as shown in Figure 7.8. This I-shaped bar indicates the insertion point where you can insert new text into your document. When you move the mouse pointer outside the document page, it reverts back to an arrow. Also, when a program is performing time-intensive operations, the mouse pointer might change to a busy cursor, often resembling an hourglass, or in the case of Windows Vista, a circle.

Clicking and Buttons

Most computer mice come with two buttons—one on the left, and another on the right. By default, the left mouse button and right mouse button have different functions. Some button behaviors may be different from the typical default settings if a user or administrator has customized the computer's interface.

Left Mouse Button

When you click the left mouse button, the operating system places a *cursor* (a bright and usually blinking movable indicator that marks a position where text can be added, changed, or deleted) in the precise location, initiates a task associated with the button or link, or moves the focus of the operating

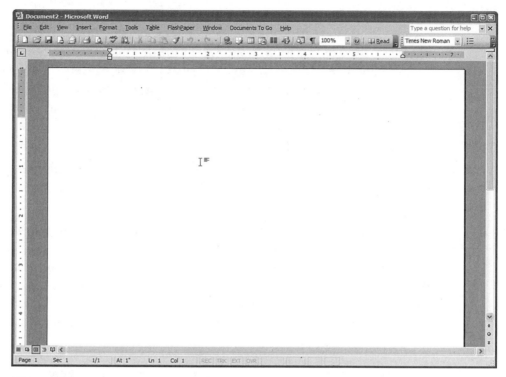

Figure 7.8 *An I-shaped bar in Word.*

system onto what you've just clicked. For example, if you click the Save button in the Microsoft Word for Windows taskbar, Windows focuses on saving the document.

Some links require that you click the left mouse button twice in rapid succession, or *double-click*, to initiate the task associated with the link. For example, if you open the Control Panel window in Windows, you must double-click one of the icons in the list of functions (such as Display) to open the associated window. This is useful if you want a user to be more deliberate in starting a task and not starting a task by accident.

You can drag icons and open windows on your desktop to other locations by moving the mouse pointer over the icon or the window title bar, holding down the left mouse button, and then moving the icon or window to different locations on the screen. This function, called *click and drag*, also allows you to move icons to other icons, such as a document into another folder. In addition, you can use click and drag functionality to click and select blocks of objects, such as text in a Word document.

Right Mouse Button

Microsoft introduced right mouse button functionality in Windows. When you click an icon, a window, or an item in the taskbar with the right mouse button, called *right-click*, a pop-up menu appears that lets you perform specific functions. Those functions can be as simple as having the ability to minimize, maximize, or close the window, or you can perform more specific functions. For example, if you right-click in a Word document, a context menu appears with options specific to the menu, as shown in Figure 7.9.

The right mouse button has become popular enough that the two Linux GUIs, GNOME and KDE, and even Mac OS X have adopted right-click functionality.

However, users may not know that right-clicking is available unless they're already used to right-clicking on objects, or they click on the right mouse button by accident and wonder how they got to the menu or option they see. As you identify your users' needs, you may want to refine those needs to determine if your users want to have right-click functionality and how to present that information so your users will know about this functionality.

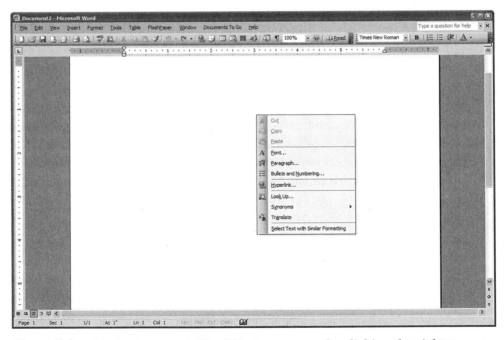

Figure 7.9   *A pop-up menu in Word that you access by clicking the right mouse button.*

Window Behaviors

No matter what GUI you use, you'll find that windows have the same behaviors that you need to adhere to when you build your user interface.

Opening Windows

You can open a window in one of four ways:

- Click on an icon on the desktop that links to the program. If the icon is a document, the program that is associated with the document opens automatically.
- Double-click on an icon or link within a window.
- Click a menu option in a program. For example, click **New** from the File menu in Microsoft Word.
- Click on a button or icon in the taskbar or Dock.

You can have more than one window open at one time. However, when you do, you run the risk of having window "pollution," where you have so many open windows at once that you can't make sense of what's going on and where. Many different windows can demand your attention, so it's important to keep everything in one area if at all possible when you create your user interface so that your users don't become confused.

One way that GUIs keep different tasks within one window is the multiple-document interface, or MDI. MDI uses tabs to keep track of separate documents within a window. In one type of MDI interface, you can click on the tab to go directly to that document without moving to a different window. Two examples of a tabbed MDI interface are the multitabbed Web browser, such as Internet Explorer 7, which keeps different Web pages in different tabs, and worksheets within a spreadsheet such as Microsoft Excel. Another form of MDI was prevalent in older versions of Windows, where the documents were displayed as movable, resizable subwindows within the master program. MDI almost went away as more powerful computers made it easier to have several open windows in the same program, but it is starting to make a comeback, as shown with Internet Explorer 7 and other modern browsers such as Netscape 8, as shown in Figure 7.10.

A window can also open a *dialog box*, which is a smaller window designed to have the user set settings and make decisions. For example, if you want to print a document in Microsoft Word, the Print dialog box appears so you can determine what printer to use, how many copies to print, and so on, as shown in Figure 7.11.

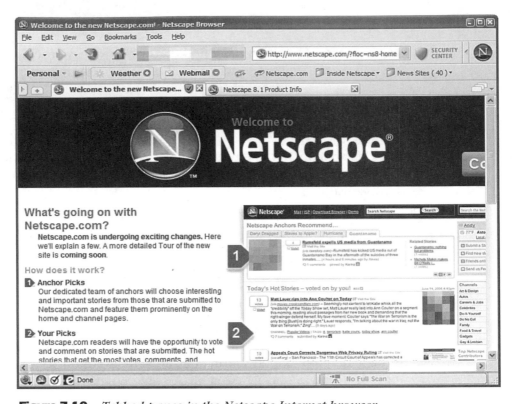

Figure 7.10 *Tabbed panes in the Netscape Internet browser.*
Netscape and the "N" Logo are registered trademarks of Netscape Communications Corporation. Netscape content (c) 2007. Used with permission.

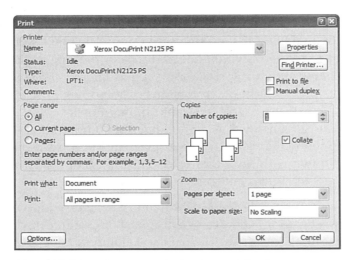

Figure 7.11 *The Print dialog box in Word.*

When you require the user to open a window, be sure that the window is for something that the user needs to do to complete the task. For example, you need to have the user specify the printer and print settings before he prints the document.

If you can have functionality appear within a primary window without making the user go to a secondary window, it is better to keep that functionality within the primary window. That will make your user's job easier. For example, when I use Microsoft Word, I can change the font on the Format menu by clicking Font and then setting the font, the font size, and other font-related features (like the font color) in the Font dialog box. However, Word contains a toolbar within the Word window so that you can change the font from within the document window, as shown in Figure 7.12.

One overarching rule applies to creating windows and dialog boxes: Be sure to provide only the information that the user needs in each window. Too many choices can overwhelm the user, or features can be buried within menus that users won't even know about because they won't know how to reach those features.

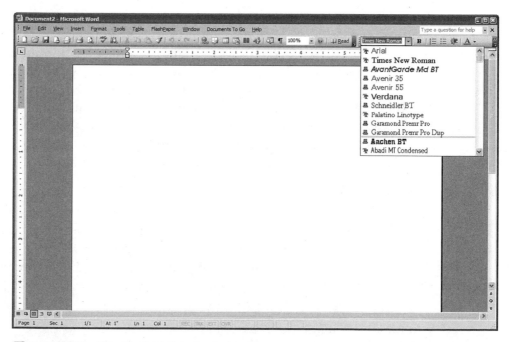

Figure 7.12 *Word's font lists in the toolbar.*

Maximizing, Minimizing, and Changing Window Sizes

You can maximize a window so that it fills your entire screen and has your full attention. For example, you may want to have a maximized window when you're writing a document so that you can stay focused on the document and not on which window to use. The Maximize, Minimize, and Close buttons appear in the title bar. In Windows, these buttons are on the right side of the title bar, as shown in Figure 7.13.

Figure 7.13   *The Minimize, Maximize, and Close buttons in a Windows title bar.*

If a window is maximized, the Maximize button in the title bar changes to the Restore Down button so that you can change the size of the window. You can change the size of the window by moving the mouse pointer to the edge of the window, holding down the left mouse button, and dragging. If you click and drag from a vertical edge, the window width changes. If you click and drag from a horizontal edge, the window height changes. If you click and drag from the corner, the width and height change simultaneously.

However, the window size of a dialog box may or may not be changeable. You can also set your window so that a user can't change its size if you feel that a window needs to be a certain size. In addition, by making the window modal, you can prevent users from switching to other windows when presented with a dialog box. This technique should be used sparingly, because UI designers often overuse modality at the expense of not allowing users to multitask within a program or between programs. During your usability tests, which you'll learn about in Chapter 9, "Usability," you'll be able to learn what window behaviors your users like and don't like in your interface.

Moving Windows Around

You can move windows around the screen so that they overlap each other; the metaphor that Xerox had when it originally developed the Alto GUI is that it wanted each window to represent an overlapping piece of paper. I don't care for overlapping pieces of paper because I tend to ignore the paper that's underneath the first sheet. A lot of people agree.

The taskbar was one way to get out from under the overlapping window problem. Another solution that Microsoft introduced was the ability to tile windows so that they appear side by side or one on top of the other. If you have four tiled windows, the windows appear in each corner. The success you have in tiling your windows depends on the screen size and resolution of your typical user's monitor. For example, if you tile more than one window side by side on a 15-inch monitor with 800-by-600 pixel resolution, you won't be able to see much in each window. Therefore, if your software application requires multiple windows to work properly, you should determine what screen size and resolution your monitors use and design your interface accordingly. You may decide to have separate windows, or an MDI approach as discussed earlier in this chapter.

Closing Windows

You close a window by clicking the Close button in the window title bar. However, you may also want to employ keyboard combination shortcuts to make it easier for users to close a window. For example, Windows uses Ctrl+W and Alt+F4 to close a file and open a program, respectively. See an example of the Word title bar menu in Figure 7.14. If your application will require a lot of keyboard use, you can include keyboard shortcuts in your user interface. They're a nice gift to your users (especially users who have disabilities), who won't have to take their hands away from the keyboard to perform tasks.

Figure 7.14   *The Word title bar menu also shows the keyboard shortcut alternative.*

Helping Users Find Information

You can give users several cues to help them find information. However, you must ensure that you use these cues appropriately and that they don't overwhelm or confuse the user.

Visual Cues

As discussed in the "Interface Behaviors" section, your mouse pointer can change shape based on where it is in the window. There are also other visual cues that appear in the window. These not only include buttons and the window name in the title bar, but can also include menu options, button bars, icons, and more.

With so many visual cues available to you as you design your user interface, it's important to adhere to the five rules of visual interfaces (Cooper and Reimann, 2003):

- **Avoid visual noise and clutter**—It's easy to overwhelm users with too much functionality in one window or too many bright colors that distract them, inhibiting their ability to make sense of it all. What's more, if some information that you provide is superfluous, the user will become frustrated.

- **Use contrast, similarity, and layering to distinguish and organize elements**—For example, make sure that buttons are lighter than the background of the window so that the users understand that they should pay attention to the buttons. You should also group related buttons together, such as buttons for saving and opening a file.

- **Provide visual structure and flow at each level of organization**—For example, if you tell Word to print a file, the Print dialog box is arranged like a grid so it's easy to find what you need. The flow of information in your windows should match the user's logical path, which is the way the eye moves. In Western countries, people read from left to right and from top to bottom.

- **Use cohesive, consistent, and contextually appropriate imagery**—If you have an icon and text in a button, the icon and text need to be consistent. For example, the Display icon should include an appropriate picture (such as a monitor) and the word *Display* underneath the picture.

- **Integrate style and function comprehensively and purposefully**—You need to be consistent when integrating your user interface style and function. If you don't do this, you will confuse the user.

Audio Cues

Today, most computers come with built-in audio cards and speakers so that you can listen to multimedia files. Today's GUIs also come with built-in sounds that you can use to alert your users to certain events. For example, if you have Outlook or Outlook Express in Microsoft Windows, you can set up Outlook to play the default Windows chime when you receive a new email message.

You should be cautious when using audio cues, such as the computer making a certain noise every time the user clicks a button. Users can quickly become annoyed with them if they happen often enough, and hard-of-hearing users won't appreciate them. To compensate for the annoyance, users might mute the volume on their computer speakers, which could defeat the purpose of other audio cues that will be important. If you do plan to use audio cues, be sure to give users the ability to turn off audio.

Pop-Up Messages

Despite their visual appeal, icons may not convey information as well as they need to. Indeed, some icons can be rather esoteric or downright confusing. One way that GUIs help bridge the gap is through the use of pop-up messages, also known as *ToolTips*. For example, when you move the mouse pointer over a toolbar icon in Microsoft Word for Windows, a small box appears below the mouse pointer that describes what the icon is used for, as shown in Figure 7.15.

The key to creating a worthy pop-up message is keeping the message as short as possible—only a few words at most—and as descriptive as possible. That's a challenge, but you're only trying to give your user a reminder of what the icon is, not an explanation of its entire process.

Figure 7.15 *A pop-up message in Word.*

Search Engines

Search engines have become common with current versions of operating systems because so many people use the Web and are familiar with using them. Programs such as Microsoft Office 2003 have a search engine text box in the upper-right corner of the application window with text inviting the user to type a question in the box for help, as shown in Figure 7.16.

Apple introduced the Sherlock search engine with Mac OS 8.5 so users could find information in files, folders, and on the Web. Google provides a freely downloadable program called Google Desktop that serves a similar function for Windows users. Windows Vista now sports search functionality in the Start menu. Depending on how your users employ the software, you may want to rely on these tools so your users can find information, or you may want to add search engine functionality from the window itself as Office does. Like Web engines, operating system search engines aren't perfect, and their functions shouldn't replace online help systems. See the next section for more details.

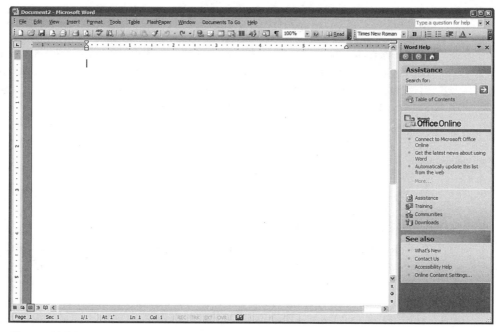

Figure 7.16   *The help box in Microsoft Word.*

Communicating with the Users

Chapter 6 discussed the fact that many users are *perpetual intermediates*, meaning that they are interested in finding the answers to their problems as quickly as possible so they can move on and finish their task. If you don't communicate effectively with your users through the interface, you'll lose them.

Making Features Easy to Find

In addition to the methods for helping users find information as described in the previous section, your user interface needs to adhere to consistency and standards in user product design. Chances are that you or someone else in your department will be responsible for designing and implementing these standards. Standards are guidelines that start with the user interface standards for software, hardware, or Web sites prescribed by the company that designs them and progress to changes that you feel need to be made. After you have the final standards for your user interface design, you need to enforce those standards consistently so your users will be able to find the information you have in the same place.

However, the fact that you have standards ahead of time doesn't mean that they won't change during the development process. Those standards could also change depending on what your users think. That is why it's so important to have usability testing, as I've described in previous chapters and in Chapter 9.

Online Help

Online help is a way to make information about using the software easily available to users. You can also include training modules and related information (such as a glossary) in the online help system. Most GUI software programs today have online help included with the system, and in most programs, you can access online help through the Help menu option in the menu bar. An online help system can make information more accessible and save your company money in printing costs—but only if you design the online help system correctly.

Users use online help primarily by searching for the term that they're having problems with, such as *printing*. That search feature is usually one of three tabs in an online help window; the other two tabs are a table of contents and a searchable index. Many companies will simply transfer a user guide to an online help system, add some rudimentary search features, and release the online help system to the masses. This is a bad idea, because users don't use online help the same way they read a user manual. Users look to online help to get answers quickly so they can move on.

Any useful online help system not only must be built to have robust search capabilities, but also have a robust index. If you plan to have an online help system, you need to develop the help system from scratch and test it for effectiveness and usefulness as you would the rest of your program. Your online help system may well be your first line of customer support. If you don't develop your online help the right way, your company will have to spend more time and money training customer support personnel.

Assistants and Wizards

Assistants and wizards help you use the application more efficiently. Assistants provide hints or ask you to provide keywords so the agent can search for an answer. You may have heard of Clippy, the online assistant for Microsoft

Office. Many users found it so obnoxious in Office 2000 and Windows XP that Microsoft made installing the Office Assistant (including Clippy) optional in Office 2003.

Figure 7.17 *Clippy, the Microsoft Office assistant.*

You may also have used wizards when you installed a program in a GUI. Wizards take you step by step through adding a program or feature in a GUI, such as when you create a home network. The wizard asks you questions at certain steps and then installs the software or configures the feature based on your information. You can also use wizards within a program. For example, Microsoft Office includes the mail merge wizard to automate a mail merging task.

The appropriateness of assistants or wizards depends on your situation. If you perform a user and task analysis, as discussed in Chapter 6, you'll learn what tasks your users will do and whether you need to include additional help in the form of assistants or wizards.

Refining the Form and Behavior

After you develop the framework definition, you're in the final stage of the Goal-Directed Design Process: refinement. It's time to refine the form and behavior of your interface, which you do by following a three-step iterative process (Cooper and Reimann, 2003):

1. **Draft the look and feel**—The designers on your team should begin to work on transferring the interfaces you created in the paper prototyping and storyboarding phase into full-resolution graphic screens that you can share with the rest of your team. Every primary view and dialog in the program should be developed so that your team can see what the interface will look like. You will likely have to go through several iterations of this step to nail down any lingering issues and put

together a final design guide that your team can apply to the rest of the program views, dialogs, and other objects.

2. **Construct validation scenarios**—You must construct validation scenarios with your program that follow up on your work with key path scenarios, because not everyone in your persona will use the interface the same way.

   Validation scenarios come in three flavors. One is *key path variants*, which are paths that split from key pathways along the persona's decision tree. For example, after the third step in the scenario, one user may decide to press Button B instead of Button A. You have to map what happens after the user presses Button B.

   The second flavor is the necessary use scenario. *Necessary use scenarios* detail all actions that must be performed, yet are performed infrequently. For example, you need to show how the user will configure the software product.

   The third flavor is *edge cases*, which detail scenarios in which users engage in optional and infrequent activities. When I played computer games, sometimes I would go off the beaten path and try to do other things, and sometimes the game would crash because the game wasn't prepared for my character to do something unexpected. Your program may crash when the user does something along the edge case as I did with the game, but edge cases are lower on the list of priorities. Of top priority is your product's ability to handle daily use and necessary cases, because if your product and interface can't handle those, it will fail.

3. **Finalize the design**—Now you're ready to finalize the design. You can create form and design specification sheets that include screen mockups and storyboards, as well as information about the personas you found, to share with other stakeholders in the company. You can also produce an interactive prototype through a programming language or on the Web, or you can create an online demonstration, to show stakeholders how the interface and the program work.

Case Study: Refining the Paper Prototype Test

Now it's time to refine the paper prototype test. In Chapter 6, you asked the 10 respondents what they thought of the system affordances and constraints and how they would resolve those constraints.

If you and Evan were producing a paper prototype test for a new application, you would have more leeway about the types of visual and audio cues as well as help features within the system. You're more constrained with an existing system, because you have to maintain existing application standards as much as possible unless the users you interview have specifically mentioned that this is a feature that possibly needs to be changed.

The current application provides one good example of a pop-up message when the user places the mouse pointer over the product name in the product availability page. This pop-up box provides brief information about the part, including the part number and the bike to which the part applies, as shown in Figure 7.18.

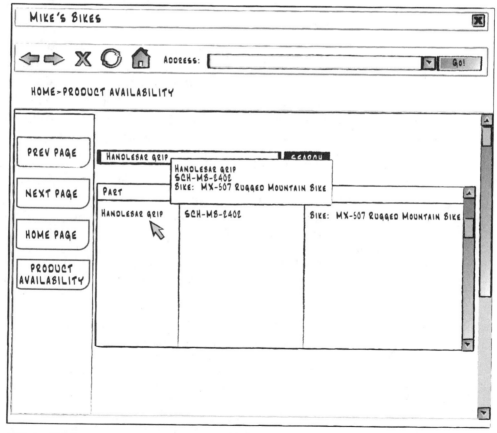

Figure 7.18   *The pop-up box with the part name, part number, and bike information.*

Therefore, if you want to add pop-up messages elsewhere in the system, such as when the user moves the mouse pointer over the new flag column in the product table to view the number of products remaining in the stores, the pop-up message box must adhere to the look and feel of other pop-up messages when you develop the product. You don't need to duplicate the look and feel of pop-up messages for the paper prototype test, but be sure to have the additional text in the pop-up message piece of the test.

If you have an existing pop-up menu, you may want to add more information in that pop-up menu as a usability enhancement. For example, when you move the mouse pointer over the product in the product table, the product table will also include information about how many stores have each product. This additional functionality meets the users' goals of getting as much information as possible as quickly as possible; therefore, you can add this additional message text as a surprise for your testers so you can get their reactions when they encounter it during the test.

The application also has several audio cues. Evan needs to be particularly mindful of these because he will be acting as the computer during the test. If the user does something to activate one of these audio cues during the paper prototype test, Evan will have to sound out those cues when appropriate during the test. For example, when the user does something wrong, Evan needs to give the system error noise (or a reasonable impression of it).

The application also includes online help text. When the user accesses online help about a new feature (such as the product availability page), you will need to show that the online help window appears. You don't need to add the actual online help text—only show that the online help text will appear when the user accesses the help system.

In sum, you need to familiarize yourself with the application so that you can accurately replicate some of the features (such as audio cues) in the test.

The application is Web-based, so you and Evan also need to be aware of Web interaction within the interface. You'll learn about applying Web interaction to your paper prototype test in the next chapter.

Summary

This chapter began by creating a list of requirements after you established personas in Chapter 6, and then designing a persona-based interaction framework. These are the third and fourth steps, respectively, of the Goal-Directed

Design Process. Creating a list of requirements is a five-step process. Your requirements list needs to pay attention to real-world requirements that will affect your design, including business requirements, customer and partner requirements, and technical requirements. You learned about the six-step process for creating a persona-based interaction framework to construct key path scenarios so that you will understand what you want users to see in your interface.

Interaction design was covered next. You learned about how to apply design principles and patterns to the four good design imperatives of being ethical, purposeful, pragmatic, and elegant. You learned about conceptual, interaction, and interface-level principles that define what a product is, how it should behave, and the interface look and feel, respectively. You also learned about identifying postural, structural, and behavioral patterns that you can apply to problems as they come up in your project.

Next, you learned about the type of postures that programs take and how to design them to match the users' work requirements. For example, you learned that the sovereign posture is for users who use a program for long periods of time. Sovereign postures include a number of tools in the user interface so that users can manipulate objects and controls.

A discussion about interface behavior followed. We discussed this behavior in the context of primary input and output devices for manipulating and viewing objects, respectively, in a desktop GUI: the mouse and the window. The "Using the Mouse Pointer" section discussed the rules for using the mouse to manipulate objects, including buttons, as well as mouse alternatives such as keyboard shortcuts. In the "Window Behaviors" section, you learned about the window manipulation rules, moving windows around, and using keyboard combination shortcuts as an alternative to closing windows.

The section on helping users find information followed. This section discussed various cues that you can employ to help people use the interface, including visual, audio, pop-up windows, and search engines. You learned about some of the drawbacks of these cues. For example, audio cues are unappreciated by users who are hard of hearing.

Next came the discussion of communicating with the users. You learned about features that make information and help easier to find, including consistently applied standards, a well-designed online help system that is designed to meet users' expectations of finding information quickly, and the use of assistants and wizards to help get users up to speed and performing tasks more quickly and easily.

The chapter ended with a discussion of the fifth and final step in the Goal-Directed Design Process: refining the program and interface form and behavior, and then finalizing the design so that you can share the information with stakeholders. You learned that you will have to go through several iterations of drafting the look and feel, and then you construct the validation scenarios that show how different people in a persona use the interface. At last, you finalize the design and share it with different stakeholders in the company.

Review Questions

Now it's time to review what you've learned in this chapter before you move on to Chapter 7. Ask yourself the following questions, and refer to Appendix A to double-check your answers.

1. Why do you need to plan for real-world requirements?
2. Why are paper prototyping and storyboarding important when constructing key path scenarios?
3. What are the three levels of design principles that guide you toward minimizing the work of the user?
4. Why is it important to create patterns?
5. What are the four desktop-based GUI postures?
6. What application characteristics make up an auxiliary application?
7. What happens when you click the right mouse button on an object?
8. Why should you avoid visual noise and clutter?
9. Why is it important to have a well-designed online help system?
10. What is the advantage of a pop-up menu over an icon?
11. What does the use of consistency standards in the design of your interface do for its users?
12. When should you use assistants and wizards?
13. Why should you construct validation scenarios?
14. How can you share the finalized design with stakeholders in your company?

Designing a Web Site

*"Some men give up their designs when they have almost reached the
goal; While others, on the contrary, obtain a victory by exerting, at
the last moment, more vigorous efforts than ever before."*
—Herodotus

Topics Covered in This Chapter

Web Versus GUI: Similarities and Differences

Web Myths

Web Postures

Why You Need Web Engineering

Web Standards

The Four Rules

When Do You Break the Rules?

Implementing applications on the Web has become a popular alternative to developing operating system applications, particularly if you want to develop applications for different operating system platforms.

However, a Web GUI interface has similarities and differences from a desktop GUI application that you must be aware of. Both interfaces adhere to some of the same rules, yet the Web must adhere to its own standards that are dictated by the Hypertext Markup Language (HTML), as well as related Web languages regarding the placement of text and objects on a Web page.

Technologies are beginning to blur the line between the desktop GUI and the Web, and more companies are developing Internet-enabled applications that allow users to use desktop software that interacts with the Web.

If you're going to develop for the Web, there are plenty of Web myths out there that have been dispelled. You need to know about these myths so that you're aware of what affordances and constraints you have with Web design. Like GUI interfaces, Web interfaces have different postures for different types of Web sites.

Web engineering is an integral part of Web design. Without the programming and database development behind the interface, you won't be able to create an effective Web site if you want to include e-commerce, Web form(s), or user databases with your Web site.

You should also understand Web standards and the four rules of Web design. The rules don't apply all the time, so this chapter tells you when it's okay to break the rules.

Web Versus GUI: Similarities and Differences

When you design for the Web, you need to be aware of the differences between desktop GUI interfaces and Web interfaces. They contain different types of constraints.

GUI Rules

A GUI contains a specific set of rules for how the user interacts with the computer. Following are these rules:

- A desktop metaphor uses icons to represent files and programs.
- The mouse (or an alternative device such as a trackball) and keyboard can be used to manipulate objects.
- Windows allow you to view and manipulate data within each window.
- The arrangement and storage of windows allow you to work on more than one program at once.
- Rigidly enforced standards ensure that windows look and feel reasonably the same. This cuts down on the learning curve needed to learn a new program because the interface is similar.

Web Rules

Web sites also have rules, some of which overlap with GUI rules:

- The Web uses a specific program called a browser that runs in the GUI to access the Web site. Therefore, when the user accesses the site, the user is required to open a window and use the mouse to manipulate objects there.

- The Web is constrained by requirements in HTML and other Web languages regarding placement of objects on a Web page. Although new Web technologies (such as Adobe's Flash animation software) are blurring the line between the desktop and the browser, most people still use browsers; therefore, browsers still constrain Web design.

- The look of a Web page is constrained by a set number of colors and fonts that all Web browsers can display, called *Web-safe* colors and fonts. Using Web-safe colors and fonts, the look of the Web page will look reasonably the same way on all computers running all available browsers. The Amazon Web site uses Web-safe colors and fonts, as shown in Figure 8.1.

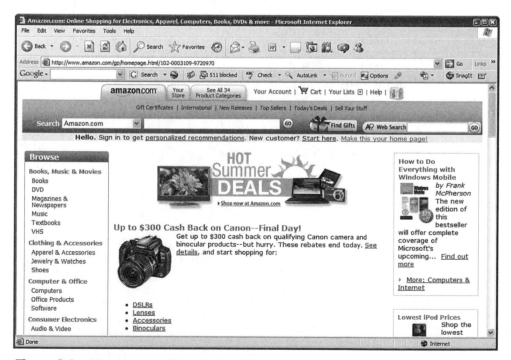

Figure 8.1 *The Amazon Web site has Web-safe colors and fonts.*
© Amazon.com, Inc. or its affiliates. All Rights Reserved.

The look of a Web page is not constrained by rigid standards, although there are generally accepted usability conventions that you should adhere to for the look and feel of a Web page. I'll discuss these standards in more detail later in this chapter.

Internet-Based Applications

The GUI desktop and the browser have been blurring as more and more users equate the desktop computing experience with the Web experience. People are using technologies such as the Java programming language, the ActiveX and PHP scripting languages, Adobe's Flash animation software, AJAX and Dynamic HTML, and even more proprietary solutions such as Microsoft .NET languages and related software to create richer, more interactive Web applications.

These technologies make it easier than ever to create a Web-centric application that's available from the desktop and transparent to the user. That is, the user will not be able to tell when the application is accessing the Web to exchange information with online resources such as one or more databases. The user will be able to use the desktop GUI to manage online resources without having to use a browser, and your Internet-centric application will have a richer interface and richer feedback than a Web interface.

Therefore, you will find that both GUI and Web affordances and constraints will apply in those situations. Be aware that many affordances and constraints in designing an Internet-based application will depend on the technologies you use to build your application. As always, consult your personas and find out whether an Internet-based application is the path that your users want you and your project team to take.

Web Myths

There are plenty of myths about Web site design, and if you adhere to any of them, you'll make your users' experiences worse rather than better. And that will translate into people leaving your site and not coming back.

This group of myths comes from several different sources, including Cooper and Reimann (2003), Web sites that discuss Web myths, and your author. These myths fall into several different categories:

- Usage
- Design
- Accessibility

Before you design for the Web, be aware of these myths so that you can dispel them in the planning stages.

Usage

Web usage myths have only grown over the years, and a lot of frustration about using the Web has come from misconceptions about how to use the Web. Before you design for the Web, understand the myths about how people use it. (The myths are bold, and the truth appears after the myth.)

- **A Web interface is easy to use**—If all you have is a static Web page with some text and a few links, this may be true. However, in recent years, the Web has become much more interactive, including forms, frames, scripts, and other embedded applications that have made Web interface design as complicated as interface design for a desktop application. Web interfaces don't yet provide all the rich feedback and flow of a desktop application, so there are also design constraints of which designers must be aware.

- **The Web and Internet are one and the same**—The Web is only the graphical interface that allows people to share information over the Internet. The Internet is a network that can transfer large amounts of data including multimedia files, email messages, and newsgroup messages.

- **Web design is all about browsers**—Technologies are already expanding Web technologies beyond the browser and onto the desktop as well as to other devices. For example, Adobe's Rich Internet Applications use Flash to create a Web site that looks and functions much more like a desktop, as discussed in the previous section. There are already Web-enabled connections for searching the Web built into Windows Vista. And my Palm Treo already connects to the Web to use Web-based applications that exchange data between the Web site and the Treo.

- **People are patient, and they will stay on the Web site to explore**—Some users are online to research, but many visitors to your Web site go there because they want specific information about something you offer. They don't want to spend time reading through long HTML pages or clicking through a large number of links to try to find what they want.

Design

Some of my business clients have believed in the following Web design myths. My business designed several Web sites for clients who believed that visitors expected some design features listed here only to realize later that their customer base really didn't care for it. (In some cases I had to report feedback, and in other cases I had to put my foot down, which lost me a couple of clients.)

- **Designing for the Web is different from designing in other media—** Yes . . . and no. It's true that designing for the Web is different. You do have a different flow of information. And there are some constraints in Web design that are similar to GUI design and some that are quite different, as the previous section discussed. However, designing for the Web still means that you have to take care to prepare. You still have to interview users and learn about the behaviors they're looking for to make your Web site user friendly.

- **Animation and a lot of graphics are a necessity—** The Web provides opportunities for you to add graphics and animation, but you must be polite to your users in that you shouldn't overwhelm them with Web graphics. Like a newspaper or any other print medium, you need a good balance between graphics and text. Of particular note is the animated graphic, which can get your users' attention but can also serve as a distraction when the user is trying to see something else on your Web site. Too many graphics or animated graphics can also distract users from what you want them to see on a Web site. In the end, the user will become annoyed and likely won't return to your site. Further, overuse of cutting-edge graphical technologies can prevent users of some Web browsers from using your application if those browsers don't support these technologies.

- **Background sound is a necessity on a Web site—** You can embed sound files to play in the background when users visit your Web site. However, this can quickly become annoying, especially if users can't turn it off short of turning the volume on their speakers to 0 or mute. Listening to the same melody over and over again can quickly become tiring.

What's more, if your application depends on sound, you might be excluding users from your user base who might have hearing difficulties.

- **Content is all that matters in Web design**—When you design for the Web, you're not just designing Web pages that have static content that you want people to read. You're designing a system that includes the form that information takes, the behaviors of your system and how the Web site flows from one page to another, and the content itself. And if the content is not easy to access, users will become frustrated and dissatisfied with your application.

- **Presentation is the only thing that matters, not any "plumbing" behind the scenes**—When you create a Web site, obviously you want your Web site to look good, all the links to work properly, and your interface to be accessible by all visitors to your site. However, after you start adding forms, scripts, or other Web application code that changes your Web site into a Web application, you need to build code behind the scenes using languages such as PHP and Java. And if the infrastructure of your site is not solid, you can risk usability problems, or worse, data or privacy loss for your users.

- **Plumbing is something you can do by yourself**—It's easy to produce the visible pages of your Web site because the rules are straightforward, and if you have merely an informational Web site, usually Web pages are all you need to design. If you are designing a Web application, however, unless you have a lot of expertise in the code required to make your site transactional, you should hire qualified companies to come in and do the work for you. Even though code packages are available for things like e-commerce, you may have some integration issues with your site that you may need someone else or another company to look at. Web development is still far from trivial and should be entrusted to those who are experienced with Web technologies.

Accessibility

Your site will be available to millions of potential viewers, and those viewers have different computer setups that are as individual as they are. Therefore, it's important to be aware of Web site accessibility myths and what the truths are.

- **All I have to do is design for the most popular and most recent browser, and everyone will be able to see my site**—Not everyone uses the latest version of Microsoft Internet Explorer, which as of this writing is the most popular browser with about 90 percent market share. People use a variety of other browsers on a variety of platforms that you must take into consideration. For example, you may have users who use Firefox in Windows, Netscape in Linux, and Safari in the Mac OS.

- **Accessible pages must appeal to the lowest common denominator version of a browser**—HTML, the language for designing Web pages, contains backward compatibility when it comes to accessibility features. The most current version of HTML, version 4.0, is supported by all major browsers, and all current versions of Web design software such as Dreamweaver and FrontPage support HTML 4.0 development. Version 4.0 of HTML is backward compatible with versions of HTML going back to Version 2.0, so you don't need to worry about designing a Web site or application using an earlier version of HTML. However, the same isn't true for many other web technologies outside of HTML. For example, there are numerous differences in JavaScript in various Web browsers.

- **Accessible pages have to be text only**—You can still have different colors, graphics, and other materials such as multimedia clips on your Web site. However, you need to have alternative tags, or ALT tags, attached to every graphic and multimedia object on the Web site, as discussed in more detail in Chapter 2, "Concepts and Issues." Users should have alternate ways of using the site that do not depend on sophisticated audio or visual effects.

- **Accessible pages don't have to make graphics accessible for people who can't see them**—The Web is a multimedia environment. People who are sight impaired can still experience Web sites through accessibility features available through their operating system. If you know that you'll have sight-impaired users visiting your Web site, you may also want to have audio links so those users can listen to features on your site.

Also note that roughly 25 to 30 percent of users don't load images on their Web sites for reasons that include sight impairment, bandwidth issues, concerns about viruses, and frustration with the prevalence of image-intensive commercial advertisements. Although the use of broadband connections like

DSL and cable is growing, there are still quite a few people accessing the Internet through dial-up connections, and of those people, you'll probably have quite a few who don't want to spend the time waiting for an image to load. Having an ALT tag attached to a graphic or multimedia object will give your users an idea of what you're trying to communicate through the graphic or object.

Web Postures

In Chapter 7, "Designing a User Interface," you learned about the postures in a desktop GUI application. To review, there are four types of postures in a desktop GUI application (Cooper and Reimann, 2003):

- **Sovereign**—An application that keeps the user's attention for long periods
- **Transient**—A task-specific, need-based application that the user uses occasionally
- **Daemonic**—An application that usually doesn't interact with the user and runs in the background
- **Auxiliary**—An application that exhibits the characteristics of both sovereign and transient applications

Do these postures also apply to Web sites? Yes, but because Web sites have different functionality, they have different names. What's more, different types of Web sites require different postures.

Different Types of Web Sites

There are three different types of sites you can create for the Web. These sites have different names from the postures for GUI applications (Cooper and Reimann, 2003):

- **Informational sites**—These do not require complicated transactional features. Informational sites are as advertised: they provide information that the user can search for by clicking on links to go to other pages within the site, and these pages contain more information. The MSNBC News Web site is an informational site, as shown in Figure 8.2.

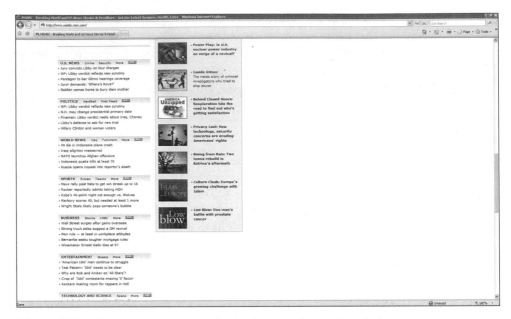

Figure 8.2 *The MSNBC News Web site is an informational site.*

- **Application sites**—These require a significant level of data transactions using scripts that manipulate that data behind the scenes. The user will never see what level of data is being transacted. The transactions can be as simple as the user filling in contact information in a form and sending the data in an email message or as complex as a full-scale e-commerce system where data has to be stored in a database and data on the site must be updated dynamically. The Amazon Web site, shown in Figure 8.3, is an application site.

- **Portal sites**—These provide information for the user about things happening with the company and links that tell the user how to get somewhere else. These sites are connected to services such as AOL and Yahoo!, as well as portals that are available through the browser, such as the Netscape portal for the Netscape browser, as shown in Figure 8.4, and the MSN portal for Internet Explorer.

The types of postures for each of these sites depend on the type of Web site you're creating—some sites include more than one posture (Cooper and Reimann, 2003).

Figure 8.3 *The Amazon Web site is an application site.*

© Amazon.com, Inc. or its affiliates. All Rights Reserved.

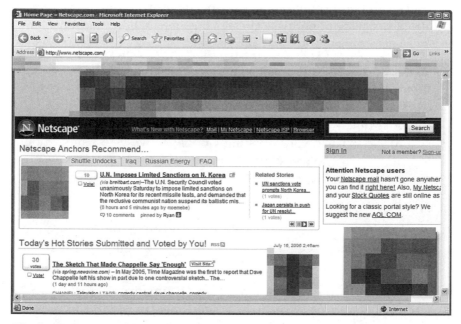

Figure 8.4 *The Netscape portal site.*

Informational Sites

Informational sites have both sovereign and transient posture characteristics depending on what you're displaying.

An informational Web site has a sovereign posture if there is detailed information displayed on the user's screen. Unfortunately, it's difficult to know what sort of display resolution the user will use to view a site. The standard maxim for Web sites is to design for a size slightly smaller than Super VGA resolution, or 800 × 600 pixels. This ensures that everyone can see the text on the screen, but it could also mean users will have to keep scrolling down to read all the information on the screen.

If screen resolution is a significant concern, make it a point to ask your users during the interview process what screen resolution they use. Then you can determine the screen resolution from the primary persona. Otherwise, if you design your site for a larger resolution and users complain, you will have to spend time and money changing the site or potentially lose current and prospective customers.

If your primary persona doesn't access your site often, your site has a transient posture. A good example is the Microsoft Windows Update Web site, which users don't visit often unless they need a critical update or they want to see about installing noncritical updates for their Windows installation.

Good navigation is always a rule, but it's especially important for transient sites because people don't want to keep clicking the same links to get to their desired page. Many sites use *cookies*, which are small text files that Web sites place on your computer, to store your site preferences and load them the next time you access the site. For example, the Google News site allows you to personalize your opening Google News Web page. Google saves the information in cookies so that your personalized Google News page appears the next time you open the site.

Application Sites

Application sites can also have different postures, but because the interaction is more complex, the postures can differ depending on the needs of the primary persona.

For example, if the application is for consumers only, such as an e-commerce site that customers visit on an occasional basis, the site must include elements of sovereign and transient postures. E-commerce sites need to have sovereign elements because they usually have a variety of products to choose from, and people want to compare different products and read about what each product does. Application sites also have a sovereign posture if the user uses the application site regularly, as does the owner of a business who needs to check the inventory on his Web site every day.

However, the site must also reflect a transient posture to users because they generally don't visit application sites every day. The transient posture on an e-commerce site includes a shopping cart that is always visible (sometimes with the current items in the cart listed as well), good navigational aids, as well as the use of cookies to tell the system what the user last viewed or making suggestions about similar products.

Cooper and Reimann (2003) suggest that transient Web applications should follow the same guidelines as transient GUI applications. However, they list several other guidelines you should be aware of:

- Clearly telegraph the application site's functionality. Make affordances obvious and visible, such as the ability to find a certain type of clothing by clicking a link on the page. You can also give hints if necessary, such as a reference in the text or in the ALT text that's associated with a photo. For example, if you have a photo of a sweater, as soon as the user moves the mouse pointer over the photo, she'll see text that reminds her to click the Sweaters link to find more sweaters.

- Make the application site simple, direct, and to the point. Remember that users have set goals when they visit your site, and you need to tell the users just enough so that you meet their needs. If you become too verbose or try to add too much functionality, you'll lose their interest.

- Make the application site fit in the users' mental models and flow in the context of the Web site. When you develop the site, pay close attention to the workflow of your Web site and what your users expect the site to be. For example, if your site is a clothing store, be sure that the site constantly reinforces the fact that you can buy different types of clothing in your online store. If you have a different application from your store site that isn't in line with what you're trying to sell, you run the risk of making that link look like an advertisement. Web users have long been desensitized to Web ads, particularly banner ads that you've probably seen at the tops of pages.

- For e-commerce sites, employ transactional features as much as possible to reduce confusion. This is especially true of the checkout process, which is usually the most confusing and frustrating part of e-commerce. However, if you carefully create the flow and design of the process to include clear input, instructions, and feedback, as well as a clear start-to-finish process, you will have happier customers and a more successful e-commerce site.

- Plan carefully regarding access to user data. Most transient Web applications can't save user data on the client side, so if you need users to log into a particular area on your page (or to the remainder of the Web site), make this functionality as seamless and obvious as possible. For example, you may have a user ID and password so the user can log into the preferred customers' page.

  Fortunately, modern Web browsers (like Internet Explorer) help users by allowing them to save their user ID and password information so they will only have to enter the ID without having to remember the password. You may also want to provide information to your users about creating a secure password.

- Make application sites with a sovereign posture nearly indistinguishable from similar desktop sites. The Rich Internet Application is one such example; with it, people can develop Web interfaces using Flash that look and behave similar to the user's desktop. Like desktop applications with sovereign postures, a sovereign application site should consist of full-screen applications with controls and objects that the user can easily access to gain as much control over the interface as possible.

Web Portals

You probably have heard about "portal" Web sites, which provide a lot of information in one location. There are several different types of portals you may encounter on the Web (Cooper and Reimann, 2003):

- **Consumer oriented**—These provide access to content and functionality related to a specific topic or a group of topics. For example, the MSN.com portal (shown in Figure 8.5) has content related to news and weather headlines as well as links to other services such as the Web search feature at the top of the page.

- **Enterprise portals**—These provide information you can access for company information and business tools. For example, Web site hosting

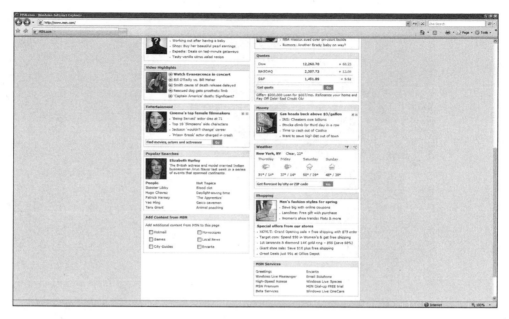

Figure 8.5   *The MSN.com portal.*

services allow you to log into your site remotely using an enterprise portal, an example of which is shown in Figure 8.6. After you log in, you can make changes to your site such as add an e-mail address or look at your statistics.

- **Environmental portals**—These are Web sites where actual work is done. The portal that the Web site hosting service offers is an excellent example. The hosting service environmental portal shown in Figure 8.7 allows hosting customers to make changes to their service information by accessing tools that are represented by icons and menu choices.

Figure 8.6   *An enterprise portal for accessing a hosting service control panel.*

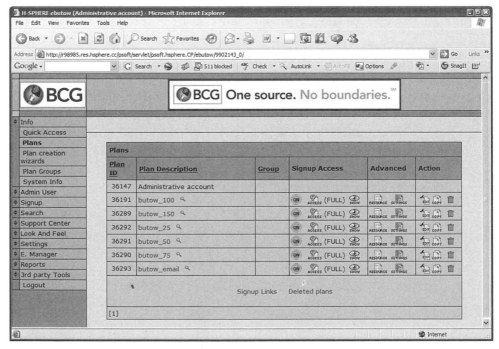

Figure 8.7   *An environmental portal for the hosting service.*

Consumer and enterprise portals usually have a transient posture, because users go to the portal to find something they want, and as soon as they click on the link they want, they're out of the portal. Within an environmental portal, however, you're running a number of individual program elements simultaneously. These elements also have two postures: auxiliary and transient.

Most environmental portal elements have an auxiliary posture because they usually present sets of information that the user wants constant access to. For example, in the case of a Web site hosting service portal, the user will want access to her list of e-mail addresses. The environmental portal also includes transient elements that are used for short periods when the user needs it, such as submitting a support ticket to the technical support staff at the hosting service.

Why You Need Web Engineering

Web design is not just the design of Web pages, but the design of a Web system. This holistic approach reflects that Web design now involves Web sites interacting with Web applications. Web applications involve many transactions based on the interactivity between the visitor and your site. If you require this sort of work, you need a Web engineer to work with your designers to create an integrated, holistic system that works the way you and your visitors expect.

"Back-End" Programming

Web sites provide information through a Web browser and connect to other sites using links. Web applications, on the other hand, can produce Web pages that change depending on the input they receive from the visitor. That can include the number of shirts the user wants to order from your e-commerce site or the type of catalog the user asks for when she fills out an online form requesting more information from your company.

Much of the functionality of Web pages happens out of the visitor's sight. Web application programming is also referred to as *back-end* programming. The *front end* is what the user actually sees, while the heavy lifting goes on in the back. Web pages and Web services work in a two-way, content-to-transaction relationship. The content can drive the transaction, such as on an e-commerce site, but the transaction can also drive the content.

Form Processing

One example of content driving the transaction is a Web site form, an example of which is shown in Figure 8.8. This form contains one or more text boxes that allow the visitor to type information into the boxes and then click a button at the end of the form to send the form information to the server. If the back-end programming considers that the visitor completed all appropriate fields satisfactorily, it processes the form and sends it to its intended recipient(s) via email.

The transaction can also drive the content, because after the Web site has completed the transaction, the programming directs the posting of a thank-you message on the Web site.

One other variable that you must be aware of is security. All current browsers provide pretty good security so people can't hack into the form and steal credit card numbers and other sensitive information. When you work with a Web engineer, be sure that he is up-to-date on security issues and programming—or find another engineer who is. You can have only one Web page that

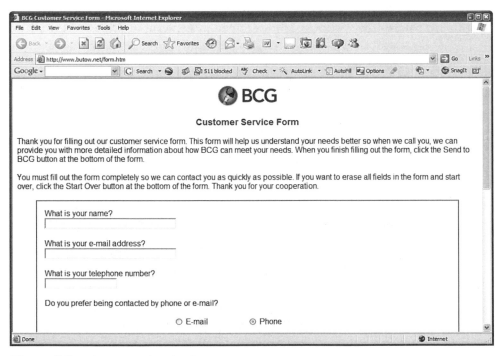

Figure 8.8   *An example of a form.*

takes sensitive information, but if this Web page is not secure, visitors will not give you their information. If visitors do give you their information and that information is stolen, you could face serious legal issues.

Databases

Back-end Web programming commonly interfaces with databases, which hold information about data that the Web visitor may be interested in. For example, an e-commerce Web site usually contains information about products for sale. The database then drives the content, because the Web site displays the number of products available as well as how many products are available for purchase (or if the company is sold out).

The visitor can order one or more products and specify how many of each product to order. After the visitor enters his shipping and credit card information, the database updates the information, processes the order, and tells the Web site to display a thank-you page. When the database changes, the back-end programming automatically changes the quantity of products available and may or may not reflect this updated quantity on the Web site.

Web Standards

Like a user interface, a Web interface must be consistent across all pages of the site, because that consistency gives your visitors the impression that the site is part of a unified whole. (Yes, it's that holistic idea again.)

Colors and Text

Colors and text are still limited by browsers. Computer users have different fonts installed on their computers. They also display different ranges of colors. For example, my computer can show more than 4 million colors on the screen, but another person's computer may only be able to show 65,536 colors. Although browsers and Web design software such as Adobe's Dreamweaver let you create any colors you want in your Web site, you should design your Web site for the least common denominator when it comes to text and graphics. That denominator is the Web-safe set of several common fonts and a set of 256 colors that all browsers can display. Also, be careful to avoid colors that might have cultural implications, or colors that might cause a problem for colorblind users.

Also, design your site so that visitors can read the text on your site properly. What looks cool to you may look to a visitor like you're trying to give her a seizure. It's important to keep the issues of contrast and simplicity in mind. For example, you should have a black font on a white background for the best contrast. You should also consider what font is the most readable. Many people find the Arial font to be more readable onscreen than Times New Roman.

What's the point of designing to the "least common denominator" for your visitors? Keep in mind that you want your site to look the same across all browsers; differences could result in your site not looking the way you intended. For example, if you use a font not on your visitor's computer, the visitor's computer may show a different font that wrecks the spacing on the site—or it may not show the site at all. If the visitor's computer can't view one or more of the colors that you have on your site, that computer will display a color that it thinks is the next best thing—and your visitor may be surprised at the color he sees. For example, if you attempted to use a red color to indicate a serious condition, but the color substituted by your computer does not convey the importance, you won't get your message across.

Also, be sure to use tasteful colors and fonts. If you use a lot of bright colors, colors that don't coordinate well together, or fonts that are whimsical and unprofessional, it can reflect on the perception that your users have of your company.

Graphics

If you've done any Web surfing, chances are that you've seen examples of bad graphics on a site. The telltale signs of bad use of graphics can include one or more of the following:

- Flashing text, a flashing block of text, or both. These are generally used in banner advertisements that users have grown accustomed to ignoring.
- Animated graphics that distract the user from looking elsewhere in the text.
- Too many graphics within an area of the page that not only distract you from looking at any text on the site, but result in frustration because all the graphics compete for your attention at the same time.
- Graphics that are pixelated and jagged.

Your site should avoid using your graphics badly. Above all, however, your site should have only enough graphics on the page to communicate to the user effectively.

In some cases, you may only need one graphic for your company logo. If you have an e-commerce Web site, it should have a limited number of graphics spaced out so the user can see what the product is but not be overwhelmed with so many graphics in one area of the page. Amazon.com is a company that does this well on its home page. The Amazon site has numerous graphics hawking various wares, but the graphics are spaced well apart and combined with text, and the text and graphics blocks are separated by a healthy amount of white space.

Navigation

Your site should be easy to navigate—meaning that if you don't have links to other related pages of your site readily available so visitors can get back to where they were, your visitors will become frustrated and leave. If you're selling things on your Web site, users leaving can mean lost business for you. And if you don't have visitors on your site, what's the point of having a Web site in the first place?

Bread Crumbs

As part of having good navigation, your site needs to include links that take users back to the home page or a higher-level page (such as a shopping cart) on each subpage. These *bread crumbs* can be links that appear on the page, as shown in Figure 8.9. Alternatively, you can have a navigation bar or area that appears the same way on each page for your visitors' use.

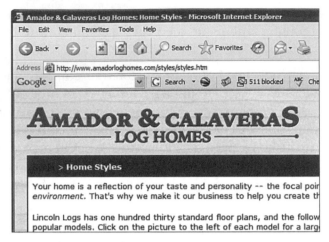

Figure 8.9 *A bread crumb on a Web site that leads the user back to the home page.*

The Four Rules

You should adhere to four rules when you design a Web site so that your site is as usable as possible: keep your site simple, keep it consistent, keep it current, and keep navigation to three clicks.

Keep It Simple

From the previous section, you probably got a good idea that your Web site should be as simple as possible, whenever possible. There are exceptions, as I'll detail in the next section, but you should make your layout as easy as possible. Also, remember from Chapter 7 that the readers' eyes in Western countries follow from left to right, and from top to bottom. However, this may not always be the case, so my advice from Chapter 7 applies—you should perform a user and task analysis of your users to find out where they're coming from and what they're looking for on your site.

Keep It Consistent

As with a user interface, your Web site interface must be consistent across all pages. If your Web site suddenly changes its look, users may become confused and think that they're on a completely different site. In the case of your user interface for a software application, such a tactic would result in calls from other customers. In the case of a Web site, visitors will simply leave and never return. To help keep sites consistent, it's beneficial to have one person responsible for reviewing the look of all the pages on the site.

Keep It Current

If you don't have current information on your site that keeps your customers coming back to see what you're up to, your visitors will get bored and leave. If they see a date or language on the site that proves that the site is badly dated—and in the Web world, one to two months qualifies as dated—they will assume that there is no reason to return to your site for updated information. Or they may get the impression that your company doesn't care about serving its customers.

Keep Navigability to Three Clicks

One of the golden rules about Web site design is the three-click rule: the user should be able to find what he wants on your Web site in three clicks. If the user can't find the information he's looking for in three clicks, you may need to change your Web site structure accordingly.

When Do You Break the Rules?

The rules in the previous section are not unbreakable. Sometimes you need to break the rules when they don't suit the needs of your company or your users.

Breaking GUI Rules

You may need to break GUI rules if there are already standards in place that the organization is currently using. For example, if the company produces software that has a specific user interface that the customer is already used to or requires, you should design your user interface to that standard.

Your user testing may also determine that, although your user interface meets the specifications for the GUI, the users find the interface to be cumbersome in places. In that case, you need to determine what the users would like to see changed and determine if you can make those changes.

Breaking Web Rules

You may have so many options available that the three-click rule doesn't apply. For example, if you have an e-commerce site, users may have to click more than three times to get to the product they're looking for. If the site were redesigned to adhere to the three-click rule, users would be faced with a product page that would overwhelm them with choices, and they would become so confused that they would decide not to bother.

If you're going to use a complex transaction that requires a richer interface, such as the Rich Internet Application that was discussed earlier in this chapter, many Web rules may not apply to your project.

If you have an existing company intranet that connects to a separate program, such as the Web-based component of Microsoft Outlook so you can schedule meetings and contact people from a Web application, and your Web site has to follow those standards, other Web standards may not apply to your site.

You may also need to break the rules to meet the standards set by the rest of your organization. For example, the Web site may need to look and act a certain way, and you may need to include features that already exist on the current Web site into your new Web site so that both sites appear to be the same.

Case Study: Interface Navigation Features

The database application that you're updating for Mike's Bikes contains a Web-based interface for easy integration into Mike's Bikes intranet so that everyone can access the application through the Web browser. In the previous chapter, we discussed the need for you and Evan to review the entire interface to ensure that the computer (played by Evan) in the paper prototype test accurately reflects the current look and feel of visual and audio cues.

Those visual cues also include the colors and navigation of the interface. Fortunately, you have a color laser printer, so when you take the screen shots for the paper prototype test, you have full color versions of the screens available for your testers. When you add new screens for testers to look at, you and Evan also decide to use multicolor pens that reflect the colors in the pages as much as possible so the test is as consistent as possible.

You must also be aware of the interface navigation features. The current application for Mike's Bikes includes breadcrumb navigation on each page as well as a navigation menu button bar at the left side of the screen so the user can move to each page easily, as shown in the figure. Your new screens need to implement these features, and because the navigation bar has a new menu button for the product availability page, you need to add the Product Availability button to all the screen shots in the paper prototype test (see Figure 8.10).

Although you don't need to be detailed in the paper prototype, such as making the new Product Availability menu button the same color as the rest of the buttons in the test, there are times when you will have to use a different color to make a point. For example, in the Mike's Bikes application, you will add a

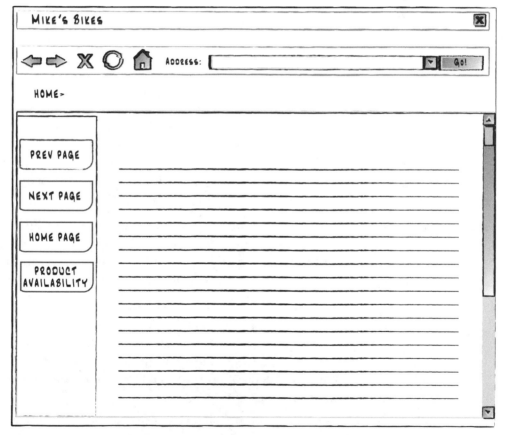

Figure 8.10　*The new screen with the Product Availability button.*

new Web site Ordering button in the product table that is a different color from the other buttons. You will have to use a marker with the color to make this button (in this case, yellow) contrast with the adjacent button so that the Web site Order button stands out. Figure 8.11 is in grayscale, but you can see the difference between the lighter color and the darker color of the adjacent button, enabling the lighter Web site Order button to get the user's attention.

Figure 8.11   *The Web site Ordering button is in a different color.*

The paper prototype test will tell you if the color you have chosen is acceptable to the testers. Speaking of the test, it's time to give your test a run with just you and Evan. Then you need to prepare for the real test, as described in the next chapter.

Summary

This chapter began with a discussion of the similarities and differences between the Web interface and the GUI interface and how technology is blurring both interfaces to make desktop interfaces Web capable. Those technologies include the Java programming language, the ActiveX and PHP scripting languages, Adobe's Flash animation software, AJAX and Dynamic HTML, and even more proprietary solutions such as Microsoft .NET languages.

Next, you learned about Web myths in terms of usage, design, and accessibility so that you can be aware of them. After each myth, information followed that dispelled these myths so you can provide truthful information if any of these myths come up for discussion during the development process.

Following that was the discussion about Web postures and the types of postures that are available for all three types of Web sites: informational sites, application sites, and portal sites. You learned that the type of Web site you create determines the type of postures you design, and the type of postures in turn (along with the needs of your primary persona) determine what features you should include in the Web site.

The section on why you need Web engineering discussed the design of a Web system and how Web sites today use dynamically generated Web pages and interactions between the front end that Web site visitors see and the back-end programming that makes the Web site functional and usable. You learned that the content can drive the transaction, such as on an e-commerce site, but it can also drive the content. One example of content driving a transaction is a Web form. The transaction can also drive the content, because after the Web site has completed the transaction, the programming directs the posting of a thank-you message there.

Web standards were covered next. You learned about the three areas of Web standards that you must pay attention to: colors and text, navigation, and leaving bread crumbs. You learned about how to use colors and text for maximum readability, and avoid certain graphics such as flashing text and animated graphics that distract the user from your message. As part of your site navigability, you learned that you should have links to other pages of your site as well as bread crumbs that take your user back to the home page or to a higher-level page.

The four rules of Web design followed: keep it simple, keep it consistent, keep it current, and keep navigability to three clicks. The chapter ended with a discussion of when to break the rules, such as if your company already has existing rules, if you want your interface to be consistent with another tool you use, and if your user testing reveals usability problems that need to be corrected in the interface, even though the correction violates the rules.

Review Questions

Now it's time to review what you've learned in this chapter before you move on to Chapter 9, "Usability." Ask yourself the following questions, and refer to Appendix A to double-check your answers.

1. What are the similarities between GUIs and Web interfaces?
2. Are GUIs and Web interfaces becoming more or less similar? Why?
3. Why do you need to know about Web myths?
4. What three categories do Web myths fall into?
5. Why is it important to know about Web postures?
6. What are the three different types of Web sites?
7. What are the three types of Web sites you can create?
8. What is an example of content driving a transaction?

9. What is an example of transaction driving content?

10. Why must you limit your color and font choices?

11. What are the four telltale signs of poor use of graphics?

12. Why should you adhere to the four rules of Web design whenever possible?

13. What is the three-click rule?

14. When do you break the Web design rules?

Usability

"Supposing is good, but finding out is better."
—Samuel Clemens

Topics Covered in This Chapter

Selecting Techniques for Your Usability Test

Defining Your Usability Test

Conducting the Usability Test

Analyzing and Presenting Usability Test Results

After you design your software, hardware, or Web user interface, it's time to put your interface to the test by letting users preview it and provide feedback so you can make changes as needed before you release it to the public.

You need to start by selecting techniques for your usability test. You will run into resistance, and this chapter discusses the different questions you may be asked and gives you some answers that you can give in response.

When you know what technique you want for your usability test, you need to define your test to determine what information you need from the users and how you will gather that information.

After you design the initial test, you need to conduct a pilot test that will allow you to hone your observational and interviewing skills. When you've worked out the kinks, you're ready to conduct the real test.

When the test is over, it's time to crunch the data and prepare a report and presentation for your stakeholders that tells them what you found and gives them your recommendations for improving the interface and the overall product.

Selecting Techniques for Your Usability Test

You can use several techniques for conducting your usability test (Hackos and Redish, 1998). Depending on your situation, you can use one or all usability techniques to get the information you need to make your product or documentation better.

Observing, Listening to, and Engaging Users

One of these techniques is to go onsite to visit the users in their natural habitat. You may run into resistance when you propose a site visit, especially if the trip to the customer costs money. If you do encounter the following questions (Hackos and Redish, 1998), which are fairly common, you can counter with the following arguments:

- **Why go at all?**—We must challenge or verify our assumptions. After all, we haven't seen how our customers work, and we may be surprised by what we find out. That information will affect our product and its documentation.

- **This is a new product, so why go out and test it?**—We can challenge our assumptions to see how well the new product will fit in the customer's workflow and how users approach new products, which will make the implementation process smoother.

- **We're just changing one part (or feature), so why look beyond that?**—Usability studies onsite can obviously affect the change in that one part. What's more, the change in that one part could affect the users' workflow, so there needs to be a holistic analysis of the change in that one part.

- **What will we learn from only a few users?**—Usability testing studies by Neilsen (1993) and Virzi (1992) have shown that testers can glean a high percentage of user needs from a sample of six to eight individuals from each user group. Beyond eight users, we see repeated patterns with a few minor variations. Testing a small group not only brings us the information we need to analyze, but it is also cost effective.

- **Why not use the customer information we already have?**—We need to test how well customers think *this* product functions, not what customers are doing now or have been doing.

As I said in Chapter 3, "Making the Business Case," be sure to perform a return on investment (ROI) analysis, and include any site travel information in your cost estimate.

When you observe users in their natural environment, you should adhere to the following rules as you plan for any type of site visit (Hackos and Redish, 1998):

- Plan ahead. Understand the site visit issues and objectives.
- Select users to represent the diversity in the user group.
- Treat the users as partners.
- Watch, listen to, and talk with users. Usually, do this one at a time, and observe their work as they work in their own environment.
- Make the conversation concrete by talking about what the users are doing or just did.
- Take your cues from the users. You should also share your emerging understanding with the users to ensure that you are correctly interpreting what you see and hear.

If you also bring this information—particularly a plan for the site visit—to your decision maker, it will help make your case even stronger.

Other Methods of User Interaction

There are other methods of user interaction that you can employ either in place of or in tandem with site visits (Hackos and Redish, 1998). These methods, which will be familiar from related concepts in earlier chapters, include usability evaluations away from the customer site as well as more traditional marketing techniques:

- **Usability roundtables**—The customers come to your site and bring their work with them so you can use the work as the context for evaluating your product's usability.
- **Controlled usability evaluations**—You can predesign your usability test and then conduct that test in a controlled environment, such as a laboratory with computers that have your product installed on them.
- **Focus groups**—You can bring your customers to your site and facilitate a group of 8 to 12 people (the typical size for a focus group) to obtain

attitudes, reactions, and opinions about your company's products, ideas, and customer requirements.

- **Bringing users to requirements-gathering sessions**—The product development team interviews the users to find out what they want to see in the product.

- **Include one or more users on the design team**—Having users on the design team can help further users' goals and desires throughout the production life cycle.

- **User surveys**—You can conduct user surveys as discussed in Phase 3 of the Usability Engineering Life Cycle (UEL) and apply this information to future versions of the product.

- **Meeting users at trade shows**—Trade shows and other professional association meetings can be great venues for gathering user information.

Each of these methods has drawbacks, generally falling into three categories: bias for lack of adequate feedback, lack of information provided by users, and misunderstandings. These misunderstandings are caused by confusion, miscommunication, or not being able to see how the users actually use the product.

There is no one best way of conducting a usability test. However, observing and engaging users onsite have been shown to be the most effective ways of gathering usability information from users (Hackos and Redish, 1998).

Defining Your Usability Test

The first step in the testing process is to define and plan your usability test. If you don't know how you are going to test and what you are testing for, then you will be wasting the time of a lot of people—not to mention the company's money. You should keep good written records of what you are testing, the responsibilities of project and usability team members, and the decisions the team makes.
—Dumas and Redish, 1999

Dumas and Redish (1999) identify five tasks that you must complete as you define your usability test:

1. Define your goals and concerns.

2. Determine who your test participants are.

3. Select, organize, and create test scenarios.

4. Determine how you will measure usability.

5. Prepare your test materials.

The following sections describe the tasks to complete (Dumas and Redish, 1999).

Goals and Concerns

After you have determined who your users are, you have to make choices when you create your test—for example, whether you want your usability test to be geared toward advanced users or the majority of users classified as intermediate. You create your goals by starting with general goals, and from there you build specific goals. These goals can come from several sources:

- Your task analysis and quantitative usability goals, such as those you developed in your paper prototype.

- Timely issues, such as having to produce a usability study to resolve a dispute about whether to add a feature.

- A heuristic analysis or an expert review, such as concerns from an internal customer (for example, marketing) that need to be addressed.

- Previous tests of this product or other products. One test may provoke concerns that require another test.

Picking Your Test Participants

You must be choosy when you determine who you want to participate in your usability test. When you create a persona, as you learned about in Chapter 6, "Analyzing Your Users," you're determining the characteristics that you want each user in your test to fit into. You need to think about two types of characteristics: those that all users share, and those that may cause differences between the users. Following are the decisions you need to make when determining characteristics:

- Users' experience with computers or the product you're testing.

- Users' work experience

- Users' experience with your product
- Users' experience with similar products

You should think broadly about your users when creating profiles. Following are some examples of thinking broadly:

- Consider new hires who are just coming into the job.
- Think about new customers who will be using the product.
- If the product is used internally within one group, think about what other groups in the company may be using the product in the future.
- Think about differences within a category. For example, younger users may adapt more quickly to new technology than older ones.

From here, you can create groups and even subgroups of users who share the same characteristics so you can, for example, learn if there are differences between subgroups toward a new feature in your program.

Selecting, Organizing, and Creating Test Scenarios

Unfortunately, you can't test every possible task that the user could do with the product. So how do you narrow it down? Use tasks that

- Probe potential usability problems
- Are suggested from your concerns and experiences
- Are derived from other criteria
- The user will do with the product

As you select tasks, you must also keep in mind how long the task will take for the user to do and what hardware, software, procedures, and other information are needed for the user to do the task. You should write down your tasks by giving each task a number and description (just as you did with paper prototyping). Each task should show the time it will take, the hardware and software needed, and the high-level instructions and procedures required to complete the task.

You can use a scenario to tell participants what you want them to do during the test. A scenario describes the task in a way that helps bridge the task (which is artificial) with what the user would be doing in the world. For example, "You have three new hires. Add accounts for them."

A good scenario has the following characteristics:

- It's short.
- It's in the user's words.
- It's unambiguous.
- It gives participants enough information to do the task.
- It's directly linked to your tasks and concerns.

Your tasks and scenarios don't have to be written. You can have human actors playing different roles, such as customers, support staff, or supervisors. You can also have the participants stop between each task, such as after a longer task or if you want to distribute a printed questionnaire to all participants after each task. However, you must provide audio cues to tell the participants to stop and start again because participants may become focused on the task and won't remember when to stop and start.

Determining How to Measure Usability

Usability measures two dimensions:

- **Performance measures**—These are quantitative measures of specific actions and behaviors that you observe.
- **Subjective measures**—These are people's perceptions, opinions, and judgments.

In the case of performance measures, you can easily log each time a user exhibits a certain behavior during the test, like expressing frustration. Subjective measures are harder to quantify unless more than one participant tells you the same thing, such as that the email button is hard to find on the page. There are commercially available programs for logging usability data, or you may want you or a programmer on your product team to create a program that meets your specific needs. If you can't use a computer-based program, you can create a printed form to use.

As you create your logging form, you need to set criteria for performance measures. A typical criterion for performance measures is a four-point scale, which forces a choice toward positive or negative because there is no strictly neutral response. This four-point scale, in fact, has three passing grades and only one failing one. You must also set performance measures that are directly tied to your general and specific concerns. For example, if you're concerned about how easy it is for a user to read a message, some of the measures you may want to add include the time it takes for the user to perform the task and the time it takes for the user to recover from errors.

You'll want to follow the same performance measures for most tasks in the same test whenever possible to get a good idea of how users perform. However, different tasks within a test may require different performance measures. For example, a function that is available in one Web page may not be available in a sublevel Web page, so you wouldn't log errors for that function in that sublevel page.

You may also have to take into account the test situation, such as whether the participants have to read the instructions for each task. If you're testing the time it takes users to complete a task, you have to add to the total time it takes the users to complete the task to account for the test situation. For example, you should add 30 seconds to the beginning of the test so the testers have enough time to read and absorb the task instructions.

Preparing Test Materials

Before you test, you must prepare legal forms for the treatment of human participants. As the tester, you are responsible for the following:

- Creating a legal form that correctly states each party's rights
- Ensuring that all test participants have read and understand the form
- Observing or witnessing all participants signing the form

You should consult with your company's legal department or attorney (if possible) to produce these forms and possibly present them to your participants. If you are required to explain and present these forms, do so in a neutral but friendly tone.

You should also have a testing script so that you test all users in all groups the same way. If you remember standardized testing from high school, you'll remember that all the teachers followed the same script to ensure that everyone was tested the same way so as not to skew the results and to make sure that all tasks were completed at the same time. The script should also include a checklist so you know that everything has been completed. If you have other team members with their own checklists, you must ensure that they have completed their checklists.

You may also want to distribute written questionnaires before the test, after each task, or at the conclusion of the test to get the following information from your users:

- **Pretest**—Gather information about the participant's background.
- **Posttask**—Gather judgments and ratings about each task.
- **Posttest**—Gather judgments and ratings about the test.

Written questionnaires are useful and efficient because you ask all participants the same questions, and you don't forget to answer the questions. However, you must ensure that all the questionnaires ask the right questions so that you get the most effective answers. For example, if you want to ask a question about the difficulty of completing a task, it would be more effective if the question asked participants to rate the difficulty on a scale from 1 to 5 (5 being very difficult) rather than being close-ended.

Conducting the Usability Test

It's time to assess your preparations by first conducting a pilot test to see how well it works. After you have conducted the pilot test, you need to learn how to take proper care of your test participants before you start your actual usability test.

Conducting a Pilot Test

You should conduct a pilot test before you conduct the real usability test (Dumas and Redish, 1999). A pilot test allows you to "debug" your test and find out if there are any initial problems with the product or Web site you're testing, its documentation, its test methods, and its test materials. Following are bugs you can encounter during the pilot test:

- The participant can't perform a task because of a bug in the hardware, software, or Web site.
- The participant uses a procedure that you didn't anticipate to complete the task.
- The participant only finishes a portion of the tasks.
- The participant keeps making the same mistakes.

- The participant doesn't have the materials needed to complete the task.
- A question or answer confuses the participant.
- Instructions in the documentation confuse the participant.
- The participant can't complete a task because of basic usability problems with the product.

Always conduct the pilot test exactly as you will conduct the full usability test, and use one test participant who represents the users you want to test. By mimicking the same conditions in the full usability test, your pilot test will give you the most accurate results. The pilot test will also let you test the way you approach your users.

To give yourself enough time to make any necessary changes, schedule the pilot test two days before the live usability test. That will give you a full day (and perhaps longer if you schedule the pilot test in the morning) to make any changes without feeling the pressure of an immediate deadline. If the pilot test exposes problems that require more substantive changes, you can also determine whether to escalate the issues.

Honing Your Observation Skills

From your pilot test, you will get clues that will help you hone your skills, especially if you're going onsite at a customer's location to view how users work and use your product. Many factors go into a successful site visit (Hackos and Redish, 1998). Before you go to the user site, keep the following in mind:

- Don't arrive unannounced. Always arrange the logistics of your visit with the managers and users onsite, and let them know what you'll be doing in general terms.
- Work through channels, including managers and unions, where necessary.
- Work with the other site to schedule your site visit at a mutually agreeable date and time.
- Confirm the visit with a fax as soon as it's arranged and with a follow-up call the day before your visit.
- Ask for directions to the site if necessary. You don't want to be late.

- Practice setting up any equipment at your headquarters to work out any setup bugs before you set up the equipment at the customer's site.

When you arrive, do the following:

- Greet the manager and the users, as well as the users' colleagues if they share space.
- Ask for permission to set up your space and the audio and visual equipment, if needed.
- Verify the expectations about how long you're visiting and what your agenda is for the visit.

Do the following while you are onsite:

- Make the visit as cooperative as possible. Ensure that you build a good relationship with the users, and help them feel reassured when necessary. However, also be sure to let the users know that you're interested in seeing how they do things, not to be an expert to explain how to do something.
- Be flexible about users' schedule and needs, such as restroom breaks.
- Be sure that your language is friendly but neutral.
- Take a lot of notes. You can never take enough notes.

When you leave, do the following:

- Thank the users and the managers.
- Give the users a gift, even if you are paying for the visit.
- Pack up quickly and quietly.

After you leave, be sure to send a thank-you note to the users and the managers.

Writing Notes

When you take notes as an observer, write them on a form that ensures that you capture the important information about what the users are doing and that you answer the question you have. Although the form should be specific to your usability needs (and perhaps customized further to meet the needs of the users you're testing), it should include the following:

- The project name
- The observation form number, because you may interview more than one user during your visit
- The name of the observer
- The date of the observation
- The page number of the form and the total number of pages in this observation form
- The user's goals
- The user's task
- Notes about the user
- Notes about the environment
- The situation at the starting point of the task
- The time the task started
- Observations about the user during the task
- The time the task stopped
- The situation at the end of the task
- The end points of the task that will show that the usability goal has been met

You should also write down inferences and questions about the users and the task during the observation. Ask questions during the observation so you can get as much information as possible.

Honing Your Interviewing Skills

You can interview the users as they are performing the task, but you can also determine both from the users you're interviewing and from the pilot usability test what interview methods and skills are best for your site visit. In addition to obtaining information while the users are performing the task, which is called a *concurrent, contextual interview*, you can also perform one or a combination of the following types of interviews (Hackos and Redish, 1998):

- **Immediate recall interview**—Record what the users do, and then talk about what they did at the completion of the task.
- **Cued recall interview**—Record what the users do, and then talk about it sometime later, perhaps with the assistance of video playback.

- **Process interview**—Interview users individually or in groups to understand an entire process or workflow.

- **Ethnographic interview**—Interview one user first as a key informant, and then later interview others and conduct observations with discussion during the observations.

- **Cued recall or discourse-based interview with artifact walkthrough**—Collect artifacts from the user and then construct an interview around the artifacts.

- **Critical incident interview**—Interview users about specific situations when you can't observe them yourself.

- **Group interview or focus group**—Interview users individually or in groups about attitudes, desires, preferences, and so on.

- **Usability roundtables**—Interview users away from their work site.

- **Customer partnering**—Work with a group of users over time, with interviews as one of the techniques.

No matter which interview process you decide to use, you should always keep three things in mind when you interview:

- Treat the users as partners, not as research subjects.
- Presume that the users know a lot about their work.
- Listen far more than you talk. As the old saying goes, you have two ears and one mouth, and you should use them proportionally.

Fundamental Skills

Within this overall three-point philosophy about interviewing, there is a set of fundamental skills you should adhere to so you can get the most out of your interviews:

- Set expectations about your respective roles and knowledge.
- Plan the questions or issues for site visit interviews ahead of time.
- Know what you are trying to learn.
- Realize the power of different types of questions to get the answers you're looking for. For example, you may want to ask general questions or specific questions at different points during the test to get the answers you need.

- Ask neutral questions instead of leading or blaming questions.
- Respect silence, and let your users think about their answers (or their questions) if they have to.
- Watch body language and other signals from users, and be cognizant of cultural differences.
- Capture exactly what the users say.
- Stay close to your site visit plan.
- Give users the opportunity to answer the questions you didn't ask.
- Treat users' questions with respect, and always promise that you will take the users' concerns, requests, praise, and other comments to the appropriate people. Then keep that promise.

An Ongoing Relationship

Sometimes your interviews may require you to create an ongoing relationship to track the progress of a product or document. As users progress from beginner to expert, they go through several stages (Kuniavsky, 2003):

1. They makes mistakes.
2. They create mental models of how the product operates or how the document reads.
3. They set expectations as their familiarity with the product or documentation grows.
4. They form habits that may or may not be efficient ways of completing a task.
5. They form opinions, which they can change as they acquire more experience with a product. They may like or dislike a particular feature or subsystem.
6. Finally, they develop a context for the product in terms of their goals, their job, and the relationship to other tools. This can result in a product becoming indispensable or relegated to a bookshelf or drawer to collect dust.

There are a number of methods for obtaining usability information over a longer period of time (Dumas and Redish, 1999):

- Have the users fill out a diary questionnaire form, which contains several questions. The tester sends a new form to the users on a regular basis either on follow-up site visits, by email, by fax, or even by regular mail. The form can have many of the same questions as well as several specific questions so you can get answers.

- Create an advisory board that meets regularly so users can provide direct feedback to the project team.

- Telescope the research by bringing together users with different experience levels so you can see how different issues affect users.

- If you're looking at the usability of a Web site, you could capture user login information to create some metrics that answer questions such as what page the users spend the most time on.

Caring for the Test Participants

You need to ensure that you take care of your test participants. When you start the test, you need to ensure that your testers are comfortable and that you're calm and focused on them. A checklist can help keep you and your testing team on track and ensure that you create a rapport with your testers from the beginning (Dumas and Redish, 1999).

Some of that rapport can include small talk and having the testing staff and testers introduce themselves by providing information about their jobs, their organization, and what they want to get out of the test. You should also talk with participants about the environment, and if you have a videotape, show it. If you have a testing room either at the user site or your own, you should show users the room and introduce them to any monitors who will be watching them and working with them throughout the test.

Conducting the Real Test

As you go through the test, remind your testers to think out loud whenever possible (Dumas and Redish, 1999). Thinking aloud helps focus the testers' thoughts and helps them understand what they're thinking. The success rate for thinking aloud can vary because some testers are more willing to share their thoughts than others.

Sometimes testing can go awry. Following are some common situations and what you can do in response (Dumas and Redish, 1999):

- A tester refuses to participate in the test any longer. In this case, you should clearly understand why he doesn't want to participate. If you can't alleviate this situation, you must let that tester leave.

- A tester is so nervous that he cannot continue with the test. You may want to take a short break and talk with the nervous tester one on one to see if you can resolve the problem. If not, you may have to let that tester go.

- A tester is not qualified to participate in the test. You will usually learn if a tester isn't qualified in the pretest questionnaire, but you may find out during the test. In any case, you have to immediately let the tester go.

- A tester is taking too much time to complete a task. Before the test starts, you should be clear that the testing group will move on to the next task even if one or more testers haven't completed the task. Also, make sure to point out that the timing problem isn't with the tester, but with the product. If a tester is taking too long, it can be an indication that the interface is difficult to use.

- If the product equipment or software fails, you should move the group to another room and explain what is happening while your other team members try to figure out what's happening. If you decide to stop the test, you must determine whether to reschedule.

- A tester is frustrated or nervous because the product is hard to use. In this case, you may want to talk with the affected tester one on one so you can determine if he wants to continue. You should point out that the difficulty he's having is quite valuable, and his feedback is needed to resolve the problems.

Note that if you're compensating testers, you'll have to determine how to compensate any who leave on a case-by-case basis.

During the test, you should always observe problems and create a problem list. Those on your testing team should also create a problem list because everyone has a different perspective on what's happening. Write down your observations, your hypotheses about the actions you observe, and your interpretations. Keep your observations as neutral as possible, and record all user problems. That way, you'll get a complete list without discounting anything. After you write down all your problems, you may want to discuss some of them with your testers to get more information. After the test, you should talk with your testing and project teams about what you found.

Some of the information in this chapter repeats what has been covered in earlier sections and chapters, but now you should see how all the information fits together so you can conduct your usability test. After you complete your usability test, you must analyze and present your data and then recommend a plan of action, as we'll discuss in the next section.

Analyzing and Presenting Usability Test Results

A usability test generates a lot of data that you need to go through (Dumas and Redish, 1999). After the test, your data can include one or more of the following:

- A list of problems from the test
- Quantitative data on times, errors, and other performance measures, including subjective ratings on questionnaires
- Testers' comments from logs, notes, and questionnaires
- The testing team's written notes
- Background data on the participants
- Videotapes of the test, perhaps from several different viewpoints in the room

Analyzing and Presenting the Data

The first step in analyzing the data is to tabulate and summarize quantitative data. This is something you can do with any spreadsheet program. You can also compile all the comments into a word processing program. More powerful software programs such as the ones found in Microsoft Office let you link your spreadsheet in Excel to the document in Word. When the spreadsheet is updated in Excel, it is automatically updated in Word.

After you have entered all the data, you can analyze it for trends and surprises. Spreadsheet programs are also useful in calculating statistical information about the data, such as the mean score for a question in a questionnaire. However, as Mark Twain said, there's always the problem of "lies, damned lies, and statistics," especially when it comes to inferential statistics. Inferential statistics take a sample from a larger set of data and make inferences about the larger data from the sample. This approach contrasts with descriptive statistics, which describe a set of data, like the average time it takes to complete a task.

A useful technique for processing data is *triangulating* it (Dumas and Redish, 1999). This involves looking at all the data together to see how each set of data supports the other sets. Each apex contains a different set of data:

- The problem list
- Quantitative data from logs and questionnaires
- Testers' comments and the testing team's observations

You measure the data against your usability goals and the quantitative criteria you set before the test to determine what the problems are inside the triangle.

You may find some surprises that warrant further research. For example, you may find that one user had different reactions to several questions. Perhaps that user felt that performing a task was a lot harder than the other respondents thought. Because the number of users in a usability test is small, you should always treat this outlying data seriously. If the outlier may represent a large group of potential users, the data may suggest that you need to schedule another usability test with more users like the outlier to see if the problem is with that set of users or is confined to that one user for some reason.

Dumas and Redish (1999) recommend that you adhere to the following guidelines to make statistical analysis as relevant as possible:

1. Use inferential statistics only if you understand how to apply and interpret them.
2. After you employ a statistical test, carefully explain what the test means.
3. Describe your interpretation of key data values when you don't compute statistical tests. This description will provide your readers with some guidance on the accuracy of "eyeball" tests.

Both your quantitative data analysis as well as the qualitative data from feedback and notes will help you organize the information into two areas (Dumas and Redish, 1999):

- **Scope**—How widespread is the problem? It's best to organize problems into general groups that indicate a significant problem that's backed up by more specific results from the test. For example, a general group can be lack of user feedback produced by a program, and the specific results that support this group can include comments from testers about times when the program wouldn't give them any feedback after they performed a task.

- **Severity**—How critical is the problem? You can set up severity criteria as you analyze the data, or you can do so before the test takes place. It's up to you to determine the criteria that are both easy for you and the people who will be reading your usability report to understand. For example, you could have a five-point scale where problems rated 1 are "show stoppers" that prevent completion of a task and need the project team's immediate attention, and problems rated 5 are problems that the project team may want to look at in the next version.

The Report

Research is not an exact science, and there is bias in all facets of research. When you present your report, be sure to start with two questions in mind (Kuniavsky, 2003):

- **What are the data collection problems?** You should acknowledge the problems with the data collection up front so no one in your audience points out a fundamental flaw in collecting data that could doom your effort.
- **What are the limitations of the analysis?** This book has discussed some of these limitations. You should explain why you decided on the subsets of data to analyze.

By addressing these questions first, you can minimize any issues and not only help the data become clearer, but also lend weight to your arguments.

The type of report you create depends greatly on the audience. You may be presenting to one or more groups within your company, so your report language needs to be tailored for one or more of these audiences (Dumas and Redish, 1999):

- **Engineers**—Engineers are problem solvers, so your report and recommendations need to focus on solutions.
- **Virtual designers**—Virtual designers are problem solvers, too, so designers are also most interested in solutions.

- **Marketing**—The report should focus on reasons behind people's choices and the mental model of the users.
- **Upper management**—The expectations of managers vary, so you should know the agendas of the managers involved in the review and approval of the report. You may also want to contact the managers directly to briefly discuss what's important to them.

In addition, you should determine what format these audiences expect. You may need only a Word file attached to an email message and send the message to the appropriate people, or you may give your presentation at an executive board meeting and therefore need a printed paper report to present to board members. If you want to ensure that your format is acceptable, send a draft to the intended recipient(s) and get feedback.

After you have established the formats, you need to categorize the report's information in the most effective manner for your audience. You may also want to produce several versions of the report depending on your audience (Dumas and Redish, 1999). For example:

- The abridged report contains only need-to-know information that's time critical. You may want to send this via email so that this information is available immediately.
- The general report contains all the need-to-know information plus the should-know information that's available to everyone.
- The complete report contains need-to-know, should-know, and nice-to-know information so that everyone is aware of not only what needs to be done, but also some of the subtle feedback you received that your project team may want to implement (as part of the nice-to-know information).

Write your report in newspaper style—that is, structured like a newspaper story where the first sentence contains the most important fact, and the least important information is saved for last (Dumas and Redish, 1999). Break out the report into several sections or chapters, such as these:

- Procedures
- Evaluator profiles

- Observations
- Evaluator quotes
- Conclusions
- Recommendations

Begin the report with an executive summary that summarizes the information in the report on one page so people who don't want to read the report can get a broad idea of what's in the report and what your recommendations are.

The Presentation

When you get ready to give your presentation, adhere to the following guidelines for making that presentation successful (Dumas and Redish, 1999):

- Prepare your audience so they're in a mindset that helps them understand the information they're about to receive.
- Pick your points carefully. In formal presentations, you don't have unlimited time to make all your points, so make sure the must-know topics are covered.
- Use real examples to make your points. You may want to use video clips if you videotaped the usability test, or use participant names and quotations.
- Emphasize the user market's perspective when you present the results so that you illustrate the differences between the users' ideas and the project team's ideas.
- Use terminology sparingly, and only after you define the term, to prevent confusion in your audience.
- Use numbers carefully. Make sure presentation of numbers is backed up by hard data, because people see numbers as an absolute representation of an idea.
- Leave one-third of your time for questions.

After you set up your presentation, practice. It's best if you can practice in front of someone else, especially someone who is similar to your audience members.

Preparing a Highlight Presentation

You may not be able to give a formal presentation. What's more, some people may never read the report because they're too busy. The development of multimedia technologies has made it easy not only to create a video presentation, but also to publish that information in a streaming video file that you can attach to an email message or post on the company intranet. For example, when I worked as a contractor at Hewlett-Packard (HP), I created streaming audio and video files using software that was available for $50, which was within the manager's discretionary budget for his department. The manager liked the production so much that we placed the file on our group page within the HP intranet.

There are advantages and drawback to making a highlight tape or streaming video file (Dumas and Redish, 1999):

- The tape or file will provide viewers with all the data they will need about the test. However, you will have only 20 to 30 minutes to make your presentation, so viewers won't be able to see all the exceptions and caveats in the report. Viewers also won't be able to ask questions in real time, although you could invite them to contact you via phone or email.

- Pictures and sound convey to people images that are more vivid and longer lasting than what they read in a report. Even so, your audience expects to see fast, snappy video pieces and may become bored quickly by a video highlight presentation.

- The video presentation may be your only way to present your report to important stakeholders. Yet there is no guarantee that people who have access to your highlight presentation will see it, in contrast to the captive audience you would have in a formal presentation.

When you create your video, write down your plans using the following criteria:

- **Scope**—Illustrate the most pressing problems and the most important recommendations for improving the current design. Keep it brief so you don't dilute your message.
- **Objective**—Determine your objective for the video.
- **Audiences**—Who is the audience for the video?

- **What they will do with the information**—What do you want the audience to do with the information presented in the video?
- **Constraints**—How long will the video be, what needs to be added into the tape, and what are the deadlines?

Note that you may also need to buy hardware and software to produce your video, which could be another impediment. If you already took videos of your usability test and you have the video equipment to produce video and audio recordings of yourself or another person as the narrator, chances are that your company has the hardware and software you need to produce the video.

Changing the Product and Process

After you've imparted your information to the project team, how do you turn that information into action so you can improve the usability of your product and the process? You can be most helpful to managers, developers, and other stakeholders—especially those who are resistant to change—by keeping three things in mind (Dumas and Redish, 1999):

- Keep open communication throughout the project. Work with all stakeholders from the beginning. If you're open and up front with them, they'll be more likely to come on board.
- Help your stakeholders organize the required changes. By structuring the problem and recommendations in a way that's easy to find and use in the report, you will go a long way toward convincing stakeholders to implement the changes.
- Be realistic in your recommendations for changes. Time and money constraints may require you to negotiate ways to fix the problem. However, don't settle for the word *can't* when you hear it—keep making the business case, and let people know what will happen if the changes aren't made.

These three guidelines also hold true for changing processes, because usability testing can well expose process defects that are leading to usability problems in your test(s). If you find that you need to change processes, your role goes beyond just testing the product—you're now a change agent for the entire organization. And when you change the processes for the company, you're helping not only to improve usability for one product, but for all future products that the company produces.

Case Study: Implementing the Paper Prototype Test

You've interviewed your testers and reviewed the existing applications. Now it's time to create the draft of the paper prototype test, place the materials in the binder, and then have Evan conduct the pilot test.

In this pilot test, Evan will give the test to you, one observer, and one note taker as he will give it to the testers in the actual test. The remaining observers and note takers you hired will be observing the pilot test and will provide feedback about that pilot test in the debriefing session immediately following the test.

The pilot test is originally scheduled to run for 65 minutes with a 10-minute introduction at the beginning of the test, which includes an introduction of the primary persona and a 10-minute question and answer session afterward. Based on the information you have gathered, you have come up with nine tasks for the project team to test:

- Searching for a product or customer using the Search box
- Viewing the product or customer information in the appropriate page
- Navigating to another page from the Product/Customer Information page
- Displaying parts supply information in the Product Availability page
- Accessing help from the Product Availability page
- Viewing part unavailability alerts in the Parts Maintenance page
- Viewing defective part alerts in the Parts Maintenance page
- Opening the parts supplier Web site from the application
- Calling the parts supplier from the application through the user's VoIP phone

Each task will take no more than 5 minutes, so this will leave 45 minutes for the remainder of the test. Evan has the test binder ready (including the task sheets) as you and the other two pilot testers sit around a round table to take the test. The observers are Ann and Sam, and the note takers are Debbie, Jim, and Robyn. Ann and Jim took part in the pilot test as the testers.

The note takers and observers will be in corners of the room and out of the way of Evan and the other testers (see Figure 9.1).

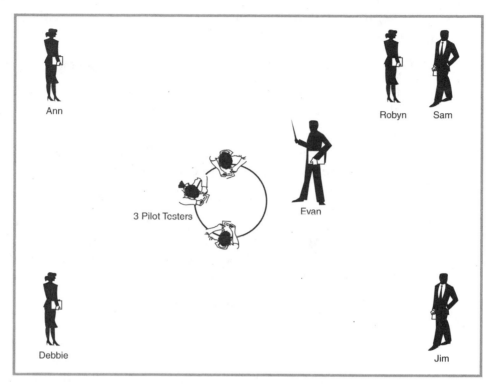

Figure 9.1 *Positioning of the "computer" and observers.*

When the test starts, Evan shows the primary persona based on user feedback so the testers know where the paper prototype options are coming from. He then gives some brief instructions for the test:

- Testers must show, not tell.
- Evan clarifies that it's okay to write on the prototype, but writing replaces typing, not clicking.
- Evan is the computer. To make sure the computer is behaving properly, bring on 2–3 college interns as note takers/observers. Have them observe and take notes about the interactions between the user and the computer (Evan). These notes will be part of the debriefing process that you, Evan, and the note takers and testers will go through after the test.
- If there is an unanticipated user action, Evan will note it or even mock up a new screen on a piece of paper quickly to reflect it.
- If the paper prototype crashes, we'll take a break.

After the pilot test, you, Evan, and the observers and note takers share your information and thoughts about the test.

You: "I want to go last. I want to hear what you thought of the test."

Ann: "I thought the test went well, but Evan was a bit rushed, so we didn't finish the last test until 2 minutes before the end of the testing session."

Jim: "I agree, and I think we need to add about 30 minutes to the test so Evan will have enough time to complete the test."

Evan: "You don't think the time should be extended to 15 minutes?"

Ann: "I think 30 minutes is about right, especially because our discussion about using the product availability page went too long. If you make changes to the product availability page, especially putting more information on the page, I think you'll alleviate that problem."

Robyn: "Especially if Evan needs to answer questions. I think he did a great job of that during the test."

Debbie: "Evan, you did a great job with the audio cues that were the same as the current application, which Ann noted during the test. That helped the testers follow along and know when the users did something right or wrong."

Evan: "This was a great test. I think we can tweak the interface a little bit per Ann's suggestion and then run the real test.

Sam: "Giving an extra 30 minutes should cover any problems the testers find about the test, especially if they want to use the Q and A time to make suggestions."

You: "I agree. I think we need to include a group of sticky notes for people to write down their suggestions, and then we can add more sticky notes from the observers and testers to make a to-do list for a follow-up session."

Evan: "I'll talk to Mike and get permission to extend the session to 95 minutes and have a second paper prototype test."

You: "Be sure to tell him that we may need a third paper prototype session depending on what happens with the second paper prototype test. And then we'll need to conduct a usability test when the draft of the application is ready for testing. Please work with Mike on the schedule, but if he has any problems, have him contact me."

The interview with your pilot test team happened 6 weeks ago. You and Evan went through the paper prototype test and a follow-up prototype test with the entire project team. Happily, those tests were finished within one work-week, and the developers implemented the team's recommendations into the draft upgrade of the application in only 12 working days.

You and Evan interviewed all members of the project team to learn how they used the draft upgrade of the application on the test site. They provided valuable information that you summarized in a report to Mike. That report included recommended changes that Mike approved. The coders made the changes quickly, and Mike approved the final changes to the application quickly.

Two days ago, the changes went online. And you visited Mike's Bikes earlier today to follow up with him about how much users like (or dislike) the changes to the system.

As you opened the door, you noticed Mike and Traci sitting around Mike's desk with big smiles on their faces. "The response has been incredible!" Mike exclaimed.

"We're already on track to exceed our ROI estimates," Traci added.

You smiled back, inwardly relieved that Mike was happy. "I'm glad you like it. Is there anything else you need?"

Mike folded his hands on the desk. "I'm glad you asked," he said. "It's time to have our customers test our new Web site that ties into our database application. When can you start usability testing?"

Summary

This chapter began with a discussion about selecting techniques for usability tests and the various types of tests available to you. There is no one best usability test; you will have to determine the best usability test for your situation. The primary usability test discussed in this chapter is observing, listening to, and engaging users. With this type of usability test, you learned that you may run into resistance and a number of questions. This chapter discussed arguments that you can use to answer these questions.

Defining your usability test was covered next. You learned about defining goals and measurements for the test, picking test participants, creating and selecting test scenarios, determining how to measure usability, and preparing test materials. When you create test scenarios, a scenario is short, unambiguous, and gives participants enough information to do the task. Although a scenario is in the user's words, it is also directly linked to your tasks and concerns.

The section on conducting the usability test followed. You learned about conducting a pilot test before the real test, honing your testing skills, and caring for the test participants. You learned that you have to conduct a pilot test to work out any problems with the test before you conduct the test with real participants. When you conduct the test with real participants, you learned that you should encourage your testers to think out loud whenever possible and what to do when the testing goes awry.

This chapter ended with a discussion of analyzing the usability test results, ways you should present the results, and ways you can present the results to your intended audience. As with a usability test, there is no one best way to present the information to your viewers—that depends on your specific situation. This chapter discussed what you need to do to create a formal presentation as well as producing a highlight presentation if you can't give a formal presentation. After you provide the information, you need to turn the information into action so you can improve not only the usability of the product, but also apply what you learned from your users to other company products.

Review Questions

Now it's time to review what you've learned in this chapter. Ask yourself the following questions, and refer to Appendix A to double-check your answers.

1. What are the three general goals that a user looks for when he uses something?
2. What are the three phases of the UEL?
3. What rules should you adhere to as you plan for a usability test?
4. What types of scenarios should you test?
5. Why should you conduct a pilot test?
6. Why is it useful to conduct a worksite visit?
7. How many users are required for a useful and valid pilot test?
8. What are the possible sources of bias in your test results?
9. How should you address the question of bias in your report?
10. How do you ensure that your project team implements your recommended changes?

Answers to Review Questions

If you want to double-check your answers to the review questions at the end of each chapter, this appendix is the place to find those answers.

Chapter 1

1. Why is it important to learn about the history of graphical user interfaces?

   Because you need to know how the GUI developed into the standard user interface that is required in most cases for finding a computing-related job.

2. Who developed the first GUI?

   Douglas Engelbart.

3. Why was the NLS so important?

   Because it was the first operating system with a GUI interface.

4. What was the first personal computer with a GUI interface?

   The Xerox Alto.

5. Why did Linux become so popular?

   Because Linux is seen as a very stable operating system.

6. What was the first Web browser with a GUI?

   Mosaic.

7. Why did Internet Explorer have such an impact on design?

   Because Internet Explorer has such a large market share and because Microsoft paused in developing Internet Explorer, which allowed other companies to produce browsers with new innovations.

8. As a user interface designer, why do you need to know how a user interface works?

   Although GUIs have great similarities, they also have a number of small differences that you must be aware of.

9. Why do you need to know about the differences between GUIs?

Because different GUIs have differences in their look and feel as well as the features available in the interface, such as the taskbar in Windows.

10. Why do you need to know about the differences between a GUI and a Web interface?

Because you have to understand how a user interface works in the operating system for which you're designing the interface.

Chapter 2

1. What is the definition of a graphical user interface (GUI)?

A GUI is a system for interacting with a computer by manipulating graphic elements and text.

2. What are the three major GUI operating systems in use today?

The three major GUI operating systems include Windows, Mac OS, and Linux.

3. What are the main parts of a GUI?

The main parts of a GUI are windows, buttons, menus, toolbars, scrollbars, and taskbars.

4. What is the Internet?

The Internet is the worldwide system of interconnected computer networks that is accessible to the public.

5. What is the World Wide Web?

The World Wide Web, also known as the Web or by its acronym WWW, is an information-sharing space on the Internet that you access through a Web browser.

6. What are the three user interface model eras?

Batch interfaces, the command-line interface, and the graphical user interface.

7. Why is Web design still a significant challenge?

Because there are still too many browser limitations.

8. Why does Web design have an impact on user interface design?

Because many people use the Web, and Web accessibility issues have forced operating systems companies to adapt.

9. What is a ZUI?

   A zooming user interface.

10. How do Dumas and Redish define usability?

    The people who use the product can do so quickly and easily to accomplish their own tasks.

11. What are the three types of usability titles or occupations discussed in this chapter?

    The three types of usability titles or occupations discussed in this chapter include usability engineers, usability scientists, and user experience professionals.

12. When do you employ quick and dirty testing?

    Usually after the product has been produced.

13. When do you employ summative testing?

    When the product reaches a certain stage of development and testers want to find out how much progress has been made in the product's development.

14. Why is the validity and reliability of user interface methods being examined?

    There aren't currently many standards for procedures, data analysis, or reporting.

15. Why is accessibility important?

    Because you need to make your interface accessible for all your potential customers or Web site visitors.

16. What legislation establishes statutory accessibility requirements in the United Sates?

    The Rehabilitation Act of 1973.

Chapter 3

1. Why is the satisfaction of customer goals important?

   Because the satisfaction of customer goals leads to the satisfaction of business goals.

2. Who are the four stakeholders in a project?

   Users, engineers or designers, sales and marketing people, and managers.

3. When should you add features and functionality into the product?

   When they blend value for the customer with value for the company.

4. Why should you start the usability process at the same time as the project design process?

   Starting the usability process at the same time as the project design gives you the ability to couch the design of not only the usability tests but also of the product interface and documentation in terms of the total user experience.

5. What should be the first topic of discussion when starting your business case?

   The benefits of good design.

6. How can you make sure that your customers' goals are satisfied by the user experience?

   By knowing the customers' needs, tasks, and goals.

7. When should you add features and functionality into the product?

   When they blend value for the customer with value for the company.

8. After you show stakeholders how good design, as well as usability design and testing, will lower costs, what do you need to show them?

   After you show stakeholders how good design, as well as usability design and testing, will lower costs, you need to show how design and testing will make the company money.

9. Why do you conduct an ROI study?

   To calculate how much a product or initiative will pay for itself over time.

10. Why should you use the Usability Engineering Life Cycle?

    Because it provides a rigorous and ongoing process to the development of your user interface and your documentation.

11. What are the three phases of the Usability Engineering Life Cycle?

    Requirements analysis; design, testing, and development; and installation.

12. Why should you get feedback during the development process?

Feedback ensures that you don't have many problems to fix once the product is out the door.

Chapter 4

1. Why should you resolve conflicts and constraints before you start the design process?

Because the result will be a better interface design that will better serve the users.

2. Why does a user interface need to be elegant?

Because all parts of the interface need to feel like they work together as part of a whole.

3. How do you bridge the gap between user and designer constraints?

Bring them up with the product development team before the design process starts. If that's not possible, get as much customer feedback as possible so you can approach designers with this feedback to better design other products.

4. Why should you use paper prototyping?

So you can learn how users interact with the design before you develop the product.

5. How do you give a paper prototyping exercise a more professional look?

You can use heavier paper or cardstock to make the prototype more resistant to wear and tear during testing.

6. What are the advantages of paper prototyping?

It provides substantive user feedback, doesn't require technical skills, facilitates communication, encourages creativity, and cuts down on misconceptions.

7. What are the disadvantages of paper prototyping?

It may not be appropriate for your situation, and there are some technical problems that can't be tested using paper prototyping, such as keyboard or mouse input problems.

8. Why does a product require good documentation?

   Because it's the first line of customer support for your business.

9. Why is good documentation design important?

   Because users turn to product documentation first to get help with a problem, and if the documentation solves the problem, that saves the company money in customer support costs.

10. Why is good design important?

    To save money, convince users to use your product, keep your existing users, and bring in new ones.

Chapter 5

1. What are affordances?

   The perceived and actual properties of something.

2. What are constraints?

   Restrictions on allowed behavior by something.

3. Why do people consider themselves helpless when they fail at a task?

   Because they blame themselves or the wrong cause, adhere to misconceptions, or practice learned helplessness.

4. What does the MBTI test do?

   Helps people identify and understand personality type preferences.

5. What are the seven stages of human action?

   Forming the goal, forming the intention, specifying the action, executing the action, perceiving the state of the world, interpreting the state of the world, and evaluating the outcome.

6. What are the trade-offs between knowledge in the brain and in the world?

   Knowledge in the world is easily retrievable as long as it's visible or audible within your visual or auditory range. You may have difficulty remembering something because of distractions, but once you do remember something, you're efficient at it.

7. What task structure is the most challenging for people?

   Wide and shallow.

8. Why must you be deliberate when you're using your conscious mind?

   Because you're relying on short-term memories.

9. Why do you transform difficult tasks into simpler ones?

   So it's as easy as possible for your brain to digest.

10. What makes up a person's conceptual model?

    A person's life experiences, beliefs, and other methods for completing tasks that the person has built up over the years.

Chapter 6

1. Why are designers still building to mechanical-age standards?

   Because that's what designers are most familiar with.

2. Who are perpetual intermediates?

   People who have enough experience with a software program or product and need specific answers to questions.

3. What questions do beginners always have?

   Questions such as "What does this program do?", "Where do I begin?", and "What do I need to do to complete the tasks?"

4. What questions do intermediates always have?

   Questions such as "How do I find this function?", "Can I undo my last action?", and "What's the command to perform this task?"

5. What are the five phases of the Goal-Directed Design Process?

   Research, modeling, requirements, framework, and refinement.

6. Why should you conduct user and task analysis?

   To get answers to questions about your users and the tasks they perform.

7. What three dimensions of information do personas connect?

   Demographics, psychographics, and topology.

8. What types of goals do users have?

   Life goals, experience goals, and end goals for using a specific product.

9. Why should you perform user and task analysis "in the field"?

   Because you need to see how users interact in the larger environment, including contact with other people and interaction with the physical environment.

10. Why should you prioritize your personas?

    Because you want to know who the primary and secondary personas are for the product; the primary persona is the primary target audience for the user interface.

Chapter 7

1. Why do you need to plan for real-world requirements?

   Because these requirements from other stakeholders will help you to refine some of the ideas you generated in the requirements process.

2. Why are paper prototyping and storyboarding important when constructing key path scenarios?

   Because you can use them to show the path of each interaction as the user completes a task.

3. What are the three levels of design principles that guide you toward minimizing the work of the user?

   The three levels of design principles are conceptual, interaction, and interface.

4. Why is it important to create patterns?

   Because you can apply those patterns to problems in your project and solve the problems more quickly.

5. What are the four desktop-based GUI postures?

   The four desktop-based GUI postures are sovereign, transit, daemonic, and auxiliary.

6. Which application characteristics make up an auxiliary application?

   Sovereign and transient.

7. What happens when you click the right mouse button on an object?

   A pop-up menu appears with options associated with the object.

8. Why should you avoid visual noise and clutter?

   Because it will overwhelm and confuse the user by presenting too much information.

9. Why is it important to have a well-designed online help system?

   Because users are perpetual intermediates who want to find things quickly, and the online help system may be the first line of customer support for the product.

10. What is the advantage of a pop-up menu over an icon?

    The pop-up menu can convey much more specific information than an icon.

11. What does the use of consistency and standards in the design of your interface do for its users?

    It helps ensure that the users can find the information they are looking for because it is always in the same place.

12. When should you use assistants and wizards?

    When your user and task analysis shows that your users will benefit from having them as part of your user interface.

13. Why should you construct validation scenarios?

    Because not everyone in your persona will use the interface the same way.

14. How can you share the finalized design with stakeholders in your company?

    By producing an interactive prototype or creating an online demonstration.

Chapter 8

1. What are the similarities between GUIs and Web interfaces?

   The Web interface runs in a browser window; therefore, it uses many GUI features like the mouse pointer to interact with the Web site.

2. Are GUIs and Web interfaces becoming more or less similar? Why?

   The line between the two has been blurring as GUIs borrow some of the look and feel of Web interfaces and Web technologies allow Web interfaces to act more like those of desktop applications.

3. Why do you need to know about Web myths?

   Because you should design your Web site to avoid these myths.

4. What three categories do Web myths fall into?

   The myths fall into the categories of usage, design, and accessibility.

5. Why is it important to know about Web postures?

   Because you need to know how to design your Web site to match how your user will use the site.

6. What are the three different types of Web sites?

The three different types of Web sites are informational, application, and portal.

7. What are the three types of Web sites you can create?

Informational, application, and portal sites.

8. What is an example of content driving a transaction?

A Web site form.

9. What is an example of transaction driving content?

The posting of a thank-you message after the Web site visitor submits a form and the program finishes the transaction.

10. Why must you limit your color and text choices?

Because these limits guarantee that all browsers on all computers will be able to see the colors and text the way they were intended to be seen.

11. What are the four telltale signs of poor use of graphics?

The four telltale signs include flashing text or a flashing block of text, distracting animated graphics, too many graphics in one area of the page, and graphics that are pixelated or jagged.

12. Why should you adhere to the four rules of Web design whenever possible?

Because it makes your Web sites as usable as possible.

13. What is the three-click rule?

The user should be able to find what he wants on your Web site in three clicks.

14. When do you break the Web design rules?

When the rules don't serve the needs of your users or the company.

Chapter 9

1. What are the three general goals a user looks for when he uses something?

The user has an easy-to-learn experience, the product solves the user's needs, and help is easily accessible.

2. What are the three phases of the UEL?

   Requirements analysis; design, testing, and development; and installation.

3. What rules should you adhere to as you plan for a usability test?

   Plan ahead; select users who reflect diversity in the user group; treat the users as partners; watch, listen to, and talk with users; make the conversations concrete; and take your cues from your users.

4. What types of scenarios should you test?

   Tasks that probe potential usability problems, are suggested from your concerns and experiences, are derived from user criteria, and that the user will do with the product.

5. Why should you conduct a pilot test?

   To "debug" your test and find out if there are any problems with the product, Web site, documentation, testing methods, and testing materials.

6. Why is it useful to conduct a worksite visit?

   To see how users work and use your product in their work environment.

7. How many users are required for a useful and valid pilot test?

   Use one test participant who represents the users you want to test.

8. What are the possible sources of bias in your test results?

   Data collection problems and limitations of the analysis.

9. How should you address the question of bias in your report?

   Acknowledge problems with the data collection and analysis limitations up front.

10. How do you ensure that your project team implements your recommended changes?

    Keep open communication throughout the project; help your stakeholders organize the required changes; and be realistic in your recommendations for changes.

B

Recommended Reading

Books

This book includes the most important, useful, and timely studies in the fields of user interface design, interaction design, and usability testing. If you're interested in going into more detail about the topics covered in this book, pick up one or more of the following books at your local bookstore:

- *A Practical Guide to Usability Testing*, by Joseph S. Dumas and Janice C. Redish, ISBN 1-84150-020-8
- *About Face 2.0*, by Alan Cooper and Robert Reimann, ISBN 0-7645-2641-3
- *Built for Use*, by Karen Donoghue, ISBN 0-07-138304-2
- *Constructing Accessible Web Sites*, by Jim Thatcher et al., ISBN 1-904151-00-0
- *Cost-Justifying Usability, Second Edition*, by Randolph G. Bias and Deborah J. Mayhew, ISBN 0-12-095811-2
- *Observing the User Experience*, by Mike Kuniavsky, ISBN 1-55860-923-7
- *Paper Prototyping*, by Carolyn Snyder, ISBN 1-55860-870-2
- *The Design of Everyday Things*, by Donald A. Norman, ISBN 0-465-06710-7
- *Usability for the Web*, by Tom Brinck et al., ISBN 1-55860-658-0
- *User and Task Analysis for Interface Design*, by JoAnn T. Hackos and Janice C. Redish, ISBN 0-471-17831-4
- *Waiting for Your Cat to Bark?*, by Bryan Eisenberg and Jeffrey Eisenberg, ISBN 0-7852-1897-1

Web Sites

There are plenty of usability-related sites and guidelines on the Web. Here are some great Web sites to start with:

- Nielsen Norman Group, www.nngroup.com/
- PaperPrototyping.com, www.paperprototyping.com/
- Research-Based Web Design & Usability Guidelines, http://usability.gov/pdfs/guidelines.html
- Society for Technical Communication Usability Web Site, www.stcsig.org/usability/
- UsabilityNet, http://usabilitynet.org/home.htm

Active Server Pages (ASP)—A technology created by Microsoft that allows Web pages to include dynamic content, often pulled from a database.

Address bar—The location in a browser where you type in the URL for the Web site you want to visit.

Aero—A graphical user interface style for the Microsoft Windows Vista operating system.

AJAX—*See* Asynchronous JavaScript and XML.

ALT—An HTML tag that provides alternative text when a Web browser cannot display nontextual elements, which are typically images.

Alto—Produced by Xerox, this was the first personal computer that had a GUI interface.

Aqua—The Mac OS X graphical user interface.

ARPANET—A computer network formed by the U.S. Defense Department Advanced Research Projects Agency in 1969. It was the forerunner of the Internet.

ASP—*See* Active Server Pages.

assistant —A program, usually embedded inside another program, that provides hints or ask you to provide keywords so the agent can search for an answer.

Asynchronous JavaScript and XML (AJAX)—A Web development technique for creating interactive Web applications.

Atlas—A software "toolkit" developed by Microsoft that is designed to ease creation of AJAX-style applications.

auxiliary—A software posture in which an application exhibits the characteristics of both sovereign and transient application postures.

batch interface—The first type of interface available for computers. These computers had one or more interfaces that let users preprogram specially formatted cards with punch holes.

bread crumbs—Links on a Web site subpage that take the user back to the home page or a higher-level page.

CLI—*See* command-line interface.

command-line interface (CLI)—Displays a command prompt that lets the user know that the computer is ready for input. The user can then type in a command using the keyboard and submit it for processing, usually by pressing the Enter key.

conceptual model—A person's idea of how he should perform a certain task based on life experiences, beliefs, and other methods that person has built up over the years.

daemonic—A software posture in which an application usually doesn't interact with the user and runs in the background.

DHTML—*See* Dynamic HTML.

dialog box—A smaller window designed to have the user change settings and make decisions.

Dynamic HTML (DHTML)—An extension of HTML that enables, among other things, the inclusion of small animations and dynamic menus in Web pages.

Flash—A multimedia authoring program produced by Adobe Systems, Inc. that is used to create content for Web applications.

GNOME—A graphical user interface for the Linux operating system.

GNU—GNU Network Object Model Environment, which is a UNIX-compatible operating system that serves as the basis for the Linux operating system.

graphical user interface (GUI)—A system for interacting with a computer by manipulating graphics elements and text. These graphics elements include windows, buttons, menus, and icons.

GUI—*See* graphical user interface.

HTML—*See* Hypertext Markup Language.

HTTP—*See* Hypertext Transfer Protocol.

hyperlink—A reference to another document on the Internet.

Hypertext Markup Language (HTML)—The coding language used to create hypertext documents for the World Wide Web.

Hypertext Transfer Protocol (HTTP)—The set of rules for exchanging files (including text, graphics, and other resources) on the World Wide Web.

Internet Explorer—A free Web browser produced by Microsoft for Microsoft Windows and Mac OS X.

Java—A platform-independent, object-oriented programming language developed by Sun Microsystems.

JavaScript—A computer language that is a subset of the Java programming language for use in Web pages to make those pages more interactive.

K Desktop Environment (KDE)—A graphical user interface for the Linux operating system.

KDE—*See* K Desktop Environment.

Linux—An operating system based on the GNU operating system.

Mac OS—The Apple Macintosh operating system, currently in version 10 (called Mac OS X).

MBTI—*See* Myers-Briggs Type Indicator.

menu—A list of commands that give you options for issuing commands to the program.

Mosaic—The first World Wide Web browser with a graphical interface.

mouse pointer—A GUI graphics feature, usually an arrow, that you manipulate directly using a mouse.

Myers-Briggs Type Indicator (MBTI)—A method of identifying and understanding personality type preferences that was developed by Katherine Briggs and Isabelle Myers.

.NET—A software development platform created by Microsoft that includes many technologies designed for rapid development of Web applications.

Netscape Navigator—The first popular Web browser for personal computers. The program is now offered by AOL for free to users as the Netscape Browser.

NLS—*See* oN-Line System.

online help—A system that provides topic, procedural, or reference information delivered through computer software.

oN-Line System (NLS)—The first graphical user interface, developed by Douglas Engelbart.

Palo Alto Research Center (PARC)—The research center operated by Xerox.

paper prototyping—A process in which you create a paper version of a software program, hardware product, or Web site so that you can learn how users interact with the design before you develop the product.

PARC—*See* Palo Alto Research Center.

PDF—*See* Portable Document Format.

personas—User models based on groupings of different user characteristics.

PHP—PHP Hypertext Preprocessor, which is programming language that allows Web developers to create dynamic content that interacts with databases.

Portable Document Format (PDF)—The de facto format for sharing, displaying, and printing formatted documents created by Adobe Systems, Inc.

portal—A site that provides information for the user about things happening with the company and links that tell the user how to get somewhere else.

posture—The stance of a product or interface in relation to the user.

principles—Design guidelines that address issues of behavior, form, and content.

return on investment (ROI)—The actual or perceived future value of an expense or investment.

ROI—*See* return on investment.

scrollbar—A widget that lets you view continuous text and graphics in a window if all the text and graphics in the area are too large to be displayed in that area.

Search Engine Software—Used to retrieve information from a database or from the Internet.

Section 508—An amendment to the Rehabilitation Act of 1973 that requires people to develop interfaces that are accessible to federal employees with disabilities.

SME—*See* subject matter expert.

sovereign—A software posture that keeps the user's attention for long periods of time.

subject matter expert (SME)—A person knowledgeable about a product, process, or topic.

TCP/IP—*See* Transmission Control Protocol/Internet Protocol.

text user interface (TUI)—A user interface that uses the entire screen area to perform tasks.

toolbar—A row, column, or toolbox that contains buttons and other widgets.

transient—A task-specific, need-based application posture that the user uses occasionally.

Transmission Control Protocol/Internet Protocol (TCP/IP)—The standard Internet data transmission protocol.

TUI—*See* text user interface.

Uniform Resource Locator (URL)—A sequence of characters that describes the location of a Web page, site, or other resource on the Internet.

UNIX—An operating system created in 1969 by Bell Laboratories.

URL—*See* Uniform Resource Locator.

usability defined by Dumas and Redish (1999)—"The people who use the product can do so quickly and easily to accomplish their own tasks."

usability engineer—A person who provides usability services.

usability scientist—A person who has formal training in usability research and development disciplines.

user experience professional—A person who is a usability engineer or usability scientist, or a person in a company, office, or department who isn't a formal usability engineer or works in a usability engineering department, but someone who does provide usability services.

Web—*See* World Wide Web.

Web browser—A software program that displays information on a Web page and lets you interact with that Web page.

widget—A component in a graphical user interface.

window—An area, usually rectangular in shape, that displays information, including user documents. The user can open or close a window, move it around on the desktop, and sometimes change its size, scroll through it, and edit its contents.

Windows—An operating system created and maintained by Microsoft. The current version of the system is Windows Vista.

Windows Vista—The latest major version of Microsoft Windows that was released in early 2007.

wizard—A GUI program that takes you step by step through adding a program or feature, such as adding a home network.

World Wide Web—An information-sharing space on the Internet that you access through a Web browser.

World Wide Web Consortium—Also known as W3C, this is the governing body for Web standards.

References

Bias, Randolph G., and Deborah G. Mayhew. *Cost-Justifying Usability, Second Edition*. San Francisco, CA: Morgan Kaufmann Publishers, 2005.

Brinck, Tom et al. *Usability for the Web*. San Francisco, CA: Morgan Kaufmann Publishers, 2002.

Cooper, Alan, and Robert Reimann. *About Face 2.0*. Indianapolis, IN: Wiley Publishing, 2003.

Donoghue, Karen. *Built for Use*. New York: McGraw-Hill, 2002.

Dumas, Joseph S., and Janice C. Redish. *A Practical Guide to Usability Testing*. Portland, OR: Intellect Books, 1999.

Eisenberg, Bryan, and Jeffrey Eisenberg. *Waiting for Your Cat to Bark?* Nashville, TN: Thomas Nelson, Inc., 2006.

Hackos, JoAnn T., and Janice C. Redish. *User and Task Analysis for Interface Design*. New York: John Wiley & Sons, 1998.

Kuniavsky, Mike. *Observing the User Experience*. San Francisco, CA: Morgan Kaufmann Publishers, 2003.

Norman, Donald A. *The Design of Everyday Things*. New York: Basic Books, 2002.

Reimer, Jeremy. "A History of the GUI," http://arstechnica.com/articles/paedia/gui.ars.

Snyder, Carolyn. *Paper Prototyping*. San Francisco, CA: Morgan Kaufmann Publishers, 2003.

Thatcher, Jim et al. *Constructing Accessible Web Sites*. Birmingham, UK: glasshaus Ltd., 2002.

Wilson, Chauncey. "Usability and User Experience Design: The Next Decade." *Intercom* (January 2005): 6–9.

Index

A

accessibility, 51
  accessibility myths (Web sites), 203-205
  operating systems, 54-55
  Section 508, 52
  Web Content Accessibility Guidelines, 52-54
Active Server Pages (ASP), 10
Address bar, 27
advanced users, needs of, 143
Aero interface, 6, 38
affordances, 127
AJAX, 13, 25
ALT tags, 204-205
Alto, 2-3
America Online (AOL), 9
Americans with Disabilities Act, 52
analyzing usability test data, 241-243
animals associated with personality types, 118
animation, Web design myths, 202
AOL (America Online), 9
Apple II series, 3
Apple Lisa, 3
Apple Macintosh, 3-4
application service providers (ASPs), 44
applications
  application sites, 206-210
  Internet-based applications, 200
  Web-based applications, 44
Aqua interface, 3-4, 39-40
Archy interface, 45-46
ARPANET, 8
The Art of Unix Usability (Raymond), 27
artifact walkthrough, discourse-based interviews
    with, 237
ASP (Active Server Pages), 10
ASPs (application service providers), 44
assistants, 190-191
assistive technologies, 51

assumptions in software design, 138
attentive interfaces, 44
audience for usability test reports, 243-244
audio information cues, 187
auxiliary applications, 175, 205, 213

B

Back button, 27
back-end programming (Web sites), 213
background sound, Web design myths, 202
backward compatibility, Web accessibility myths,
    204
Bash (Bourne Again SHell) shell, 30
batch files, 29
batch interface, 28
batch programming, 29
Bates, Marilyn, 117
beginners, needs of, 141
behavior. *See* user behavior
behavioral design patterns, 173
behaviors in GUIs, 177
  mouse pointers, 178-180
  windows, 181-185
bell curve. *See* experience bell curve
Berners-Lee, Tim, 9
beta testing, 49, 92, 102, 136
Bias, Randolph, 71. *See also* Vienna (Windows
    code name)
blaming oneself (reasons for failure), 114
blaming wrong cause (reasons for failure), 115
blogs, 104
brain-computer interface, 46
brain, knowledge in, 122-124
brainstorming sessions, 165
bread crumbs, Web site design, 217
breaking Web site design rules, 219-220
Briggs, Katherine, 115
browsers. *See* Web browsers

Bush, Vannevar, 1
business case for usability
  benefits of good design, 64-67
  framework for, 63-64
  Mike's Bikes case study, 76-82
  profitability, 67-69
  ROI (return on investment) analysis, 69-71
  stakeholder expectations, 60-63
  Usability Engineering Life Cycle (UEL), 71-72
    design, testing, and development phase, 73-75
    installation and feedback phase, 75-76
    requirements analysis phase, 72-73
business case for usability, 60
business goals, 150
business requirements, 166
buttons, 20

C

calculating dollar amount of benefit (ROI), 70-71
case study. *See* Mike's Bikes case study
CERN, 9
checklists for documentation design, 98-102
CLI (command-line interface), history of, 28-30
clicking
  clicking and dragging, 179
  left mouse button, 178-179
  right mouse button, 180
closing windows, 185
colors
  in Web site design, 215-216
  Web-safe colors, 42, 199
command-line interface (CLI), history of, 28-30
communication with users
  assistants and wizards, 190-191
  online help systems, 190
  paper prototyping advantages in, 94
  standards, 189-190
competitive temperament, 120-121
conceptual-level principles, 172
conceptual models
  creating, 127-129
  design, 74
  Mike's Bikes case study, 129-131
  mockups, 74
concurrent, contextual interviews, 236
conducting usability tests, 233
  interviewing skills needed, 236-238

observation skills needed, 234-236
ongoing relationships, establishing, 238-239
pilot tests, 233-234, 248-251
rapport with participants, establishing, 239
resolving problems during, 239-241
conscious behavior, subconscious behavior versus, 125
consistency in Web site design, 215, 218
constraints
  defined, 127
  on designers, 88-89
  on users, 88
  Web site design versus GUI design, 198-200
consumer-oriented Web portals, 210
context scenarios, 165
contextual needs, 165
contextual text analysis, 73
controlled usability evaluations, 227
cookies, 208
Cooper, Alan, 49, 86, 139-140, 143, 164, 171, 173, 209
critical incident interviews, 237
cued recall interviews, 236
cues. *See* information cues
cultural constraints, 88
current information in Web site design, 219
cursors, 178
customer partnering, 237
customer personas, 155
customer requirements, 166
customer retention, 67
customer segments, factors affecting interface usage, 93-94
customer support costs, 66
customers' goals, 150
customizability of GUIs, 31

D

daemonic applications, 175, 205
data elements, 167
data needs, 165
databases, Web site interaction with, 215
deep and narrow task structures, 124
defining usability tests, 228-229
  goals, creating, 229
  measures, determining, 231-232
  participants, selecting, 229-230

test materials, preparing, 232-233

test scenarios, creating, 230-231

demographics in personas, 147

descriptive statistics, 241

design myths (Web sites), 202-203

design team, 228

design, testing, and development phase (UEL), 73-75

design. *See* Goal-Directed Design Process; user interface design

designers

  constraints on, 88-89

  expectations of, 61

detailed user interface design, 75

DHTML (Dynamic HTML), 25

dialog boxes, 181

difficult tasks, transforming into simple tasks, 126-127

disabled users. *See* accessibility

discourse-based interviews with artifact walk-through, 237

distributions (Linux), 7

Dock in Mac OS GUI, 11-12, 39

documentation,

  defined, 48

  good design for, 96-97

  planning process, 97-103

dollar amount of benefit (ROI), calculating, 70-71

Donoghue, Karen, 68

DOS, history of CLI (command-line interface), 29

double-clicking, 179

drop-down menus, 20

Dubberly, Hugh, 86

Dumas, Joseph, 47, 228, 242

Dynamic HTML (DHTML), 25

E

edge cases, 149, 192

Eisenberg, Bryan and Jeffrey, 117, 147-148

elastic users, 149

elegant, good design as, 87, 171

embedded links, 26

end goals, 150

end user design, 149

Engelbart, Douglas, 1

engineers, expectations of, 61

enterprise Web portals, 210

environmental Web portals, 211

error messages, poor design of, 138

ethical, good design as, 86, 171

ethnographic interviews, 237

ethnography, 144

evaluating personas, 154

expectations

  of personas, 165

  of stakeholders, 60-63

experience bell curve, 140-141

  advanced users, needs of, 143

  beginners, needs of, 141

  intermediate users, needs of, 142-143

experience goals, 150

Extensible Markup Language (XML), 41

extreme usability, 152

extroversion/introversion dichotomy, 116

F

failures, reasons for, 114-115

feedback, 225. *See also* usability tests

  in conceptual models, 129

  on documentation design, 102

  feedback phase (UEL), 75-76

feeling/thinking dichotomy, 116

fingerprint scanning, 35

Firefox, 10

Flash, 13, 25

focus groups, 227, 237

fonts in Web site design, 199, 215-216

Fore, David, 86

form factor, 166

form processing (Web sites), 214-215

formative usability testing, 49

formatting conventions for documentation, 102

Forward button, 27

framework, 166-169

framework phase (Goal-Directed Design Process), 144

Free Software Foundation, 7

front end (Web sites), 213

functional elements, 167

functional groups, 168

functional needs, 165

future of user interface design, 44-46

  Mac OS, 43

  Web browsers, 43-44

  Windows Vienna, 43

G

gesture interfaces, 45
GNOME, 7, 12-13, 40
GNU operating system, 7
Goal-Directed Design Process, 49, 143-146
    framework, defining, 166-169
    refinement stage, 191-194
    requirements, obtaining, 164-166
    user and task analysis
        observing users, 152-154
        personas, constructing, 147-159
        personas, evaluating, 154
        personas, prioritizing, 154-156
        qualitative research, 146-147
goals
    constructing personas, 149-150
    creating for usability tests, 229
    of good design, 85-87, 171
good design
    designers and users, constraints of, 87-90
    for documentation, 96-103
    goals of, 85-87, 171
    importance of, 104-105
    paper prototyping
        advantages of, 93-95
        disadvantages of, 95-96
        Mike's Bikes case study, 105-110
        overview of, 91
        product mockups versus, 91
        skepticism toward, overcoming, 92-93
        storyboarding versus, 91
        wireframes versus, 91
    paper prototyping, 90
    patterns of, 172-173
    principles of, 172
Goodwin, Kim, 86
Google Spreadsheet, 44
Gore, Al, 9
graphical user interfaces. *See* GUIs
graphics
    in Web site design, 216-217
    Web accessibility myths, 204-205
    Web design myths, 202
group interviews, 237
GUIs (graphical user interfaces), 30-32
    behaviors
        mouse pointers, 178-180
        refining, 191-194
        windows, 181-185
    behaviors, 177
    defined, 18
    differences among
        Linux GUI, 12-13
        Mac OS GUI, 11-12
        Web pages, 13-14
        Web programs, 14
        Windows GUI, 11
    differences among, 10
    GUI design, Web site design versus, 198-200
    history of
        Apple Macintosh, 3-4
        Linux, 7-8
        Microsoft Windows, 5-6
        Xerox Alto, 2-3
    history of, 1-2
    operating systems, 18-19
    parts of, 19-23
    rules for interaction with, 198

H

Hackos, JoAnn, 153
haptic feedback, 36
hardware, security interfaces, 34-36
help. *See* information cues; online help systems
helplessness (reasons for failure), 115
hierarchy of functional groups, defining, 168
High-Performance Computing Act of 1991, 9
highlight presentations of usability test results,
        246-247
Hippocrates, 116
history
    of CLI (command-line interface), 28-30
    of GUIs, 1-2
        Apple Macintosh, 3-4
        Linux, 7-8
        Microsoft Windows, 5-6
        Xerox Alto, 2-3
    of Web design, 8
        Internet Explorer, 9-10
        Internet, beginning of, 8
        Mosaic, 9
        Netscape Navigator, 9
HTML (Hypertext Markup Language), 24
human characteristics of user interface design, 171

humanistic temperament, 120
hyperlinks, 25-26
Hypertext Markup Language (HTML), 24

I

I-shaped bar as mouse pointer, 178
de Icaza, Miguel, 7
images. *See* graphics
immediate recall interviews, 236
implementation model, 139
individuality constraints, 89
inferential statistics, 241
information cues
    audio cues, 187
    pop-up messages, 187
    search engines, 188
    visual cues, 186-187
informational sites, 205, 208
input methods, defining, 166
installation and feedback phase (UEL), 75-76
Intel 80386 chips, 5
interaction design, 171
    goals of good design, 171
    patterns of good design, 172-173
    principles of good design, 172
interaction framework, sketching, 168
interaction-level principles, 172
interfaces, 1. *See also* GUIs
    interface design, 49
    interface-level principles, 172
intermediate users
    needs of, 142-143
    perpetual intermediates, 140
Internet
    defined, 23
    history of, 8
Internet-based applications, 200
Internet Explorer, 9-10
interviewing users when constructing personas,
    151-152
interviewing skills for conducting usability tests,
    236-238
introversion/extroversion dichotomy, 116
intuition/sensing dichotomy, 116, 122-124
iterative conceptual model evaluation, 74
iterative design standards evaluation, 75
iterative detailed user interface design evaluation, 75

J

Java, 14, 24
JavaScript, 25
judging/perceiving dichotomy, 117
Jung, Carl, 116

K

KDE, 7, 12-13, 40
Keirsey, David, 117
key path scenarios, constructing, 169
key path variants, 192
kiosks, Section 508 accessibility, 52
knowledge in brain versus in world, 122-124
Korman, Jonathan, 86

L

left mouse button, clicking, 178-179
legal documents, preparing for usability tests, 232
Leopard (Mac OS X), 40
Level 1 design (UEL), 74
Level 2 design (UEL), 74-75
Level 3 design (UEL), 75
life goals, 149
links. *See* hyperlinks
Linux, 7-8
    as GUI operating system, 19
    interface design issues and improvements, 40
    unique GUI features, 12-13
Lisa, 3
logical constraints, 88
long-term production costs, 65

M

Mac OS, 3-4
    future of user interface design, 43
    as GUI operating system, 19
    OS X, 3-4
        interface design issues and improvements,
            39-40
        unique GUI features, 11-12
managers, expectations of, 62-63
mapping process in conceptual models, 129
Marble Answering Machine, 45
marketing people, expectations of, 62
maximizing windows, 19, 184
Mayhew, Deborah, 71

MBTI (Myers-Briggs Type Indicator), 115-117, 130
MDI (multiple-document interface), 19, 181-182
measures, determining for usability tests, 231-232
mechanical-age design, result of, 138-139
memex, 1
Mena, Federico, 7
mental model. *See* users' mental model
menu bar in Mac OS GUI, 11
menus, 20-21
methodical temperament, 119
Microsoft Internet Explorer, 9-10
Microsoft Windows, 5-6
Mike's Bikes case study
    business case for usability, 76-82
    conceptual models, creating, 129-131
    paper prototyping, 105-110
    personas, constructing, 156
    personas, constructing, 157-159
    pilot usability tests, conducting, 248-251
    refining paper prototype test, 192-194
    Web site navigation features, 220-222
minimizing windows, 19, 184
Minority Report (film), 45
Mirsky, Steve, 98
misconceptions, adhering to (reasons for failure), 115
misunderstandings in seven stages of human action, 121-122
mockups, paper prototyping versus, 91
modal windows, 184
modeling phase (Goal-Directed Design Process), 144
    personas, constructing, 147-152, 156-159
    personas, evaluating, 154
    personas, prioritizing, 154-156
Mosaic, 9
mouse pointers, 178-180
moving
    mouse pointers, 178
    windows, 184-185
MSN.com Maps, 45
multimedia products, Section 508 accessibility, 52
multiple-document interface (MDI), 19, 181-182
multitasking, 5
Myers, Isabelle, 115
Myers-Briggs Type Indicator (MBTI), 115-117, 130
myths about Web site design, 200-205

N

narratives for personas, 154
National Center for Supercomputing Applications (NCSA), 9
navigation in Web site design, 217-222
navigation buttons, 27
NCSA (National Center for Supercomputing Applications), 9
necessary use scenarios, 192
needs of personas, identifying, 165
negative personas, 156
net present value (NPV) amount, calculating, 70
Netscape Navigator, 9
NLS (oN-Line System), 2
Norman, Donald, 121, 128
notes, writing during usability tests, 235-236
NPV (net present value) amount, calculating, 70

O

obscurity in software design, 138
observation skills while conducting usability tests, 152-154, 226-227, 234-236
ongoing relationships, establishing, 238-239
online help systems, 100, 190
open-source software, 7
opening windows, 181-183
Opera, 10
operating systems
    accessibility features, 54-55
    GUI operating systems, list of, 18-19
outlines for documentation, creating, 102

P

Palo Alto Research Center (PARC), 2
paper documentation, 98
paper prototyping, 90
    advantages of, 93-95
    conducting pilot tests, 248-251
    constructing key path scenarios, 169
    defined, 85
    disadvantages of, 95-96
    Mike's Bikes case study, 105-110
    overview of, 91
    product mockups versus, 91
    refining, 192-194
    skepticism toward, overcoming, 92-93

storyboarding versus, 91
wireframes versus, 91
Paper Prototyping (Snyder), 90
PARC (Palo Alto Research Center), 2
participants in usability tests
  establishing rapport with, 239
  selecting, 229-230
partner requirements, 166
path scenarios, constructing, 169
patterns of good design, 172-173
PDF (Portable Document Format)
      documentation, 99
perceiving/judging dichotomy, 117
performance measures, 231-232
perpetual intermediate users, 140
perpetual intermediates, 189
personality types
  animals associated with, 118
  MBTI (Myers-Briggs Type Indicator), 115-117,
      130
  primary temperaments, 117-118
    competitive temperament, 120-121
    humanistic temperament, 120
    methodical temperament, 119
    spontaneous temperament, 119-120
personas
  advantages of, 148-149
  constructing, 147-152, 156-159
  evaluating, 154
  expectations of, 165
  identifying needs of, 165
  prioritizing, 154-156
  requirements, obtaining, 164-166
persuasion process in sales, 148
photographs for personas, 154
PHP, 25
physical constraints, 88
pilot usability tests, conducting, 233-234, 248-251
planning process
  for good documentation design, 97-103
  paper prototyping advantages in, 93-94
platform capabilities/constraints in requirements
      analysis, 73
platform-independent, 24
pointing devices in GUIs, 31. *See also* mouse
      pointers
pop-up menus, 20
pop-up messages, 187

Portable Document Format (PDF) documentation,
      99
portal sites, 206, 210-213
postural design patterns, 173
postures. *See* software postures; Web postures
PowerShell, 30
pragmatic, good design as, 87, 171
presenting usability test results, 245-247
primary personas, 155-159
primary temperaments, 117-118
  competitive temperament, 120-121
  humanistic temperament, 120
  methodical temperament, 119
  spontaneous temperament, 119-120
principles of good design, 172
prioritizing personas, 154-156
problem statements, 164
problems during usability tests, resolving, 239-241
process interviews, 237
product engineers/designers, expectations of, 61
product mockups, 91
production costs, 65-66
professionalism of paper prototyping, 92
profitability of usability design, 67-69
programming languages for Web pages, 24-25
project teams, 97-98
prototyping design standards, 75. *See also* paper
      prototyping
psychographics in personas, 148
psychology of user behavior
  MBTI (Myers-Briggs Type Indicator), 115-117
  primary temperaments
    competitive temperament, 120-121
    humanistic temperament, 120
    methodical temperament, 119
    spontaneous temperament, 119-120
  primary temperaments, 117-118
  reasons for failure, 114-115
  seven stages of human action, 121-122
purposeful, good design as, 87, 171

Q

qualitative research, 146-147
quantitative research, 146
questionnaires, preparing for usability tests, 233
quick and dirty usability testing, 49

R

Radio Frequency Identification (RFID) tags, 35
rapport with test participants, establishing, 239
Raskin, Jef, 45
Raymond, Eric, 27
real-world requirements, 166
Red Hat, 7
Redish, Ginny, 153
Redish, Janice, 47, 228, 242
refinement phase (Goal-Directed Design Process),
    145, 191-194
reflexive interfaces, 45
Rehabilitation Act of 1973, 52
Reimann, Robert, 49, 86, 139, 140, 143, 164, 171,
    173, 209
Reimer, Jeremy, 1
relationships, establishing ongoing relationships,
    238-239
reports, writing on usability tests, 243-245
requirements analysis phase (UEL), 72-73
requirements-gathering sessions, 228
requirements phase (Goal-Directed Design
    Process), 144, 164-166
research phase (Goal-Directed Design Process),
    144-147
resizing windows, 184
resolution of Web pages, 33
resolving problems during usability tests, 239-241
results of usability tests, presenting, 245-247
retina scanning, 35
return on investment (ROI), 69-71, 92
review process for documentation, 103
RFID (Radio Frequency Identification) tags, 35
RIAS (Rich Internet Application System), 13, 44
right mouse button, clicking, 180
ROI (return on investment) analysis, 69-71, 92
rules for Web site design, breaking, 218-220

S

sales, persuasion process, 148
sales people, expectations of, 62
scenarios, creating for usability tests, 230-231
scope of usability test data, 242
scrollbars, 22
SDIs (single document interfaces), 19
search engines, 188
secondary personas, 155

Section 508 accessibility, 52
security
    Web engineering, 214
    Windows Vista, 38
    security interfaces, 34-36
selecting
    participants for usability tests, 229-230
    usability test techniques, 226-228
self-referential design, 149
semantic constraints, 88
sensing/intuition dichotomy, 116, 122-124
served personas, 155
seven stages of human action, 121-122
severity of usability test data, 243
SGML (Standard Generalized Markup Language),
    41
shallow task structures, 124
short-term production costs, 65
simple tasks, transforming difficult tasks into,
    126-127
simplicity
    in conceptual models, 128
    in users' mental models, 139
    in Web site design, 218
single document interfaces (SDIs), 19
site visits for observing users, 226-227
smart cards, 34
Snyder, Carolyn, 90
social constraints, 88
software development
    bad behaviors of, 138-139
    phases of, 136-137
    Section 508 accessibility, 52
software postures, 173-177, 205
sound, Web design myths, 202
sovereign applications, 173, 205, 208
spontaneous temperament, 119-120
Sputnik, 8
stakeholder expectations, 60-63
Stallman, Richard, 7
Standard Generalized Markup Language (SGML),
    41
standards
    in level 2 design, 74-75
    in user interface design, 189-190
    in Web site design
        colors and text, 215-216
        consistency, 215

graphics, 216-217
   navigation, 217-222
Star, 3
Start button, 11
statistics, types of, 241
storyboarding, 90. *See also* paper prototyping
  constructing key path scenarios, 169
  paper prototyping versus, 91
structural design patterns, 173
structuring tasks, 124-125
style guide development, 75
style sheets, defining for documentation, 102
stylus, 37
subconscious behavior, 125
subjective measures, 231
summative usability testing, 50
supplemental personas, 155

T

table of contents for documentation, 103
tabs in MDI (multiple-document interface),
    181-182
tactile interfaces, 36
tangible interfaces, 45
task structures, 124-125
taskbars, 11, 23
tasks
  conceptual models
    creating, 127-129
    Mike's Bikes case study, 129-131
  scenarios, creating for usability tests, 230-231
  transforming from difficult to simple, 126-127
  user and task analysis
    observing users, 152-154
    personas, constructing, 147-159
    personas, evaluating, 154
    personas, prioritizing, 154-156
    qualitative research, 146-147
TCP/IP, 8
teams for documentation design, 97-98
technical goals, 150
technical requirements, 166
telecommunications products, Section 508
    accessibility, 52
temperaments. *See* primary temperaments
test materials, preparing for usability tests,
    232-233

test scenarios, creating for usability tests, 230-231
testing methods. *See* usability testing
testing scripts, preparing for usability tests, 232
tests. *See* usability tests
text in Web site design, 215-216
text user interface (TUI), 30-31
thinking/feeling dichotomy, 116
three-click rule, 128, 219
time constraints, 89
toolbars, 11, 21-22, 26
ToolTips, 187
topology in personas, 148
Torvalds, Linus, 7
touch interfaces, 36
trade shows, meeting users at, 228
training costs, 66
transforming difficult tasks into simple tasks,
    126-127
transient applications, 174, 205
  application Web sites as, 209-210
  informational Web sites as, 208
  portal sites as, 213
triangulating data, 242
trough (of scrollbar), 22
TUI (text user interface), 30-31

U

UEL (Usability Engineering Life Cycle), 71-72
  design, testing, and development phase, 73-75
  installation and feedback phase, 75-76
  requirements analysis phase, 72-73
UNIX-based CLIs, 30
URL (Uniform Resource Locator), 24
usability design
  business case for, 60
    benefits of good design, 64-67
    framework for, 63-64
    Mike's Bikes case study, 76-82
    profitability, 67-69
    ROI (return on investment) analysis, 69-71
    stakeholder expectations, 60-63
    Usability Engineering Life Cycle (UEL), 71-76
  connection with user interface design and
    usability testing, 60
  defined, 47
  importance of, 59
  types of, 48-49

Usability Engineering Life Cycle (UEL), 71-72
  design, testing, and development phase, 73-75
  installation and feedback phase, 75-76
  requirements analysis phase, 72-73
usability engineers, 48
usability goal settings in requirements analysis, 73
usability roundtables, 227, 237
usability scientists, 48
usability services, 48
usability tests, 49-50
  analyzing data, 241-243
  changes based on, 247
  conducting
    interviewing skills needed, 236-238
    observation skills needed, 234-236
    ongoing relationships, establishing, 238-239
    pilot tests, 233-234, 248-251
    rapport with participants, establishing, 239
    resolving problems during, 239-241
  conducting, 233
  connection with user interface design and
      usability design, 60
  defining
    goals, creating, 229
    measures, determining, 231-232
    participants, selecting, 229
    participants, selecting, 230
    test materials, preparing, 232-233
    test scenarios, creating, 230-231
  defining, 228-229
  paper prototyping. *See* paper prototyping
  presenting results of, 245-247
  techniques for, 226-228
  types of data from, 241
  writing report on, 243-245
usage myths (Web sites), 201-202
usage patterns, discovering, 144
user and task analysis
  defined, 50
  Goal-Directed Design Process, 49
  observing users, 152-154
  personas, constructing, 147-159
  personas, evaluating, 154
  personas, prioritizing, 154-156
  qualitative research, 146-147
  trends in, 50-51
  usability testing, 49-50

user behavior
  conceptual models
    creating, 127-129
    Mike's Bikes case study, 129-131
  conscious versus subconscious
      behavior, 125
  knowledge in brain versus knowledge in world,
      122-124
  psychology of
    MBTI (Myers-Briggs Type Indicator), 115-117
    primary temperaments, 117-121
    reasons for failure, 114-115
    seven stages of human action, 121-122
  task structures, 124-125
  transforming difficult tasks into simple tasks,
      126-127
user goals, Goal-Directed Design Process, 143-146
  framework, defining, 166-169
  refinement stage, 191-194
  requirements, obtaining, 164-166
  user and task analysis, 146-159
user interface design. *See also* GUIs; user interface
      models
  accessibility issues
    operating systems, 54-55
    Section 508, 52
    Web Content Accessibility Guidelines, 52-54
  accessibility issues, 51
  communication with users
    assistants and wizards, 190-191
    online help systems, 190
    standards, 189-190
  connection with usability design and testing, 60
  framework, defining, 166-169
  future of, 44-46
    Mac OS, 43
    Web browsers, 43-44
    Windows Vienna, 43
  good design. *See* good design
  GUI behaviors, 177
    mouse pointers, 178-180
    refining, 191-194
    windows, 181-185
  human characteristics of, 171
  information cues
    audio cues, 187
    pop-up messages, 187

search engines, 188
visual cues, 186-187
interaction design
  goals of good design, 171
  patterns of good design, 172-173
  principles of good design, 172
interaction design, 171
issues and improvements
  Linux, 40
  Mac OS X, 39-40
  Web interfaces, 41-42
  Windows Vista, 38-39
issues and improvements, 42
requirements, obtaining, 164-166
software postures, 173-177
user interface models
  batch interface, 28
  button interfaces, 37
  CLI (command-line interface), history of, 28-30
  GUI (graphical user interface), 30-32
  security interfaces, 34-36
  tactile interfaces, 36
  telephone user interfaces, 37
  touch interfaces, 36
  TUI (text user interface), 30-31
  types of, 27-28
  Web interfaces, 32-35
user profile in requirements analysis, 73
user surveys, 228
users. *See also* user interface design
  behavior
    conceptual models, 127-131
    conscious versus subconscious behavior, 125
    knowledge in brain versus knowledge in world, 122-124
    psychology of, 114-122
    task structures, 124-125
    transforming difficult tasks into simple tasks, 126-127
  constraints on, 88
  expectations of, 61
  experience bell curve, 140-141
    advanced users, needs of, 143
    beginners, needs of, 141
    intermediate users, needs of, 142-143
  goals, Goal-Directed Design Process, 143-146
    framework, defining, 166-169
    refinement stage, 191-194

requirements, obtaining, 164-166
  user and task analysis, 146-159
  interviewing when constructing personas, 151-152
  observing, 152-154, 226-227
  users' mental model
    bad software development behaviors, 138-139
    implementation model versus, 139
    phases of software development, 136-137

V

validation scenarios, 192
validity of paper prototyping, 92
videos, Section 508 accessibility, 52
Vienna (Windows code name), 43
views, defining, 167
visibility in conceptual models, 129
vision statements, 164
VisiOn, 5
visual information cues, 186-187
voice mail hell, 37

W

W3C (World Wide Web Consortium), Web Content Accessibility Guidelines, 52-54
Web, 9, 23
Web-based applications, 44
Web browsers
  Address bar, 27
  defined, 23-24
  Firefox, 10
  future of user interface design, 43-44
  Internet Explorer, 9-10
  Mosaic, 9
  navigation buttons, 27
  Netscape Navigator, 9
  Opera, 10
  toolbars, 26
  Web accessibility myths, 204
Web Content Accessibility Guidelines, 52-54
Web engineering, 213-215
Web interfaces, 32-35, 41-42
Web postures, 205-207
  application sites, 208-210
  informational sites, 208
  portal sites, 210-213
Web programs, unique GUI features, 14

Web site design
  defined, 49
  GUI design versus, 198-200
  history of, 8
    Internet Explorer, 9-10
    Internet, beginning of, 8
    Mosaic, 9
    Netscape Navigator, 9
  hyperlinks, 25
  interaction with Web sites, 199
  myths about, 200-205
  programming languages for, 24-25
  resolution of, 33
  rules for, breaking, 218-220
  Section 508 accessibility, 52
  standards
    colors and text, 215-216
    consistency, 215
    graphics, 216-217
    navigation, 217-222
  three-click rule, 128
  unique GUI features, 13-14
  Web engineering, 213-215
  Web postures, 205-207
application sites, 208-210
    information sites, 208
    portal sites, 210-213
  Web-safe colors/fonts, 42, 199, 215
  Web sites as documentation, 101
wide and deep task structures, 124
widgets, 19
Wilson, Chauncy, 47, 50
Windows, 5-6
  as GUI operating system, 18
  history of CLI (command-line interface), 29
  unique GUI features, 11
  Windows Vienna, 43
  Windows Vista, 38-39

windows
  behaviors of, 181-185
  closing, 185
  defined, 19-20
  moving, 184-185
  opening, 181-183
  resizing, 184
wireframes, paper prototyping versus, 91
wizards, 190-191
work re-engineering, 74
World Wide Web, 9, 23
World Wide Web Consortium (W3C), Web Content
      Accessibility Guidelines, 52-54
world, knowledge in, 122-124
writing
  notes during usability tests, 235-236
  reports on usability tests, 243-245
WWW (World Wide Web), 9, 23

X-Y-Z

X Window system, 9
Xerox
  Alto, 2-3
  PARC (Palo Alto Research Center), 2
  Star, 3
XGA resolution, 33
XHTML, 41
XML (Extensible Markup Language), 41

zooming interfaces, 45
ZUI (zooming user interface), 45

THIS BOOK IS SAFARI ENABLED

INCLUDES FREE 45-DAY ACCESS TO THE ONLINE EDITION

The Safari® Enabled icon on the cover of your favorite technology book means the book is available through Safari Bookshelf. When you buy this book, you get free access to the online edition for 45 days.

Safari Bookshelf is an electronic reference library that lets you easily search thousands of technical books, find code samples, download chapters, and access technical information whenever and wherever you need it.

TO GAIN 45-DAY SAFARI ENABLED ACCESS TO THIS BOOK:

- Go to **http://www.awprofessional.com/safarienabled**
- Complete the brief registration form
- Enter the coupon code found in the front of this book on the "Copyright" page

If you have difficulty registering on Safari Bookshelf or accessing the online edition, please e-mail customer-service@safaribooksonline.com.

Addison
Wesley